HUMAN SEXUALITY AND THE MENTALLY RETARDED

Human Sexuality and the Mentally Retarded

Edited by

FELIX F. DE LA CRUZ
GERALD D. LaVECK

*National Institute of Child Health
and Human Development
National Institutes of Health*

BRUNNER/MAZEL, *Publishers* ● NEW YORK

SECOND PRINTING

Copyright © 1973 by Brunner/Mazel, Inc.

Published by
BRUNNER/MAZEL, INC.
64 University Place, New York, N. Y. 10003

Library of Congress Catalog Card No. 72-92057
SBN 87630-063-8

MANUFACTURED IN THE UNITED STATES OF AMERICA

PROCEEDINGS OF A CONFERENCE ON HUMAN SEXUALITY AND THE MENTALLY RETARDED

Sponsored by

The National Institute of Child Health and Human Development, United States Department of Health, Education, and Welfare
Public Health Service
National Institutes of Health
Bethesda, Maryland

PROGRAM PLANNING COMMITTEE

Cochairmen:

Robert W. Deisher, M.D.
Felix F. de la Cruz, M.D., M.P.H.

Members of Committee:

Michael J. Begab, Ph.D.
W. Roy Breg, M.D.
Philip Corfman, M.D.
Paul H. Gebhard, Ph.D.
David L. Joftes, Ph.D.
John W. Money, Ph.D.
Murry Morgenstern, Ph.D.
Sidney H. Newman, Ph.D.
Sheldon C. Reed, Ph.D.
Theodore D. Tjossem, Ph.D.

Contents

BACKGROUND PAPERS

CONFERENCE PARTICIPANTS

ROBERT ATHANASIOU, Ph.D.—Department of Psychiatry and Department of Obstetrics and Gynecology, The Johns Hopkins Hospital, Baltimore, Maryland 21205.

MEDORA S. BASS, M.A.—Consultant on Retardation, Department of Education, Planned Parenthood of SE Pennsylvania, Ardmore, Pennsylvania 19003.

MICHAEL J. BEGAB, Ph.D.—Head, Mental Retardation Research Centers, Mental Retardation Program, National Institute of Child Health and Human Development, National Institutes of Health, Bethesda, Maryland 20014.

ELIZABETH M. BOGGS, Ph.D.—Past President, National Association for Retarded Children, R.D. #1, Hampton, New Jersey 08827.

W. ROY BREG, M.D.—Assistant Medical Director, Southbury Training School, Southbury, Connecticut 06488.

DEREK L. BURLESON, Ed.D.—Director of Education and Research Services, Sex Information and Education Council of the U.S., New York, New York 10023.

ROBERT A. BURT, J.D.—Professor of Law, University of Michigan Law School, Ann Arbor, Michigan 48108.

DAVID GORDON CARRUTH, M.S.W.—Division of Child Health, Department of Pediatrics, University of Washington, Seattle, Washington 98105.

GERALD R. CLARK, M.D.—President, Elwyn Institute, Elwyn, Pennsylvania 19063.

ROBERT W. DEISHER, M.D.—Director, Division of Child Health, Department of Pediatrics, University of Washington, Seattle, Washington 98105.

FELIX F. de la CRUZ, M.D., M.P.H.—Special Assistant for Pediatrics, Mental Retardation Program, National Institute of Child Health and Human Development, National Institutes of Health, Bethesda, Maryland 20014.

ROBERT B. EDGERTON, Ph.D.—Associate Professor, Department of Psychiatry and Anthropology, University of California at Los Angeles, Los Angeles, California 90024.

SETSU FURUNO, Ph.D.—School of Public Health, University of Hawaii, Honolulu, Hawaii 96822.

PAUL H. GEBHARD, Ph.D.—Director, Institute for Sex Research, Indiana University, Bloomington, Indiana 47401.

PARK S. GERALD, M.D., Chief, Clinical Genetics Division, Children's Hospital Medical Center, Boston, Massachusetts 02115.

GERALD GINGRICH, Ph.D.—Division of Family Study, University of Pennsylvania School of Medicine, Philadelphia, Pennsylvania 19104.

MR. RUSSELL GOODMAN—Family Life Development Specialist, Community Resources Section, Department of Public Welfare, St. Paul, Minnesota 55501.

SOL GORDON, Ph.D.—Professor of Child and Family Studies, College for Human Development, Syracuse University, Syracuse, New York 13210.

RICHARD GREEN, M.D.—Associate Professor of Psychiatry in Residence, UCLA School of Medicine, Los Angeles, California 90024.

JUDY E. HALL, Ph.D.—Staff Psychologist, Center for Development and Learning Disorders, University of Alabama in Birmingham, Birmingham, Alabama 35233.

DONALD W. HELBIG, M.D.—Assistant Director, Division for Program Development and Evaluation, International Institute for the Study of Human Reproduction, Columbia University, New York, New York 10032.

MR. JEROME HELLMUTH—P.O. Box 356, Bainbridge Island, Washington 98110.

J. HELWEG-LARSEN, M.D.—Rigshospitalet, Copenhagen, Denmark.

ELSIE D. HELSEL, Ph.D.—Washington Representative, United Cerebral Palsy Associations, Inc., Washington, D. C. 20001.

WARREN R. JOHNSON, Ph.D.—Professor of Health Education, Director, Children's Physical Developmental Clinic, University of Maryland, College Park, Maryland 20742.

C. C. LI, Ph.D.—Department of Biostatistics, Graduate School of Public Health, University of Pittsburgh, Pittsburgh, Pennsylvania 15213.

MR. RICHARD A. LIPPKE, Formerly, Deputy Executive Director, Secretary's Committee on Mental Retardation, Department of Health, Education, and Welfare, Washington, D. C. 20201.

MISS JANET MATTINSON—Institute of Marital Studies, Tavistock Institute of Human Relations, London, N.W. 3, England.

HAROLD MICHAL-SMITH, Ph.D.—Professor of Pediatrics and Psychiatry, Associate Director, University Affiliated Institute for Mental Retardation, New York Medical College, New York, New York 10029.

JOHN W. MONEY, Ph.D.—Associate Professor of Medical Psychology and Pediatrics, Departments of Psychiatry and Behavioral

Sciences and Pediatrics, Johns Hopkins University and Hospital, Baltimore, Maryland 21205.

MURRY MORGENSTERN, Ph.D.—Associate Director, Division of Psychology, University Affiliated Institute for Mental Retardation, New York Medical College, New York, New York 10029.

EDMOND A. MURPHY, M.D.—Division of Medical Genetics, Johns Hopkins University School of Medicine, Department of Medicine, Baltimore, Maryland 21205.

JOSEPH R. NAROT, D.H.L.—Rabbi, Temple Israel, Miami, Florida 33132.

SHELDON C. REED, Ph.D.—Director, Dight Institute for Human Genetics, University of Minnesota, Minneapolis, Minnesota 55455.

ALBERT REICHERT, M.D.—Superintendent, Rainier School, Buckley, Washington 98321.

IRA L. REISS, Ph.D.—Professor of Sociology, Director of the Family Study Center, Department of Sociology, University of Minnesota, Minneapolis, Minnesota 55455.

MRS. JEANNETTE ROCKEFELLER—President's Committee on Mental Retardation, Washington, D. C. 20201.

G. ALLAN ROEHER, Ph.D.—Director, National Institute on Mental Retardation, York University Campus, Toronto, Ontario, Canada.

PHILIP ROOS, Ph.D.—Executive Director, National Association for Retarded Children, Arlington, Texas 76011.

SALERNO, LOUIS, M.D.—Professor of Obstetrics and Gynecology, New York Medical College, New York, New York 10029.

BRIAN G. SCALLY, Ph.D.—Consultant Psychiatrist, Eastern Special Care Management Committee, Northern Ireland Hospitals Authority, Muckamore Abbey, Muckamore, County Antrim, Northern Ireland.

RICHARD H. SPITZ, M.D.—Clinical and Research Associate, Reproductive Biology Research Foundation, St. Louis, Missouri 63108.

MR. HARVEY A. STEVENS, Program Administrator, Waisman Center on Mental Retardation and Human Development, University of Wisconsin, Madison, Wisconsin 53706.

GEORGE TARJAN, M.D.—Professor of Psychiatry, Program Director of Mental Retardation, Department of Psychiatry, Neuropsychiatric Institute, UCLA, Los Angeles, California 90024.

THEODORE D. TJOSSEM, Ph.D.—Program Director, Mental Retardation Program, National Institute of Child Health and Human Development, National Institutes of Health, Bethesda, Maryland 20014.

JEROME WALLER, Ph.D.—Department of Biostatistics, Graduate School of Public Health, University of Pittsburgh, Pittsburgh, Pennsylvania 15213.

RICHARD E. WHALEN, Ph.D.—Chairman and Professor, Department of Psychobiology, University of California, Irvine, California 92661.

CONTRIBUTING AUTHORS (not at Conference)

V. ELVING ANDERSON, Ph.D.—Dight Institute for Human Genetics, University of Minnesota, Minneapolis, Minnesota 55455.

HENRIK HOFFMEYER, M.D.—Head, State Psychiatric Hospital, 2600 Glostrup, Denmark.

GERALD D. LaVECK, M.D.—Director, National Institute of Child Health and Human Development, National Institutes of Health, Bethesda, Maryland 20014.

RICHARD SARKIN—The Johns Hopkins University, Baltimore, Maryland 21218.

CAROL K. WHALEN, Ph.D.—Program in Social Ecology, University of California, Irvine, California 92661.

CONFERENCE STAFF

BETTY BARTON—Chief, Scientific Conference Branch, National Institute of Child Health and Human Development, Bethesda, Maryland 20014.

KATHRYN CLOSE—Science Writer, 2500 Wisconsin Ave., Washington, D. C. 20007.

MERYOM LEBOWITZ—Conference Assistant, National Institute of Child Health and Human Development, Bethesda, Maryland 20014.

DIANNE SAVILLE—Secretary to Dr. de la Cruz, National Institute of Child Health and Human Development, Bethesda, Maryland 20014.

CAROL ANN ZIMMERMAN—Secretary, Mental Retardation Program, National Institute of Child Health and Human Development, Bethesda, Maryland 20014.

Preface

ON NOVEMBER 7-10, 1971, specialists in various aspects of mental retardation, human sexual development, and sex education met in Hot Springs, Arkansas, to discuss what is known and what needs to be known about the place of sexuality in the development and behavior of the retarded. The conference was sponsored by the Mental Retardation Program of the National Institute of Child Health and Human Development and was attended by individuals representing the fields of biology, medicine, psychology, anthropology, sociology, genetics, education, theology, social work, and law.

The participants discussed human sexuality, in its broadest context, which is considered important for the development of an individual, regardless of his intellectual or physical capabilities. With the concept of "normalization" as the underlying assumption of the entire discussion, the participants reported what sometimes seemed to be conflicting theories and findings on the intensity of the retarded person's need for, and his ability to exercise control over, his sexuality. However, when differences in degrees and types of retardation and variations in individuals within these types were taken into consideration, the conflict tended to diminish.

For the past several years there has been an increasing realization that the mentally retarded have the right not only to proper education, decent care, and to experience a happy and meaningful life, but also to develop and nurture a human relationship including sexual expression. This publication contains discussions covering various aspects of human sexuality, including impediments to and consequences of sexual expression. We hope that this volume will give us a better understanding of one of the basic needs of the mentally retarded and guide us in developing programs to help the retarded in expressing those needs with a minimum of undesirable consequences.

FELIX F. DE LA CRUZ
GERALD D. LAVECK

Greetings from the President's Committee on Mental Retardation

JEANNETTE ROCKEFELLER

IT IS A PARTICULAR PLEASURE for me to extend formal greetings from the President's Committee on Mental Retardation. We are all deeply concerned with both knowledge and myth. How, in the special circumstance of the mentally retarded, do we separate fact from myth? Separating piece by piece, what intelligent courses of action are open to us? And then, finally seeing a potential breakthrough, how do we mobilize the necessary public awareness and concern to move ahead?

I think it is paradoxical, but frustratingly true, that the science of social attitudes is far less exact than the science of medicine. Across history, it has been written that what man does not understand, he resists. And nowhere has this been better evidenced than in his regard for his own fellow creatures.

Yet, when given understanding, we have seen great human compassion and the capacity for change. Our struggle now is toward a confluence of these characteristics, compassion and change, relative to the mentally retarded. What are the rights of the mentally retarded? How much freedom are they entitled to as private individuals? At what point and to what extent does the so-called normal element of society impose its judgment in such questions and then pursue what have been and what will be the consequences of wrong judgments both in the lives of the retarded and in society itself?

You, as professionals, know best of all there will be no final, perfect answers. But, also as professionals, you find nowhere an option to discontinue the search.

We come to this conference from many different places and represent many different disciplines. And yet, I believe it is correct to say that a common motivating conviction does exist and will sustain your deliberations for the next few days. Whatever we do not know about the mentally retarded may represent tragically needless restrictions upon already restricted lives.

We know that as rapidly as myths can be disposed of both in public attitudes and in the continuing evolution of professional enlightenment, then to the same degree can the capacity for usefulness and happiness and fulfillment be enlarged for the mentally retarded.

In extending these greetings, I can tell you that the President's Committee looks forward with keen interest to a report of your activities and findings here. It is in that spirit that I convey to you the very best wishes of my colleagues, and I am certain of many others, for a most successful and certainly a rewarding conference.

HUMAN SEXUALITY AND THE MENTALLY RETARDED

Some Thoughts on Sexual Taboos and the Rights of the Retarded

JOHN W. MONEY

Johns Hopkins University and Hospital

TWO INCIDENTS IN MY EXPERIENCE have left an indelible impression on me. One of them occurred about 15 years ago when I was taken by a friend in Singapore to visit a leper colony across on the mainland. There I learned from the superintendent that he had allowed people in the colony, some of whom were very badly mutilated by their disease, to form conjugal units and live together in little housekeeping huts on the grounds instead of in the big hospital-like buildings.

I had been impressed by an apparent serenity among the people there. This impression was confirmed by the superintendent who said that having a regular sex life and the tenderness and affection of a sexual partner had, indeed, provided comfort and consolation to people who were doomed to spend the rest of their lives in the colony.

The superintendent had imposed only one rule on these conjugal couples: that if their life together resulted in an offspring, the child would have to be placed out of the colony for adoption. This policy derived from the fact that an infant is likely to contract the disease only if he lives with affected persons over an extended period of time. At that time the superintendent had access to neither information nor equipment regarding birth control.

Some years later I visited the Maryland State institution for the retarded at Rosewood. There I found that in the houses for inmates of various ages the black attendants had adopted what I considered to be a wise policy toward the sexual friendships of people who were living under extraordinarily unpleasant, crowded conditions. Whereas the cultural background of white attendants probably would have dictated that any kind of sexual expression among their charges be severely punished and, if possible, suppressed, these black attendants simply decided that it was necessary for nature to have its proper expression. And since the people in their care were obliged to live in a sexually segregated environment, it was inevitable and understandable that they would have their sexual relationships homosexually.

In this huge institution there was an almost complete lack of privacy. Consequently, any sexual activity going on was likely to be seen. I think that sexual activity *per se* was not so important to the inmates of this institution as the opportunity for two people to build a relationship of affection and tenderness that could be expressed occasionally in sexual activity. The pairings were recognized as special sexual friendships by all the other inmates in the building and by the staff as well.

Here again, as in the Singapore leper colony, the opportunity to develop a sexual relationship permitted a degree of tranquility in the confined people that would otherwise not be present.

I refer to these experiences to stress my belief that there should be greater understanding of the importance of allowing to the mentally retarded an opportunity for expressing tenderness, affection, and love even to the point of sexual activity. In other words, I would like to see something done in recognition of the conjugal rights of mentally retarded persons, even for those whose intellectual deficit is so great that they are unable to live at home or anywhere in the outside world.

I realize that many people see in this suggestion a problem involving decisions about sterilization and other steps to prevent breeding in those retarded persons who are either incompetent to look after children or likely to transmit a genetic defect. However, I do not see that such decisions pose a problem any more serious than other important decisions that have to be made in the practice of medicine. I do not believe that there would be great difficulty in setting up an appropriate jury system for making such decisions for the benefit of the people concerned.

I have interviewed retarded people who are managing to live at home but who would not be able to look after children, or would run the risk of transmitting a genetic disease if they reproduced. I have found that when they understand these issues they usually decide in favor of sterilization so that they can accept the possibility of romance and sexuality in their adult lives.

Explicit Teaching

Teaching sex education to the retarded may require teaching the actual positions in coitus—through the use of pictures in books and films. This type of teaching is actually done for paraplegics in Minnesota through a film that shows them how to overcome their sexual handicaps. However, most of us are extremely inhibited with regard to pictures of sex. The prevalence of this inhibition is most evident, of course, in the anguish with which society encounters the question of pornography.

Inhibitions against Pictures

This brings me to my next point, an examination of why our society has always had this extraordinary prejudice against pictures of sex—this cultural prohibition against the graven image below the belt. I state it thus because, in testifying in several pornography trials, I have tangled with society's attempt to achieve a clear definition of pornography through Supreme Court rulings. As a result, I have decided that in our society the current definition of pornography stems from the feeling, "Thou shalt not look at the sex organs." This attitude parallels the traditional prohibition in the Moslem faith against the graven image of the face.

The Supreme Court definition of pornography is a threefold one. It tries to define pornography in terms of prurient appeal without defining the word "prurient," which simply means "itching." That leaves any expert completely at a loss in trying to interpret what is and what is not pornography.

So one turns to the second criterion in the current legal definition: representations of sex are pornographic unless they have some social value or at least are not utterly without redeeming social value. That is an impossible criterion for a precise interpretation. There is always somebody who finds some point of redeeming social value in almost anything. Even cancer has redeeming social values to cancer researchers.

So one turns to the third criterion of pornography: representations of sex are pornographic if they are completely contrary to the social standards of a community today. That sounds reasonable enough. One could use the Gallup poll to find out what the standards of a given community are. But let me remind you that in the heyday of the Inquisition there were villages in southern Germany in which every living female was burned as a witch. There are times, apparently, when the prevalent community standards can be judged by a small minority as absolutely wrong.

Those who engage in sex education of the mentally retarded must deal with the extraordinary inhibition regarding pictures of sex which has been inculcated in all of us and which is the cause of a great deal of anxiety about what kind of pictures should be shown to the people receiving sex education, and how explicit they should be. For example, should sex education material include pictures of sexual intercourse?

Most people who have not yet thought through this issue avoid dealing with it. When the SIECUS book on sex education[1] was in manuscript, it contained a set of line drawings showing positions of sexual intercourse. Even though it was difficult to figure out what the lines represented, the final verdict was not to publish the drawings since they portrayed the coital position. So in 1969 the book came out without them.

However, a great deal has been happening recently in the courts to lift taboos against the graven image of the sex organs. It is not clear at this stage whether society began to change first and then the commercial people providing the erotic materials began to follow, or whether something happened within the publishing trade that began to change society. It may be that history had reached a certain point at which changes began coming from both directions.

The fact is that some of the major dealers and distributors of pornography saw the chance for making money. Then, to their own surprise, they became civil rightists. The more they were harassed by the government, the more they decided people had the right to look at any pictures they wanted to see. So, with their lawyers, these dealers in pornography have served as a kind of vanguard for publishers in opening the way to illustrating material about sex. Gradually, as the publishers of pornography have tested each case in the courts, the respectable publishers of medical books have gained the freedom to present the kind of illustrations in their books that they formerly avoided.

From this standpoint, the existence of pornography has been helpful to sex educators. It can also be helpful in providing a direct confrontation with sex. Viewing of pornographic pictures requires a person not only to think about the whole issue of pornography in our society, but also about the possible value of pictures of sex in our professional activities.

Of course, pornography as it has been tested in the courts includes written pornography as well as pictorial pornography. However, by far the majority of the cases have involved picture books of sex, a fact which led to my theory that our major inhibition against sex has to do with the graven image rather than with the written narrative.

Nature's Own Pornography

In what I call nature's own pornography shows, I refer particularly to the sexual imagery spontaneously presented to a boy in wet dreams and masturbation fantasies as he develops into adolescence and manhood. There is an important difference between the sexes in this regard. I have run into very few examples of adolescent girls, either in my work in sex education or any-where in the professional literature, who have reported experiencing spontaneous images equivalent to the vivid, natural visual erotica that boys experience in adolescence. The Kinsey studies indicated that women are more likely to have vivid sexual imagery in their dreams rather later in life.[2] The visual image in the male seems to be an important part of nature's plan with regard to sexual arousal, for in human beings the initiation of sexual arousal from a distance is through the eyes. In many other species the sexual attraction of the male toward the female is through the nose by way of the sense of smell stimulated by a pheromone, an odoriferous substance secreted by the female.

Recently, Michael and his colleagues in London showed that there is a chemical substance released in the vagina of the female rhesus monkey at the time of ovulation and that this substance acts as a pheromone, attracting the male.[3] We still do not have information to indicate whether or not pheromones play a part in sexual arousal in the human species. Even if they do, the fact remains that boys and men are girl-watchers in a very different way than girls and women are boy-watchers. The woman, while not unresponsive to the visual erotic image, depends more on tactile stimulation for sexual arousal. Men are also responsive to tactile stimulation.

Although some writers on the subject used to say that women are not sexually aroused by visual images at all, the more recent studies of reactions to slides and movies of a sexual scene indicate that women are aroused to some extent by pictures. Even so, there are differences between the reactions of men and women to such material.

For example, if a man is sexually aroused by seeing a movie of sexual intercourse, he will probably mentally take the female in the picture down from the screen to become the object of his own sexual expression.

However, if a woman is aroused by the same movie, she is more likely to project herself up onto the screen into the position of the woman in the picture, experiencing in her fantasy something of the same type of experience that the woman in the picture is having. She may even take home a few pointers on how to improve her own sexual behavior next time she is in a sexual relationship with her chosen partner.

The foregoing example illustrates that a very different psychological mechanism is at work in the reaction of the sexes to the same stimulus. Further exploration of differences in male and female responses to erotic pictures may help us to understand more about sex differences, including differences in the reactions of women and men on juries in sex cases.

The Source of Taboos

Why does our society have such strong taboos against erotic pictures? A good deal of the answer to that question is lost in history. But I can make one or two guesses. Let me give the background to my guessing.

Having lived with the Aborigines in Arnhem Land on the north coast of Australia, I have learned that these people do not have strict taboos around sex. In fact, if young children play coital thrusting movements together as they are going to sleep around the campfire—a rare occurrence—the reaction of the older people who see it is to think that it is cute, to laugh, and then to pay no more attention to it.

The great taboo among these Aborigines is against the use of the vocal organs, not the sexual organs. There are certain people in their clan relationships whom a person is not allowed to speak to.

For example, a boy cannot speak to any woman or girl who could eventually bear a child who would be marriageable to him (nor could the woman speak to him). Likewise, a girl cannot speak to any woman who could become her mother-in-law. A mother-in-law, in this totemic sense of relationships, is a person whom one must respect. And the respect is so important that one must never look at her and never talk to her. All communication with her must be through an intermediary.

There are many other major taboos around the world, for example, food taboos and taboos relating to how one deals with the dead. In general, however, a society gives only one major taboo a prominent place in its culture. If the society has another taboo, it usually plays only a minor role in the culture.

What is the function, then, of the major taboo? I think one might justly speculate that in prehistoric times the rulers of growing cities and towns decided that they could control their subjects more effectively if they made them feel guilty about something when they were little children. If you instill a sense of guilt into your children about one of the ordinary functions of the human body, then you have a weapon, guilt, which you can forever use over them.

The Importance of Nonjudgmentalism

Everyone who is working in the field of sex education has to go through a special developmental process of his own to achieve an ability to be nonjudgmental about the sexual behavior of other people. It is the same type of nonjudgmental attitude that a medical specialist in venereal disease must achieve. The physician may have very firm standards of his own about taking the risk of contracting venereal disease, but he does not pass judgment on the patient in his clinic even though the patient has contracted the disease for the third or fourth time. He simply gives the necessary treatment.

I am not recommending indiscriminate sexual behavior to anyone. Everybody has to develop his own standards about appropriate sexual behavior. The mentally retarded also have to develop their own moral standards, and we have to help them do so. But in order to help we have to be capable of professional nonjudgmentalism so that we do not seal off any possibility of communication with those we are trying to help. If we do have a judgmental attitude, we will not be able to conceal it and those we are trying to help will not feel free enough to be able to accept any of our help.

For example, anyone at Rosewood, the Maryland institution I referred to earlier, who had strong moral objections to homosexuality could not deal with the people locked up in sex-segregated cottages for whom the only possible relationships of tenderness and affection must be of a homosexual nature.

Only if one can be completely nonjudgmental about sex can one think clearly about the wisdom and possibility of making proper arrangements for conjugal living where mentally retarded members of the two sexes can become true partners.

An effective educational experience in achieving nonjudgmentalism is the experience of frankly examining visual and narrative erotic publications and sexual movies. Every person seriously concerned with sex education and the mentally retarded owes it to himself or herself to have this frank experience. Only with such frankness can one's talk about sex education avoid being talk exclusively about reproduction and sexual hygiene, and become also honest talk about love, the human relationship, and the joy of having sex together.

(To illustrate his points Dr. Money showed 115 slides depicting sexual representations from pre-Columbian Peru to contemporary Denmark, and a brief movie of heterosexual love and coitus.—Eds.)

REFERENCES

1. BRODERICK, G. B. & BERNARD, J. (Eds.): *The Individual, Sex and Society.* Baltimore, The Johns Hopkins Press, 1969, 406 pp.
2. KINSEY, A. C., POMEROY, W. B., MARTIN, C. E., & GEBHARD, P. H. (Eds.): *Sexual Behavior in the Human Female.* Philadelphia, W. B. Saunders Company, 1953, 842 pp.
3. MICHAEL, R. P., KEVERNE, E. B., & BONSALL, R. W.: Pheromones: Isolation of male sex attractants from a female primate. *Science*, 172:964-966, 1971.

PSYCHOSOCIAL DEVELOPMENT
AND
SEX EDUCATION
(Session One)

1

The Psychosexual Development
of the Retarded

MURRY MORGENSTERN
New York Medical College

WHO TODAY WOULD TAKE exception to Wordsworth's lines, "The child is father of the man"? Yet, it is not so long ago that few people believed that any child, normal or retarded, had an early or present sex life. Before Freud, no mention was ever made of or thought given to the young child's developing sexual feelings. Whatever ideas children entertained about sex were trapped under layers of voluminous petticoats and stiff breeches, until suddenly, by some mysterious mechanism, these insentient young things reached pubescence or adolescence and became young men and women with new feelings about sex and new sexual powers. In all these magical proceedings, little thought was given to the process of sexual growth in either the normal or retarded child. In fact, the retarded child was either very carefully hidden at home or shunted off to an institution, a forgotten member of the family, neither mentioned, recognized, nor considered. He or she was a familial disgrace, condemned to concealment and oblivion.

Before the turn of the century, scientists in our country were interested in changing sexual feelings, but in adolescence only. G. Stanley Hall in the early 20th century introduced the subject of sexuality in adolescence into the professional literature but made no mention of earlier psychosexual development.[1] Of course, pubescence or adolescence had always been of great interest to societies. It was ceremoniously heralded by song, dance, and ritual in many countries and cultures, as though, like Rabelais' Gargantua, it came to life fully grown without an antecedent history. In this country, puberty seemed to emerge as a sudden spectacular event, proclaiming the child's discard of youthful toys, games and clothes and the abrupt assumption of adult responsibilities and sexuality.

That the march toward sexuality in childhood was overlooked seems particularly strange as scientists in this country and elsewhere were always looking for cause and effect and other relationships. One only has to remember phrenology, the study of head bumps, and its supposed relationship to character, Jung's personality types, Berman's assumptions about glandular secretions, personality, character and sexuality to see the oddities in scientific thinking. Berman, an endocrinologist who made many controversial statements, maintained that the rise and fall of Napoleon's pituitary duplicated the rise and fall of his political and military history.[2]

It was Freud, of course, who aligned childhood with a natural psychosexual development that takes place throughout life from the moment of birth to death. He postulated that the roots of pubertal sexuality reside in the newborn infant. But by sexuality Freud did not mean the orgiastic revelries imagined by our Victorian ancestors. To him sexuality meant the growth of love for self and for others and the development of energies destined eventually for adult sexual activity, as well as for overall wholesome and fruitful productivity.[3]

Freud gathered his knowledge from his neurotic adult patients, but he never maintained that sexuality is a sudden eruption of sexual feelings that come at a scheduled time of life. On the contrary, he underlined the continuity in sexual development from infancy to adulthood. He pointed out that sexual attraction and feelings flourish in all children from birth on, just as muscles, bones, vision, and language ability grow, blossom and bloom.

Though Freud's theory of sexuality may not be accepted in its entirety today, it is impressive for its description of human devel-

opment through psychosexual stages, and for its inclusive terminology. Freudian nomenclature has been accepted by psychiatrists,
psychoanalysts, sociologists, cultural anthropologists, and other behavioral scientists.

Freudian concepts do not apply exclusively to one class, race,
or ethnic group. On the contrary, they bring the young of the
whole world under the common growth pattern composed of
psychosexual developmental stages, each with individual characteristics, leading eventually to adult sexuality. In short, according
to Freudian psychology, each boy or girl goes through a series of
five psychosexual stages from infancy to sexual maturity: the oral,
the anal, the phallic, the latency, and the genital stages. This
developmental schedule is everyone's heritage, be he normal,
exceptional, handicapped, or retarded.

Within broad limits, the retardate's development follows the
same schedule as the normal person's, except that the retarded
child requires more time to advance from one stage to another,
and because of his deficits and smaller store of capacities, has less
tolerance for stress, more readily accessible masses of anxiety,
weaker ego strength and far poorer relationships to people and
objects. The retarded child may never be as completely attuned
to people, as responsive to the environment, or as capable of love
as the normal child, but this may be as much the result of his
living experiences and overall deficits as of developmental omis-
sions. There may be many developmental gaps which prevent
some areas from ever reaching the usual degree of maturation, but
the retardate's irregularities in development are not capricious
vagaries of chance or the result of individual differences. On the
physical level, interference with the retardate's growth and development is attributable to chromosomal anomalies, inborn errors
of metabolism, genetic aberrations, cortical insults, and the like.
On the psychological level, interference with development is attributable to insufficient ego, indifference to environment, environmental deprivation, inability to shift thinking, and lack of
discrimination of self.

In the beginning of life, the infant, retarded or normal, has to learn about forces in the outer world that are beyond his control. The newborn child is preoccupied with his own immediate needs. His emotional attention is riveted on feeding, evacuation, sleep, and avoidance of pain. The longer the hours of sleep, the better the quality of food, the surer the elimination of discomfort, the more satisfied the baby, especially if the ministrations to his comfort by his mother or other external figure are accompanied by pleasurable touch and tenderness. This external figure, the baby originally sees as part of himself. Sullivan believed that the child under a year old is only vaguely conscious of time, place, and people.[4]

In addition to sensuously enjoying touch experiences, the baby learns gradually to love and to realize he is something apart from his mother. He experiences both tension and relaxation. Recognition of the world outside himself comes when his needs are not self-gratified and an external agent, whether mother or nurse, allows a lapse of time before gratifying them. In the course of this long maturational process, the young child begins to realize that neither he nor the external agent can control all his whims and desires. Acceptance of this strengthens the normal ego. For the retardate, slower than the normal child in motor, mental, and social development, it is undoubtedly harder to forego ideas of infantile omnipotence and ideas of unilateral self-containment.

The retardate's ego is too weak to learn to withstand the need pressures, to recognize infantile vulnerability or lack of omnipotence, and to adjust to the pressures of outside reality. His fragile ego and the perilous developmental state leave him feeling vulnerable and frustrated and may impede the development of a mutually trusting relationship between himself and the mothering adult. Slowness in ego development and in other developmental processes usually results in deviancy in the child's involvement with things and people and limitations on his ability to manipulate, to explore, to learn, and to love.[5]

Object indifference may result from the child's failure to learn to assess himself properly in his environment or to allow the existence of objects other than himself. Only he exists. He fails to grasp the idea that his mother is not an extension of himself or that the care she provides is not an attribute of himself. Retardates who thus fail to respond to the environment tend to remain unattached to things and to people and to remain uncommunicative. They tend to be loners or unattached wanderers who dart and flit around without meaning or goals, aimless, undirected, rudderless.

On the other hand, some retardates desperately hang onto objects for protection. For them the object remains the protector long after the normal child has given up his need to carry a favorite blanket or a teddy bear as a talisman. The retardates who need toys or other objects as talismans are unaware of their dependency and cannot differentiate between the objects' functional use and their personal need for something to hold on to, preferably something rather than someone. Any object that catches their interest becomes emotionally invested and animated.

Crises in ego development can occur at any developmental stage and at any time in the child's life. Every change, every new maturational stage, involves an expenditure of energy and of ego strength and ego control for new learning. During early life, the retardate, like the normal child, must learn to recognize his own individuality, to accept the outer world, and his own vulnerability, and to understand the meaning of gratification delay. As he grows older, he must acquire motor skills and perceptual abilities in order to master some activities necessary for independent living. But the limitations on the retardate's capabilities prolong his dependence and add to his problem in making an emotional separation from his parents. His early experiences in connection with his daily care and training color his future view of the world and make him see it as a threatening place or as his special oyster. More frequently the former view prevails because of the deprivation and frustration arising from his deficits.

The period of latency brings other traumatic experiences that tend to weaken the retarded child's ego and bring a loss of self respect. During this developmental period the child has to find his place not only at home but also in school and in the community. He has to learn new concepts, acquire proficiency in skills that may be beyond his capacity, listen to new ideas, and witness, or be used for, various kinds of sexual investigation. Sexual drives in this period are relatively quiescent, but interest in the opposite sex, particularly during the later years, slowly begins to rise. The retarded child, however, has far less opportunity than the normal child to go to mixed parties, to begin dating, or to engage in telephone conversations with his peers.

Latency is the period when the normal child's knowledge of sex is formed by graffiti, misinformation passed on by older siblings, whispered pornography, and street talk. It is the time of parental scrutiny, accompanied by scoldings, punishment and recriminations for unacceptable language and behavior, especially for masturbation. During this stage, the retarded child, like the normal child, watches the young girl flip her miniskirt or listens to the 12-year-old newspaper boy try out his wolf whistle. The worldly-wise newspaper boy may even companionably wink at a peer who is also touched by the sight of the little girl as she tries out her newly developed provocative walk. If the retarded child is beginning to feel a quickened heartbeat as he watches a girl go through her attention-getting paces, he may have no one with whom he may share his feelings or who will watch his feigned indifference. He is far less likely than the normal boy to belong to any teams or clubs, or have friends his age in his neighborhood. Usually he has little freedom for even gazing at street sights since his parents may not allow him to spend his leisure time in unsupervised street play. Should he be daring enough to try some adventuresome sexual play in a school cloakroom or in some other secluded spot, he is more likely than the normal child to be severely punished or guarded forever after.

An 11-year-old mongoloid boy who was discovered in sexual play with another boy in the school toilet room provides a case in point. The school principal demanded immediate action from the father—transfer, institutionalization or punishment. The boy, apparently initiated to sex by older boys, denied having similar experiences with girls, but admitted that he enjoyed this experience with other boys and willingly participated when such sexual release was demanded of him in the school toilet rooms. He was severely punished by the father, who became even more irate later when he discovered his son masturbating.

Anecdotal material, observations, and parental interviews, as well as data from the Kinsey studies,[6] show that from nursery school age on normal boys tend to be sexually curious, exhibitionistic and voyeuristic. Nearly all begin to masturbate at an early age and to find innumerable situations to meet their masturbatory needs, from tight clothes to wrestling. Yet sexual behavior of this sort is generally regarded with more alarm when indulged in by the retardate.

During adolescence, the developmental task for the retardate, much like that of the normal young person, is to strengthen his sense of identity, to assume his sex role, and to achieve a measure of independence. During this period, the parents of the retardate are often thrown into crisis. They tend to feel overwhelmed by the manifestations of their child's physical and sexual growth and also by his failure to give up his dependency as a result of his problems in adaptation and social contact. Sometimes parents urge their retarded son or daughter to grow up, as though maturity could arrive on demand. Yet at the same time they prolong the retardate's need to be dependent through actions based on conflicts in their feelings about him and worry about his ability to get along in the future when they are gone or too old to care for him.[7]

In adolescence, the retardate himself begins to fight for identification with his normal peers. He wants to dress, look, and sound like the others; he wants to incorporate what he sees and hears on television about the young into his own life; he wants to date, to go to parties, to be like the boy or girl next door. To maintain the illusion of being like others, the retardate begins to brag about his dates and romances, even though he has none.

It is well known that the retardate too often sees himself as a clumsy, awkward person who cannot compete with his peers in large muscle motor activities like running or jumping, or in ordinary motor activities like cutting or wrapping. Yet his school teachers and parents tend to concentrate on his need to do well in such activities to prepare for future roles. How does the retardate feel about specific roles? Does he assign specific skills to either of the sexes? Which role would he prefer for himself if he could divorce his thinking from stereotypes?

More and more people who work with the retarded have become concerned about the adolescent retardate's attitudes about himself as a person, how he sees himself as a boy or girl, man or woman, and whether his acceptance of self or lack of self-acceptance derives from his training or his defense mechanisms. Some of my own studies throw some light on some of these issues.

To arrive at some clarification of role perception among young retardates, we devised a questionnaire to be presented to a group of young retarded persons as a game called "Who Does That?" The questions pertained to specific types of activities customarily considered part of a sex role, such as cooking, repairing furniture, washing clothes, or fixing the toilet. The replies to these questions —whether "father" or "mother" or "brother" or "sister"—would indicate the subjects' knowledge and perception of sex role patterns in the culture.

Over 300 subjects from the ages of 7 to 20 with intelligence quotients between 50 and 83 were interviewed with this questionnaire.[8] In contrast to their normal peers, the younger retardates—those below 10 years of age—tended to choose the female, or the mother figure, for most activities. However, the closer the older retardate came to his normal peer in overall functioning, the higher was his percentage of sex role recognition. The questions were repeated 2 years later to many of the same subjects in the original study, as well as to new participants. The later results followed the same pattern of preference by age. That is, the younger the child, the more likely he was to assign all types of functioning to the mother regardless of the activity involved. The older retardates tended to discriminate roles more thoughtfully, but on the whole could not move away from the female role entirely; as many put the female in the leading role as differentiated between the sexes. On the other hand, 90 percent of the normal subjects of similar cultural background and age clearly differentiated the customary sex roles. Despite changing societal values and the recent tendency to fuse male and female roles in our culture, the average normal child in this sample still separated functions according to old cultural patterns.

For broader understanding, the questions were then combined in this way: "What would you rather do, cook supper or paint the house?" Again, the younger the child, the greater the need to choose work that would keep him close to the mother. Preference for feminine roles was high among the boys 10 years of age or younger and, more understandably, in the girls in the same age group.

In general, the older retarded boys were more selective in sex roles and indicated preference for those associated with males and considered more prestigious.

The identification with female work or the female role by most of the young and some of the older retarded boys suggests the retardates' dependency needs and their wish to stay close to the familiar. Retarded girls, less inclined than normal girls to be competitive with boys, have no compelling need to emulate boys. They are satisfied to keep their roots planted in the family soil.

When we examined responses of the retarded subjects who were between the ages of 13 and 16, we found that their sex role preference followed the pattern of the normal subjects who were *below* 13 years of age. Similarly, the retarded subjects from *17 to 20 years* of age showed sex role preferences like those of the normal subjects *below* 17 years of age. These results reinforce the impression that the psychosexual development patterns of retardates often come at a later chronological age than they do for normal persons.

In another study we explored the identification figures of 500 children, retarded and normal, both to get an idea of their self-image and to see whether identification figures and role preferences corresponded.[9] The findings were obtained from children's drawings of human figures, male and female. The sex drawn first was considered to be the identification figure.

A brief overview of the findings shows that the number of retardates above 9 years of age who drew the same sex first is comparable to the number of normal children 6 to 8 years old who did so. Between 16 and 18 years of age the retardates came closer to the normal young person in same-sex identification. This suggests again that added time is necessary for retardates to achieve self-identification, as well as appropriate role preferences.

Apparently, once the normal boy has lived through the Oedipal situation and has adjusted to the family love story, he is able to move with greater speed to same-sex identification. The normal girl between the ages of 8 and 11 is more mature than the normal boy of the same age and even more closely identified with her own sex. The retarded boy or girl, however, requires a longer time to develop a personal identity and to establish sex roles.

In the drawings of the younger retardates it is often very difficult to recognize any sex differences between the male and the female other than hair. Their drawings tend to be impoverished, shrunken in size, and lacking in limbs. The retarded boy, who tends to be less involved with his father than the normal boy, has no strong concrete male figure to emulate and so has to identify with stereotyped figures like the policeman, the fantasy Martian, or the protective mother.

The retarded girl, more at ease in her passive, dependent role, is encouraged to emulate her mother and to be the helper or little mother, but her drawings, too, are weak, impoverished, and poorly coordinated.

To get some additional information about the role emotional attitudes play in personal contact, we gave the Family Relations Test to 300 of the original group.[10] This is a simple test that is neither analytically deep nor statistically complicated. The emotional attitudes the test elicits include strong feelings of love and hate and milder feelings of like and dislike. It also taps feelings toward oneself and sexualized feelings related to close physical contact and manipulation.

The test material consists of a number of cardboard figures of various sizes representing members of the child's family. The most novel figure is NOBODY, whose features and characteristics apply to no one in the family. A series of statements that purport to reveal emotional attitudes are read to the child, who chooses the one he considers to reflect his feelings.

The statement may say: "This is the person in the family whom mother likes best," or "I like to be kissed by this person." The statement is written on a little card given to the child, and he places the card in a slot behind the figure he has designated to represent a particular family member.

Thus the test differentiates between outgoing feelings that originate with the child and include some other family member, and incoming feelings that make the child the recipient of someone else's feelings.

On the whole, children in the normal group indicated the existence of sexualized feelings toward and from family members— mother, father, siblings and others, in that order. These findings suggest that the normal children are closely related to their sexualized feelings and respond to others as they believe others respond to them.

In contrast, in the retarded group, the mother came last as a recipient of sexualized feelings: 47 percent indicated that sexualized feelings were directed toward the NOBODY figure; 25 percent toward siblings; and only 5 percent toward the mother. The remaining 23 percent were distributed between the father and other family members.

The retarded apparently are unable to express sexualized feelings, possibly because they do not see themselves as recipients of symbolic and concrete affection. Perhaps their inability to extend themselves and to feel like integral parts of their families keeps them from forming personal relationships. Denial and repression may be the mechanisms that retardates have to employ to avoid facing their own painful feelings.

Counselors who had examined the parent-child relationships in interviews with the parents described mothers in many of the cases as rejecting or indifferent.

Other results of this test were also revealing. Those older retardates who showed few inhibitions about their sexualized feelings toward the mother or other family members were generally more responsive to other people than the other retardates. They often volunteered information about social engagements and participation in group activities. They expressed interest in dating and marriage. Their parents and counselors more often characterized them as curious about sex and aware of themselves as people and as males or females.

For example, a 23-year-old girl, after talking about her hope that she would marry, said:

"Sometimes I'm like her," pointing to the figure representing a younger sibling, "and sometimes I'm like my aunt," pointing to another figure. "Is it because I'm still a baby, like my mother says?" Apparently, this young woman was aware of conflict between the childlike and the more mature interests within herself.

In this group of older retardates, discussions about sex and marriage often revealed a naive, innocent and natural approach. Interest in sex was not expressed in terms of intercourse, especially among the more retarded persons in the group. Though they did not seem genitally oriented, they did have boyfriends and girlfriends with whom they sought physical contact by hugging and kissing. These young people tended to see a boyfriend or a girlfriend as a companion—someone who buys you things, someone who is yours and gives you the same kind of status enjoyed by your normal siblings and peers, and especially someone to care for and be loved by.

The psychosexual development that takes place from birth to adulthood is the ripening process that gives shape, meaning and verve to sexuality and to sex. It is part of the drama of life experienced by everyone, including the retarded. What then differentiates the retardates from their normal contemporaries, from the young secretary and salesman locked in fond embrace on a park bench? Is the difference to be judged by a job or by the loving features of an imitation Rodin?

The mildly retarded young person who is on the threshold of adulthood is likely also to be groping for self-expression, but he tends to be more literal minded, poorly aware of his own identity, more evasive or more given to denying his limitations, less in touch with his own peers, and poorer in ego strength and control than his normal peers.

Would his picture be more alive and buoyant if he were given the same opportunities that normal young people have to experiment socially, vocationally, educationally, and sexually? Would such opportunities bring him closer to the average functioning individual?

Before reaching conclusions about the sexual behavior of retardates, perhaps we should pay more attention to their need to have wider opportunities, to form relationships, to date, to become engaged, to marry, and, if desired, to enjoy homosexual experiences. Perhaps, too, we need to understand better the meaning of love, to distinguish between romantic love, sex, and marriage, to identify the necessary components of each kind of sexual relationship. Does the relationship include cognitive facilities, measurable indices of demonstrable sexualized feelings, passionate physical drives and responses, emotional acceptance of an enduring friendly relationship between two people, or a combination of these elements?

Society's changing sexual mores and the demands of young people for greater freedom to make their own decisions may lead to other problems among the retarded. Perhaps, in demanding new solutions, the future will bring greater consideration for the retarded as potential workers, citizens, parents and lovers.

REFERENCES

1. HALL, G. S.: *Adolescence.* New York, Appleton, 1909, Vol. 1.
2. BERMAN, L.: *The Glands Regulating Personality* (Rev. ed.). New York, Macmillan Co., 1928.
3. FREUD, S.: *The Basic Writings of Sigmund Freud.* New York, Modern Library, 1938, 1001 pp.

4. SULLIVAN, H. S.: *Interpersonal Theory of Psychiatry*. New York, Norton & Co., 1953, 393 pp.
5. HUTT, M. & GIBBY, R.: *Mentally Retarded Child: Development, Education and Guidance*. Boston, Allyn & Bacon, 1958.
6. KINSEY, A., POMEROY, W., & MARTIN, C.: *Sexual Behavior in the Human Male*. Philadelphia, W. B. Saunders Co., 1948, 804 pp.
7. MORGENSTERN, M.: Sex Education for the Retarded. *PCMR/Message 21*, Aug. 1969.
8. MORGENSTERN, M.: Unpublished data.
9. MORGENSTERN, M.: Unpublished data.
10. BENE, E. & ANTHONY, J.: *Manual for Family Relations Test*. London, National Foundation for Educ. Research in England and Wales, 1957.

2

Sexual Behavior of the Mentally Retarded

PAUL H. GEBHARD
*Institute for Sex Research
Indiana University*

WHEN PLANS FOR THIS CONFERENCE were being discussed, I recalled that in the course of interviewing subjects for various research projects the Institute for Sex Research had accumulated a number of case histories of persons whose intelligence was substantially below average. This recollection prompted me to volunteer to review the accumulated data and present a paper on the sexual behavior of the mentally retarded. Subsequently, when I began to comprehend the nature of the data, I regretted my offer.

The first step was to cull from the Institute's files the case histories of persons who were clearly retarded and whose retardation had been measured by some IQ test. The decision to use data only from persons for whom IQ test scores existed immediately reduced the potential sample to persons who were institutionalized when interviewed. From these, only persons with an IQ of 70 or under were selected for study. Persons whose IQ was 70 or under at the time of the interview, but who had previously had a higher IQ score, were excluded. In brief, the sample consisted of persons who had always been retarded.

The sample consisted of 84 white males. Forty-six had IQ scores between 61 and 70; twenty-three between 51 and 60; thirteen between 41 and 50; and two between 31 and 40. Only three of these people had more than grammar school education: two had attained the ninth grade and one the twelfth. The majority had not completed grammar school; their formal education ended between the fourth and seventh grades.

All the persons in the sample had reached or passed puberty. One-quarter were between 11 and 15 in age, another quarter between 16 and 20, and nearly a quarter between 21 and 30. The remainder consisted chiefly of persons in their thirties and forties (see Table 1).

The sample derived primarily from penal institutions. Nineteen retardates were interviewed in California prisons, another 19 in an Indiana prison, and 18 in an Ohio facility for juveniles. Twenty-six others, most of them in their teens and early twenties, were interviewed in a Michigan institution for the mentally retarded. One person was interviewed in a Maryland prison and one other was in an Indiana high school.

Since the time spent in institutions was an obvious variable, I calculated the percentage of postpubertal life these persons had spent in institutions. The results showed a bimodal distribution: 35 persons had spent 0 to 10 percent and 20 had spent all or nearly all (91 percent or more) of their postpubertal lives in institutions. The remaining cases were scattered between these two extremes.

Clearly, the sample is both fortuitous and biased. At best it could be said largely to represent a group of the mentally retarded whose behavior was sufficiently irresponsible or criminal to result in incarceration. However, the aim of this presentation is not to offer an adequate sample of some defined larger population. The aim is to salvage some case-history data on the sexual behavior of some mentally retarded persons and to compare these data with the data on a group of normal men of lower socioeconomic status in the hope that the findings will provide useful ideas for designing future research on the sexuality of the retarded.

The comparison group consisted of 477 white males of grammar school or high school education who had never been convicted of a crime, imprisoned, or sent to a mental institution. This group

TABLE 1

SAMPLE DESCRIPTION

Item	Cases	Percent
Age		
11-15	21	25
16-20	21	25
21-25	14	17
26-30	6	7
31-35	9	11
36-40	3	4
41 plus	10	12
IQ		
61-70	46	55
51-60	23	27
41-50	13	15
31-40	2	2
Percent of post-pubertal life in institution		
0-10	35	42
11-30	8	10
31-50	7	8
51-70	10	12
71-90	4	5
91-100	20	24
Source		
Institution for retarded	26	31
Juvenile facility	18	21
California prisons	19	23
Indiana prison	19	23
Miscellaneous	2	2
Ever-married	21	25

is the control group used in the Institute's volume, *Sex Offenders: An Analysis of Types.*[1]

Prepubertal Sexual Activity

The average (mean) age at which the retardates reached puberty was 13.3 years. This is younger than the age for white males of all educational levels (13.6)[2] and younger than the males of the control group (13.8). This precocity, if it is actual and not merely an artifact of imprecise recollection, is curious.

Two-fifths of the retardates had engaged in prepubertal heterosexual play, a proportion well below the 52 percent of the control group. The retardates involved had begun such play at an average age of 8.3 years. The play consisted of touching genitalia in 71 percent of the cases, vaginal insertion of finger or object in 41 percent, mouth-genital contact in 6 percent, and coitus or attempted coitus in 65 percent. In the group among the controls who had engaged in prepubertal sexual play, the proportions were similar for touching genitalia (72 percent) and mouth-genital contact (4 percent), but lower for actual or attempted coitus (38 percent).

About the only interpretation one may make from these findings is that retardation seemingly has no pronounced effect on prepubertal heterosexual play except that it may increase attempts at coitus among those who engage in such play.

Prepubertal homosexual play presents a different picture. The incidence was higher in the retarded group: 50 percent reported homosexual play as opposed to 41 percent in the control group. Similarly, the incidence of touching genitalia was higher in the retarded group (81 percent of those who engaged in homosexual play versus 67 percent in the control group) as was the incidence of mouth-genital contact (26 percent vs. 14 percent) and anal coitus (29 percent vs. 22 percent). In brief, relatively more of the retardates than controls had engaged in homosexual play before puberty and in doing so more had employed manual, oral, and anal techniques. The greater prevalence of prepubertal homosexual play among the retarded was probably the result of early institutionalization.

On the whole, these retardates did not seem to have been sexually exploited by adults in childhood. Only three (or 3.6 percent) had had sexual contact with an adult male before puberty, a proportion almost identical with that in the control group (3.7 percent). Three retardates, including the one who had had contact with a male, had had sexual contact before puberty with an adult female, as compared with 2.2 percent in the control group.

Forty-eight percent of the retardates reported having engaged in prepubertal masturbation, as compared with 33 percent of the control group. The difference may in some obscure way be linked with the retardates' greater tendency to homosexuality. The Institute's volume on sex offenders notes that prepubertal masturbation was more common among homosexual than heterosexual offenders.

Masturbation

Masturbation after puberty is such a universal experience for males that an "ever-never" comparison is meaningless. Among the retardates, 94 percent reported the experience; the controls reported 93 percent.

However, substantial differences showed up between the two groups in the incidence of masturbation among the never-married at various age-periods (see Table 2). For example, between puberty and age 15, 93 percent of the never-married retardates had masturbated, but only 81 percent of the never-married controls had done so; between the ages of 16 and 20, 92 percent of retardates had masturbated as compared with 86 percent of the controls. Between ages 21 and 25, 90 percent of the retardates and 69 percent of the controls had masturbated. In older age-periods after 21-25, the differences lessen but the mentally retarded continue to present the higher incidences. For example, in age-period 31 to 35, four-fifths of the unmarried retardates were masturbating compared to only about two-thirds of the controls.

The average (median) frequencies of masturbation for the never-married retardates ranged from once a week to once every two weeks from puberty to age 25, frequencies definitely lower than those of the controls. The frequencies for the retarded in age-periods 26 to 30 and 31 to 35 are based on too small a number of individuals for an average to have meaning, particularly since the number includes three extreme cases.

TABLE 2

MASTURBATION AMONG NEVER-MARRIED MALES

N=number in total group who had reached or passed the designated age-period.

Item	Total	Pub-15	16-20	Age-periods 21-25	26-30	31-35
Incidence						
Retarded	94%	99% (N=80*)	92% (N=62)	90% (N=31)	79% (N=14)	88% (N=9)
Control	93%	81%	86%	69%	67%	67%
Frequency (median) per week						
Retarded		1.00	1.60	0.50		
Control		1.94	1.63	1.46		
Average (mean) age began						
Retarded	13.5 yrs.					
Control	14.0 yrs.					

Fantasy	None	Heterosexual	Homosexual
Retarded	21.5%	57.0%	24.0%
Control	10.8%	99.0%	8.0%

* Four individuals did not reach puberty until after age 15 and hence do not appear in the puberty-15 age-period.

Fifty-seven percent of the retardates who masturbated reported having heterosexual masturbatory fantasies, a much smaller proportion than the control group's 99 percent, a difference indicative of the greater homosexual orientation of the retarded group. The same explanation accounts for the fact that more of the retarded reported having homosexual fantasies: 24 percent as opposed to 8 percent of the control group. More retardates than controls reported masturbation without fantasy: 21 percent against 11 percent. This difference may reflect a lack of imaginative capacity in the retarded—a condition one would expect.

Orgasm in Sleep

Nearly three-fifths (58 percent) of the mentally retarded subjects had experienced orgasm in sleep—a low incidence even considering the relative youthfulness of the group. The retardates also began having such orgasms later than the controls, the average age at first experience being 17.1 for the retarded and 15.2 for the controls.

In any 5-year age-period, fewer of the unmarried retardates were experiencing orgasm in sleep than unmarried controls. For the retardates, the proportion having this experience from puberty to age 15 was 34 percent; from age 16 to 35 it was 57 to 68 percent; and for ages 35 to the mid-forties, it was 75 percent, but this last figure may be meaningless because of the small size of the sample. In any case, all the percentages for the retarded are from 7 to 21 percentage points lower than those for the controls. Clearly, incarceration and isolation from heterosexual activity did not produce a compensatory high incidence of orgasm in sleep.

The frequencies of orgasm in sleep are also uniformly less among the retardates than among the controls. For the retarded, they were once a month to once every three weeks during the ages of 16 to 45. The equivalent figures for the controls were once in three weeks to once in two weeks.

Thus, mental retardation seems to correlate with a low incidence of orgasm in sleep, a later age at first experience of the phenomenon, and lower frequencies.

The nature of the dreams that generally accompanied orgasm in sleep differed in the two groups only in relation to homosexuality. Only 9 percent of the control group had homosexual dreams resulting in orgasm; 22 percent of the retardates had such dreams. Again, this difference is probably a consequence of the homosexuality engendered by institutionalization.

Premarital Petting

Premarital petting, roughly defined as anything short of coitus but more than a formal goodnight kiss, had been almost universally experienced in the control group, 95 percent having engaged in it (see Table 3). Only 77 percent of the retarded had had this kind of experience. This difference is primarily the result of institutionalization, as the following figures demonstrate. Among the retardates between puberty and age 15 who had spent one-quarter or less of their postpubertal lives in institutions, 83 percent had had petting experience, but among retardates in the same age group who had spent over three-quarters of their lives in institutions, only 43 percent had had such experience. The figures for retardates aged 16 to 20 with equivalent institutional experiences are 100 percent and 45 percent, and for those aged 21 to 30, 100 percent and 50 percent.

The age of the retardates at their first petting experience ranged from 11 to 22, the average being 14.9, a figure not far from the average of 15.3 for the control group.

Figures on petting in specific age-periods clearly reveal the heterosexual handicap suffered by the retarded. While 91 to 94 percent of the unmarried members of the control group petted during the age-periods 16-20, 21-25, and 26-30, only 61 to 73 percent of the retardates did so. Later in life the proportion who were petting declined for both groups. However, in the age-period 36-40 nearly four-fifths of the unmarried persons in the control group were petting, compared to only two-fifths of the retarded. A breakdown of petting experience in the specific age-periods in relation to the proportion of the subject's life spent in

TABLE 3

PREMARITAL PETTING AND COITUS WITH COMPANIONS

N=number in total group who had reached or passed the designated age-period.

Item	Total	Pub-15	Age-periods 16-20	21-25	26-30	31-35
Petting						
Incidence						
Retarded	77%	65% (N=80*)	73% (N=62)	61% (N=31)	64% (N=14)	60% (N=10)
Control	95%	59%	91%	94%	94%	88%
Average (mean) age began						
Retarded	14.9 yrs.					
Control	15.3 yrs.					
Coitus						
Incidence						
Retarded	61%	41% (N=80)	61% (N=62)	36% (N=31)	43% (N=14)	50% (N=10)
Control	80% (by age 23)	27%	61%	73%	78%	67%
Frequency (median) per week						
Retarded		0.50	0.60	1.00		
Control		0.63	0.98	1.12		
Average (mean) age began coitus						
Retarded	14.3 yrs.					
Control	16.9 yrs.					
Average (median) number of coital partners						
Retarded	5.0					
Control	7.6					

* Four individuals did not reach puberty until after age 15 and hence do not appear in the puberty-15 age-period.

institutions again shows the deterring effect of institutionalization.

The number of female partners with whom petting occurred
also varies according to the degree of institutionalization.

Premarital Coitus

Among the retardates 61 percent had had premarital coitus with
companions, not counting coitus with prostitutes (see Table 3).
The incidence figures are profoundly influenced by age and degree of institutionalization. Of the retardates aged 15 and under
who had been institutionalized for less than 25 percent of their
lives, 58 percent had experienced coitus as compared with only
14 percent in the same age group who had been institutionalized
for 75 percent or more of their lives. The equivalent figures for
those in the 16 to 20 age group are 78 and 33 percent, and for
the 21 to 30 age group, 83 and 50 percent. In each age group the
incidence of premarital coitus for those who had spent less than
a quarter of their lives in institutions was close to the incidence
among the controls.

Those who did have premarital coitus began at a remarkably
early age, the average (mean) being 14.3 years—one year after
puberty, and almost three years earlier than the mean age for the
control group. This finding suggests either poor impulse control
or a failure to internalize social restraints. This interpretation is
strengthened by another finding showing a high incidence of
incest: of the 51 males who had had premarital coitus with companions, eight had had coitus with cousins, one with his sister,
and one with his mother.

The median frequencies of premarital coitus for retardates who
had had the experience were usually only moderately less than
the frequencies in the control group. Between puberty and age
15, the median frequency figure for retardates was 0.5 per week
while the frequency for the controls was 0.6. In the period between 16 and 20, the figures were 0.6 and 1.0, respectively, and
in the period between 21 and 25, 1.0 and 1.1.

The number of coital partners ranged widely. The median number for the retardates was 5, while for the control group it was 7.6. Slightly over one-quarter of the retardates had had premarital coital experience with only one or two companions.

One might assume inadequate contraception would be typical of the retardates. However, only seven men reported being responsible for premarital pregnancies—14 percent of those who had had premarital coitus with companions.

Coitus with Prostitutes

Among the retardates, 31 percent had had premarital coitus with prostitutes. While this figure is less than the 48 percent for the control group, one must recall that the retardate sample contains a larger proportion of young persons. In an analysis of the degree to which the retarded depended upon prostitutes for premarital coitus, a curious polarity came to light: the individuals either had little prostitute experience (one-third or less of their coitus) or a great deal (over one-half)—no one fell in an intermediate category. Forty percent of the retardates who had experience with prostitutes had had half or more of their premarital coitus with prostitutes. Four men had relied upon prostitutes exclusively. None of the four had married.

Of the 21 retardates who had been married at some time (designated as "ever-married" in the data), six (29 percent) had had coitus with a prostitute while still married. All of these men had also had premarital experience with prostitutes.

Sixteen of these 21 ever-married retardates had been widowed, separated, or divorced. Of these, 10 (63 percent) had had coitus with prostitutes after the termination of their marriages. Seven of these 10 had never had coitus with a prostitute prior to the termination of their marriages. Only three of the 10 had had half or more of their postmarital coitus with prostitutes, and all three of these persons had had no previous experience with prostitutes.

In brief, although a few individuals did rely heavily upon prostitution, we can say that prostitution was only moderately important in the lives of the retardates in the sample, and that they did not depend upon it to a greater degree than normal persons. Note that Kinsey found a far higher incidence of premarital coitus with prostitutes among the grade school and high school educated than is found in the retardates.[3]

Marital Coitus

Twenty-one men, or 25 percent of the sample, had married. Eleven had married once, nine twice, and one three times, making a total of 32 marriages. Of these marriages, only eight were intact at the time of interview. In other words, three-quarters of the marriages had terminated. Twenty marriages (63 percent) had ended in separation or divorce, and five (16 percent) in the death of the wife.

Ten of the 21 ever-married men had had children born of their marriages; the average number of children was 1.4. Only two men had had more than three offspring.

The median frequencies of marital coitus among the retardates and the control-group members are identical for two age-periods and not markedly dissimilar in the remaining three age-periods for which data exist. Considering the small size of the samples, the degree of similarity is rather surprising. Except for age-period 21-25 when the average was 3.5 times per week, figures for the retardates averaged about 2.5 times per week from age 16 to age 40. The average figures for the same age-periods in the control group begin at about 3.5 times per week and gradually decline to about twice a week. It seems safe to say that the frequency of marital coitus among these retardates was neither unusually high nor low.

Homosexual Activity

Owing in large part to institutionalization, the incidence of homosexual experience is markedly greater in the retarded group than in the control group: 57 percent in contrast to the control group's 34 percent (see Table 4). In the various age-periods

TABLE 4

HOMOSEXUAL ACTIVITY

N=number of total group who had reached or passed the designated age-period.

Item	Total	Pub-15	16-20	21-25	26-30	31-35
			Age-periods			
Incidence						
Retarded	57%	51% (N=80*)	46% (N=63)	38% (N=42)	23% (N=28)	23% (N=22)
Control	34%	22%	19%	13%	11%	12%
Frequency (median) per week						
Retarded		1.00	1.00	1.00	1.00	
Control		0.71	0.53	0.61	0.75	
Average (mean) age began						
Retarded	14.6 yrs.					
Control	14.7 yrs.					
Average (median) number of partners						
Retarded	6.0					
Control	3.4					

* Four individuals did not reach puberty until after age 15 and hence do not appear in the 'puberty-15 age-period.

the differences are greater still, the incidence among the retarded in each period (with one exception) being more than twice that in the control group. The differences would be even greater if the proportion of ever-married males in both groups had been equal. As it is, the incidence figures for the control group are based on never-married males. In the period from puberty to 15 years of age, 51 percent of the retardates had engaged in homosexual activity, but the incidence diminishes in successive age-periods to 23 percent in the age-period 31-35. The incidence in the control group similarly decreases with age, going from 22 percent in the younger age group to about 11 percent in the older.

An analysis of the incidence among the retardates by amount of institutionalization showed the expected trend. The influence of institutionalization toward homosexual activity increased with age. Among retardates between puberty and age 15 who had had little institutionalization, the incidence of homosexual activity is only slightly less than among those in the same age-range who had had extensive institutionalization: 67 percent versus 72 percent. Among those in the age-period 16 to 20, the difference is substantial: 45 percent versus 56 percent. None of the retardates between ages 21 and 30 who had little institutionalization were engaging in homosexual activity in that period, but each one with extensive institutionalization was doing so.

The median frequency of homosexual activity among the retardates who engaged in this practice was once a week for those in every age-period from puberty to 30—a remarkable consistency. The median frequency for the corresponding control groups varied from 0.5 to 0.7 per week. The range of individual variation was, of course, extensive. Among the retardates it ranged from once a year to once a day.

The retardates also tended to have homosexual experience with more partners. For those who had such experience the median number of partners was 6, while in the control group it was 3.4.

While the overt behavior of about 25 percent of the retardates was exclusively homosexual at the time of interview, only 4 percent of all said they were sexually attracted only to males. Despite

TABLE 5

EFFECTS OF INSTITUTIONALIZATION IN TERMS OF PERCENTAGE OF POSTPUBERTAL LIFE IN INSTITUTIONS

(Calculations not included for persons who spent 26 to 75 percent of postpubertal life in institutions.)

Age of Individual at Interview	N	Homosexual Activity	Ever-never Incidence Petting	Premarital Coitus	Frequency (mean) per week Premarital Coitus
Puberty to 15					
0-25% life institutional	12	67%	83%	58%	0.64
76-100% life institutional	7	72%	43%	14%	0.05
16 to 20					
0-25% life institutional	9	45%	100%	78%	2.51
76-100% life institutional	9	78%	45%	33%	0.95
21 to 30					
0-25% life institutional	6	17%	100%	83%	not calculated: range 1.0-15.0
76-100% life institutional	6	100%	50%	50%	not calculated: no frequency over 0.05

the influence of institutionalization, the retardates remained remarkably heterosexual in orientation, if not in behavior: only 10 percent of them were more interested in males than females. Even if one confines one's attention solely to retardates with homosexual experience, one finds that only about one-fifth preferred homosexual to heterosexual activity. Another indication of the heterosexuality of the retarded is the finding that over a third (37 percent) of those with homosexual experience had such experience only while living in institutions.

Animal Contact

Only nine of the 84 retardates had ever had sexual experience with animals (10.7 percent), a proportion less than the 14 percent for rural white males of grammar school education reported in the first Kinsey volume.[4] However, only three of these nine retarded men came from rural areas. The IQs among the nine ranged from 52 to 70. Six of them had had animal contact only once or twice, usually in adolescence. One man had had ten such experiences, and two men had had animal contact regularly up to age 20.

Response to Psychological Sexual Stimulation

All respondents were questioned about their response to thinking about women and girls, and seeing them clothed and nude. The respondents were also questioned about their reactions seeing clothed males, an erect penis, and pornographic pictures. The response categories noted were (1) greatly aroused, (2) moderately aroused, (3) slightly aroused, and (4) not aroused.

About one-third reported strong arousal from thinking of females (32 percent), seeing females (30 percent), and viewing pornography (33 percent) —essentially the same proportions as in the control group. However, there were great differences in the proportions reporting no arousal: 37 percent of the retardates said they recognized no arousal from thinking of females, 47 percent from seeing them, and 45 percent from viewing pornography. The proportions of the control group were much smaller: only 10 percent claimed little or no response to seeing or thinking of females, and 33 percent reported pornography had little or no effect. Strangely, the degree of retardation seems unrelated to the response to psychological stimulation: the responses of the 15 retardates with IQs of 50 or less were very similar to the responses of the whole group of retardates.

About all one can say is that the responses of the retarded tended to polarize between two extremes: they either reported strong arousal or none at all to the stimuli in question. In the control group, on the other hand, about two-fifths of all reported some intermediate strength of arousal. Perhaps some of the retardate's polarity in response is simply the result of a tendency in retarded persons to think in dichotomous terms rather than to cope with the more difficult concept of several levels of response.

Oddly enough, seeing a nude woman or girl was less sexually exciting to the retardates than seeing a clothed female or simply thinking of one. Only 23 percent of the retardates reported strong arousal from female nudity, and nearly two-thirds maintained they had no arousal at all.

Response to homosexual stimuli was limited. About three-quarters of the retardates reported no arousal in seeing other males; only 23 percent reported some degree of arousal. When we consider that nearly three-fifths of the retardates reported having some homosexual experience, the fact that only 23 percent reported arousal on seeing males confirms our feeling that much of their homosexual behavior stemmed from the institutional situation rather than from preference. Again the retardates displayed a polarity in their responses: they tended to report either strong arousal (15 percent) or no arousal at all (77 percent). Only a few individuals reported intermediate responses.

There were more reports of arousal in seeing an erect penis than in merely seeing another male, probably because empathy as well as homosexuality was involved. At any rate, 21 percent of the retardates reported strong arousal to this stimulus and 66 percent none at all.

Altogether, 13 retardates (nearly 16 percent of the sample) reported no arousal from any of the six types of stimuli. Their IQs ranged from 36 to 70, the average (mean) being 59.6. In other words, they were not much more retarded than the sample as a whole.

Only one person, a 17-year-old with an IQ of 36, was sexless—lacking response to any of the stimuli or experience of any overt sexual behavior. One other person, a 15-year-old with an IQ of 44, had had no overt sexual experiences but did report arousal from pornographic pictures. Another 15-year-old, with an IQ of 50, also responded only to pornography, and his only form of overt sexuality consisted of sexual dreams resulting in orgasm. These three persons were the most sexually retarded individuals in the sample.

Sexual Knowledge

Two persons, the 17-year-old with an IQ of 36 and a 15-year-old with an IQ of 49, lacked any sexual knowledge: they did not know of coitus or pregnancy. One other male, a 16-year-old with an IQ of 53, knew of coitus, but not pregnancy. All others had knowledge of both.

The median age at which retardates first learned about coitus was 10. Some learned about it as early as age 4. The most belated discovery was at age 17. Knowledge of pregnancy came slightly later, the median age being 11. A few did not know about pregnancy until they were in their later teens, and one maintained he was ignorant until he was in his twenties.

Generally, knowledge of female anatomy came later than knowledge about pregnancy. Indeed, one-quarter of the retardates had never seen the genitalia of a postpubescent female. The median age at which the retarded had seen female genitalia was 14, also the median age for first coitus and first petting.

Such sex information as the retardates possessed was derived almost exclusively from peers. When asked about the main source of their sex information, 92 percent named their friends and associates; only four listed their fathers and one, his mother. Teachers and clinicians were not mentioned.

Especially Retarded Group

In an attempt to clarify further the relationship between mental retardation and sexuality, I examined the data on the 15 persons having IQs of 50 or less. Of these, seven had been institutionalized all their postpubescent lives, two for between half and two-thirds of their lives, and the remaining six for 10 percent or less of their lives.

The responses of these people to thinking about females and to visual stimuli were, surprisingly enough, very like the responses of the retarded group as a whole. Such correspondence was a surprise, since the smallness of the sub-sample would be expected to produce some large differences.

There were a number of differences, however, in overt behavior. The incidence of masturbation was somewhat less among the especially retarded (80 percent in contrast to 94 percent in the group as a whole), but the incidence of orgasm in sleep was markedly greater (73 percent in contrast to 58 percent). As might be expected, heterosexual activity was rarer among the especially retarded: only 47 percent had been involved in petting (as opposed to 77 percent of all the retarded) and only 47 percent had had premarital coitus with companions (in contrast to 61 percent for the whole group)—a reflection of their institutionalization. Interestingly, of the eight who had coital experience (seven with companions and one with prostitutes only), seven had had coitus with prostitutes. This greater use of prostitutes, plus the relatively low incidence of petting and coitus, reflects the influence of retardation and institutionalization on heterosexual life.

In this low IQ group, the deprivation of heterosexual opportunities brought no compensatory increase in homosexuality. The incidence of homosexuality is very low: 33 percent as opposed to the 57 percent of the retarded group as a whole. Homosexuality occurred only among those who had been institutionalized all their lives.

Thus, it seems the especially retarded had less sexual activity than the group of retardates as a whole, except for orgasm in sleep, the one activity not requiring volition.

Summary

With half the sample having IQs between 60 and 70, and most of the remainder above 50, the group cannot be considered severely retarded. Consequently, one should not expect dramatic differences between the study sample and the control group. Moreover, intellectual capacity is less important in sexual expression than in most other areas of life. Even so, the data revealed significant differences between the sexual lives of institutionalized mentally retarded persons and of normally intelligent persons of comparable socioeconomic level.

The retardates had a higher incidence of prepubertal homosexual play and less of heterosexual play. The retardates also had a higher incidence of masturbation before puberty.

After puberty the retardates of every age group had a higher incidence of masturbation in every age-period, but the frequency of masturbation was lower than in the control group. More of the retardates had homosexual masturbatory fantasy, fewer had heterosexual fantasy, and more did not employ fantasy at all.

On the whole, the retardates had a lower incidence of dreams culminating in orgasm and a lower frequency of such dreams. However, the especially retarded had an incidence nearer that in the control group, possibly because of their lack of sociosexual activity. Homosexual dreams were commoner among the retarded than among the normal controls.

Fewer retardates had experienced premarital heterosexual petting, and those who had had petted with fewer females.

Fewer retardates had had premarital coitus with companions, but among those who had such experience, the frequencies were only slightly lower than those of the control group. The retardates had experienced coitus with fewer females.

As a whole, the retardates did not rely on prostitutes more than the control group, although a few depended largely on prostitutes for much of their coitus.

About three-fifths of the marriages of the retarded had ended in separation or divorce. However, during marriage the frequency of coitus with their marriage partners was similar to that in the control group.

As expected, the incidence of homosexual behavior was much higher among the retardates than among the controls and the frequencies somewhat greater. However, very few retardates were exclusively homosexual. About a third confined their homo-sexual activity to periods of institutionalization.

In response to psychological and visual stimuli, the retarded differed from the control group in having a larger proportion of unresponsive individuals.

On the average, knowledge of coitus and pregnancy seemed to be about the same in the retarded as in the control group except that among the retarded there were more cases of extreme igno-rance or belated acquisition of knowledge. Relatively fewer re-tardates had seen the genitalia of adult females.

The especially retarded, those with IQs of 50 or less, experi-enced less sexual activity with either females or males than those with higher IQs. There was no compensatory rise in masturbation, but orgasm in sleep was more prevalent.

The sexual lives of these mentally retarded persons were obvi-ously profoundly influenced by institutionalization. This finding places an enormous psychiatric and ethical responsibility upon the clinicians who determine the policies of institutions.

REFERENCES

1. GEBHARD, P., GAGNON, J., POMEROY, W., & CHRISTENSON, C.: *Sex Offenders: An Analysis of Types.* New York, Harper & Row, 1965, 923 pp.
2. KINSEY, A., POMEROY, W., & MARTIN, C.: *Sexual Behavior in the Human Male.* Philadelphia, W. B. Saunders Co., 1948, 804 pp.
3. KINSEY, *op. cit.*
4. KINSEY, *op. cit.*

Psychosocial Development and Sex Education

(SESSION ONE)

GENERAL DISCUSSION

ROBERT W. DEISHER, *Presiding*

Drs. Morgenstern and Gebhard have both shown that the mentally retarded are people who have been subjected to extreme deprivation, observed Dr. Athanasiou. He suggested that because deprivation in peer group association may have rather severe effects on the psychosocial development of retardates, sex information provided the retarded should be complemented by appropriate socialization experiences. Dr. Morgenstern agreed, adding that opportunities for such experiences ought to be a major part of any sex education program for the retarded.

The discussion turned to the retarded child's lag in sexual identity noted by Dr. Morgenstern. Dr. Green asked whether this lag could be clearly correlated with the degree of retardation. Dr. Morgenstern implied that such a correlation could not be made, for he said that the lag seems to be more in identification with sex roles and activities rather than in the realization of whether one is a boy or a girl, and that it becomes greater as the child grows older. Dr. Athanasiou suggested that this tendency for the lag to increase may derive from the difference in the way younger and older children acquire information on sex roles— younger children from their parents and older children from a peer group or an institution. Dr. Morgenstern named other factors that might also contribute to the lag: difficulties in motor

51

coordination; families' restrictions on activities; lack of social exposure. To a question about the influence of siblings, he replied that he had no specific information, but that Farber and others had made studies on the subject.

The discussion of the paper by Dr. Gebhard centered on the sampling and interviewing methods used in his study in relation to the reliability of the data. Dr. Reiss pointed out that since the experimental group was an institutionalized population some of the findings might be the result of the institutionalization rather than of the retardation. That possibility, he said, argued for an institutionalized control group. Dr. Gebhard explained that he had made a comparison, not reported in his paper, of his experimental group with a group of prisoners who were not retarded and had found that the nonretarded prisoners had experienced sexual activity much more frequently. Asked by Dr. Reiss whether the findings on these two groups showed a difference in incidence of homosexuality among essentially heterosexual persons, Dr. Gebhard replied that he had run into difficulty in matching the two groups because he did not have figures on the amount of postpubertal life the nonretarded prisoners had spent in an institution. He emphasized that his findings on institutionalized retardates may not apply to retardates in the outside world.

The question of whether everyone included in Dr. Gebhard's group was actually retarded arose when Dr. Money commented that often IQ figures recorded in prisons were untrustworthy— usually because of insufficient or inadequate testing. Dr. Boggs, on the one hand, cited an investigation, conducted as part of the George Washington University study of the mentally retarded and the law, which found that a wide discrepancy did not exist between IQs recorded in penal institutions and those recorded for the same people in elaborate follow-up clinical investigations.* On the other hand, Dr. Gordon told of studying an institution where he found that half the residents designated as retarded were not retarded at all. In regard to his study, Dr. Gebhard said

---

* Brown, B. S., and Courtless, T. F.: *The Mentally Retarded in Penal and Correctional Institutions*. Am. J. Psychiat., 124:1164-1170, March 1968.

that some of the prisoners with IQ scores in the high 60's may have been given lower IQ ratings in prison than they should have been given, for in the outside world they had been "socially functioning beings" in the sense that they were married, earned a living, and had friends.

Observing that the length of imprisonment of the experimental subjects may indicate that they had atypical behavior problems, thus making them a "highly select" group, Dr. Salerno commented that while the specific findings of Dr. Gebhard's study could not be applied to other groups of retardates, general conclusions might be drawn about the effects of institutionalization on sexual experience and behavior. Dr. Gebhard maintained that the real message of the study is that the retarded are sexual beings.

The question of whether there were any problems in taking sex histories of retarded persons was brought up by Dr. Burleson. Dr. Gebhard said that there was no problem with people whose IQs were in the 60's and 70's; some difficulty, because of imprecise recall, with those whose IQs were in the 50's; much difficulty, because of their suggestibility, with those with IQs under 50; and such great difficulty as to be impractical with those whose IQs were under 40. For persons with IQs under 60, the questions had to be carefully phrased so as not to suggest the answers and had to be repeated several times to test for accuracy of response, he said.

Dr. Deisher told of the extreme shyness encountered by University of Washington interviewers in trying to get sex information from institutionalized adolescent retardates. They seem to have acquired the idea that sex was terrible, he said, and some refused to answer even simple questions that would not be at all threatening to the average adolescent.

Dr. Morgenstern told of finding the customary sex terminology useless in interviewing institutionalized retardates. He found that many didn't even know the meaning of the word "intercourse" and that nearly all denied engaging in masturbation, in spite of the known frequency of masturbation among the institution's residents. He stressed the importance of using the vernacular in such interviews.

Blaming the reluctance to respond to questions about sex on "the problems of explosive ears," Dr. Money suggested that pictures of sexual activity be shown before interviews to let the respondents know they are perfectly safe in giving accurate information.

With regard to the reliability of the data in the Gebhard study, Dr. Gordon suggested that some parts of the data might be more accurate than others. For example, he said, the number of marriages was probably more nearly accurate than the frequency of night emissions or coitus. Part of the unreliability of the data, he said, could be attributed to the imprecision of recall and part to the sexual ignorance of many retarded persons, some of whom don't even make a connection between intercourse and pregnancy. He agreed with Dr. Gebhard, however, that the "message" of the study is more important than the precision of the data, a message phrased by Dr. Burleson as, "There is a great deal of sexual activity among the retarded."

PSYCHOSOCIAL DEVELOPMENT
AND
SEX EDUCATION

(Session Two)

3

Sex Education of the Mentally Retarded

WARREN R. JOHNSON
Professor of Health Education
Director,
Children's Physical Developmental Clinic
University of Maryland

SEX EDUCATION and education of the mentally retarded are conspicuous challenges to educators today. Dealing with these challenges rationally when they merge together is, indeed, a special challenge. Perhaps an examination of the basic anatomy of the teaching-learning process will help to put this challenge into reasonable perspective.

The teaching-learning process may be reduced to three dynamically interrelated aspects: (1) the characteristics of the learner; (2) the characteristics of the subject matter; and (3) the characteristics of the teacher. Let us consider each of these aspects with respect to sex education and mental retardation.

Characteristics of the Learner

I need not dwell on what everyone already knows about the broad range of learning capability and perhaps equally broad range of sexual vigor and interest among those people designated as "mentally retarded." However, several points would seem worth keeping in mind about the mentally retarded when discussing sex education for them.

1. Labels like "mentally retarded" tend both to create and to conceal the *individuals* under them. It is, therefore, hazardous to suppose that such a label necessarily provides any useful information when dealing with any given person, either with regard to his capacity to learn or his interest in sex. For example, it is often taken for granted that persons labeled mentally retarded are not able to benefit from education about contraception. However, Fujita and others have made a convincing case,[1] which is in harmony with my own view[2] and the view of Kempton, *et al.*,[3] that contraception education is as feasible for the retarded as other educational undertakings of importance to them. Mentally retarded persons share with the rest of mankind the usual human interest in closeness, physical contact, affection, and being in on things. The concept of appropriate time and place for various types of behavior can certainly be learned by most retarded persons.

2. Like the so-called "normal" person, the so-called "mentally retarded" person is likely to, but does not necessarily, have a strong interest in sex. Also, like the normal person, the retarded person is likely to experience great difficulty in finding ways of expressing sexual interest, since virtually all sexual expression is defined by our society as unacceptable, immoral, and probably illegal. Deviation from society's standard brings feelings of guilt, self-deprecation, and inadequacy to anyone vulnerable to the inculcation of social standards. It may also bring punishment and perhaps incarceration. Typically, the retarded, being more closely supervised and scrutinized and having less privacy than other persons, are more likely to manifest behavior which, because it is visible, is regarded as a symptom of retardation rather than of the goldfish-in-a-bowl circumstances in which the retarded commonly live.

3. The mentally retarded do indeed tend to be mentally retarded with respect to sex education. This type of retardation is, perhaps, one of the characteristics that they share most fully with the brilliant and so-called "normal." Nearly all of us are mentally retarded with regard to sex; and many intellectually bright people

are not even educable or trainable in this regard. Unfortunately, some of these sexually uneducable people are supposed to instruct or otherwise manage the lives of the retarded with respect to sex.

4. Again like the rest of us, the retarded tend to decline in level of functioning intelligence as emotional upset increases. We all tend to be less rational when dealing with things that upset us, as sexual matters and sexual language in the home or in an educational setting tend to do.

5. Like the verbally normal, the mentally retarded characteristically have to deal with a language barrier when confronted with sex education. First of all, they face the frustration of being unable to decode some important verbal messages adequately because of the unfamiliar vocabulary or complex style in which they are couched. To talk about sex acceptably, it seems, one must be skilled in circumlocution and medical terminology.

Another language barrier is the educator's resistance to vulgar language. Etymologically, "vulgar" language means language of the common people. We all understand this language, but a hangover from medieval times requires us to talk like medieval aristocrats or scholars—in Latin rather than English—when it comes to sex and elimination.

6. Mentally retarded people, like most other people, are interested in sex primarily for its potential sensual gratification. Sexual gratification usually has nothing to do with motivation to procreate; it may very well have little or nothing to do with establishing or maintaining a permanent or even long-term relationship; and it does not necessarily occur within "love" or marriage.

Masturbation may bring exquisite gratification. However, for unknown but possibly very important reasons, most people evidently get the most gratification from sex when they are in some way stimulated physically by another person, usually, but not necessarily, of the opposite sex. Relatively few people prefer same-sex contact, but many turn to this by default when sexually segregated, as in institutions and prisons.

7. The mentally retarded also share with the "normal" popu-

lation a lack of virtually anything in the way of systematic training in child rearing, or any orientation as to what having children might be all about—in either a personal or broad social sense.

Thus, it is apparent that the mentally retarded individual is in most ways not readily distinguishable from the rest of us in relation to sexuality. There does not seem to be a high correlation between sex IQ and general IQ.

Characteristics of the Subject Matter

The prime characteristic of the subject matter of sex education is that it is different. It is not treated as educational subject matter, in the same sense as chemistry and nutrition. Alchemy and sacred food taboos do not dominate instruction in chemistry and nutrition anymore. However, comparable unscientific but revered and spooky artifacts continue to plague efforts at sex education.

A number of studies have been made to determine whether people in this country—school pupils, PTA groups, school administrators, and school board members—consider human sex a legitimate subject for study in the schools.[4] The great majority of people queried have responded that they consider such education to be important and even urgently needed; but, hardly any teacher training institutions are teaching teachers in this respect on anything approaching a systematic basis. To the best of my knowledge, comparable surveys have not been done with regard to the mentally retarded or other special groups, although workers in the field of mental retardation certainly seem to feel the need for such information.

The subject of sex is, indeed, different. Whoever heard of having to poll the public, school officials, and others over the question of whether it is desirable to teach arithmetic, the history of the Napoleonic wars, or tennis? Why this dread of being caught teaching about sex, especially to children? Are we bold enough to examine this question closely? For some of our most inscrutable and ineffable tribal taboos may be at stake. The inquisitor must raise the question: whence came the strange taboo system that passes for a sexual morality and the attitudes that make a healthy sexual adjustment impossible in childhood and youth and nearly impossible in adulthood? Whence came the bizarre sex laws that glare at us suspiciously, often savagely, even in the privacy of the marriage bed? What will we say when we learn that this morality within which we aspire to live and try to require our children to live was laid down by an ancient, desperate, tribal people of the Middle East, the Old Testament Jews, who, for all of their practical wisdom, could not possibly have anticipated modern circumstances? What will we say when we learn that the early Christian fathers added to the Jewish regulations a frank hatred of sex and women? For example, the influential St. Augustine wrote that the gateway to hell lay between a woman's thighs; and it was he who permanently fixed the sex-sin-guilt association in the Christian mind. Thus became rooted the traditional view of sex, recently described by the Roman Catholic priest, James Kavanaugh, as "the chief and single sin, man's fleshy battle with the world." [5]

In due course, Henry VIII brought ecclesiastical law under the jurisdiction of civil law, and thereby provided the basis for the later transmission of Judeo-Christian morality and law to this country by the Puritans. In the sexual area, there has been no real separation of church and state in this country. The ancient religious-moral tradition is backed by many laws, some of them criminal laws requiring punishments far in excess of those imposed for crimes of violence.

In the Puritan tradition, civil war veteran Anthony Comstock rammed through Congress our present law against sending "obscene" material through the mail. This law makes sense only if you believe, as did Comstock and his backers, that pornography incites people to masturbate and that this activity gives rise to personal and social disease, insanity, death, and damnation. The continuing influence of the Puritans and Comstock is evidenced by the recent official disavowal of the report of the President's Commission on Pornography and Obscenity—which found no evidence that pornography produces ill effects on the beholder, child or adult.

Thus, historical, moral, legal, and linguistic traditions profoundly affect all efforts at sex education and often impede efforts to educate the young objectively in this area. Especially impeded, perhaps, are any efforts to teach the mentally retarded.

In sum, the subject matter of sex education can as yet scarcely be regarded as subject matter in the usual educational sense. The growing objective knowledge about sex is still so tangled up with moral theology parading as virtue, and with misconceptions parading as matters of health or decorum, that parents and teachers continue to blunder about anxiously and, for the most part, ineffectually. Only very recently have I begun to note what appear to be significant changes in teacher attitudes towards the sexuality of the retarded.

Characteristics of the Teacher

Teachers, like most other people, are likely to be conflicted and bewildered in sexual matters. I have heard William Masters state in medical meetings that sexual inadequacy is evidently epidemic in this country. It is, therefore, reasonable to suppose that many people with sexual problems of their own are creating the sexual atmosphere within which children grow up. What I call "atmospheric" sex education, whether in home, institution, or school, profoundly influences children's attitudes toward sex. Adult influences on children, perhaps by psychological osmosis, are very likely to give rise to difficult sexual adjustment. However, it has been my experience, in nearly 20 years of teaching sex education, that we tend to underestimate the potential of parents and teachers for doing a better job with more accurate knowledge and the opportunity for easy, open communication on the subject.

Teachers of sex education must go beyond atmospheric education and provide direct education and counseling. Effectiveness in this task would seem to require the teacher to have several characteristics.

1. The teacher needs to know the basics of the subject matter. It is not enough for him to be able to rap with a group of kids or adults. He must deliver an honest message. Admittedly, the long-time suppression of scholarship in this area has limited the acquisition of knowledge about human sexuality, but we know enough to be able to debunk misconceptions about menstruation, masturbation, sex play, "dirty" words, pornography, and other sexual phenomena. We also know a good deal about contraception and are learning more.

2. Any teacher must be informed about the characteristics of the particular group he is teaching. Since teachers of sex education must be prepared to teach young people of various cultural backgrounds, parents and other adults, normal and retarded persons, gearing instructions to the particular characteristics of the group is a complicated undertaking. Actually, we teachers often make the mistake of thinking more about our subject matter than about how it is perceived by our prospective learners. For example, a psychologist I know was told by the director of an inner city neighborhood center to provide a group of young girls with sex education by reading them a moralistic little birds and bees book. When she finished reading, one of the little girls asked her very seriously: "Are you trying to tell us about fucking?"

3. The teacher of sex education must have come to terms with his or her own sexuality—to have recognized not only its existence but also its full status in the functioning of his total personality. In other words, he must be able to deal directly with his subject matter and his pupils' reactions to it without having to struggle at every step with his own conflicts, anxieties and tensions. Well-informed teachers sometimes upset pupils needlessly by presenting their material in a way that lets their own negative or conflicted feelings show through. People who are caught up in personal sex problems, like sexual inadequacy or masturbatory conflicts, often convey a negative message not in harmony with the goal of the instruction.

4. The teacher must also have come to terms with the languages of sex, both the technical and the vulgar. You simply cannot teach

about the penis, testicles, labia, vagina, or clitoris if these and related words are not comprehended by the prospective learners or send an emotional shock wave through your own system. Fuck, screw, jack off, cock, pussy, wet dream, and the like are, perhaps, regrettably vulgar, but they are the dominant linguistic sex vehicles of American English. Teachers and nurses frequently flop in their efforts at sex education—that is, fail to communicate their message—because they persist in speaking a language foreign to their students. Moreover, when girls or women use the language of the people, the teacher must face up to the question of whether he believes the First Amendment applies to both sexes.

5. The teacher needs to be aware that the goal of sex education is not to eliminate all sexual responses and that sexual interest or behavior is not sinful, intrinsically evil, or sick. True, it is often necessary to exercise control over sexual behavior, even though the ultimate aim may be to produce a person capable of controlling his own behavior in appropriate ways; but that control need not convey an impression that gives rise to feelings of guilt and self-deprecation.

Some contrasting examples may clarify my meaning.

The traditional method of dealing with evidences of sexual interest was displayed by a teacher who almost savagely insisted to any boy in her class who engaged in masturbation that the practice was bad and would lead to his being institutionalized. What better way to inculcate a sense of fear and guilt? Similar scare methods were adopted by the parents of a mentally retarded boy. They made a practice of sneaking up on him to "catch him" masturbating. When they succeeded, they punished the boy, both verbally and physically. The only redeeming part of this story was the attitude of the boy's older sister, who greatly admired his continuing loyalty to one of his few pleasures in life.

In contrast, some teachers view frequent masturbation as evidence that children are probably bored. They want to know whether they are providing enough interesting learning experiences for the children. They are not horrified by evidence of sexual interest, but try to help teach the child the concept of appropriate time and place.

In another case, a mentally retarded boy masturbated to ejaculation while riding a school bus. A girl classmate became very upset on viewing the incident, and the bus driver exploded over the episode. The school authorities, however, refused to panic. A counselor told the girl's mother what had happened in a way that kept the mother from getting unduly excited. The boy's teachers then attempted to get at the meaning of his behavior. Was it an attention-getting device used by the boy because it had had successful shock value at home or elsewhere? Or did it reflect a lack of comprehension of appropriateness of time and place? The teachers are now attempting to convey to the boy that masturbation, while commonly and legally practiced in private, is severely punished when practiced in public. They have not complicated matters by introducing traditional "moral" issues.

Conclusion

Sex education for the "mentally retarded" is likely to pose an even graver problem than sex education for the "normal." Sex education for normal persons may be an unmanageable problem for many educators or parents, for the reasons I have already outlined. Teachers and parents alike may regard adding an interest in sex to the existing handicap of mental retardation as heaping handicap on handicap.

Still, the need for appropriate sex education is clearly urgent. As with most other people, a great many of the mentally retarded have in their sexuality a major resource for adding appreciably to the quality of their lives. Appropriately recognized, it can add to their guilt-free enjoyment of life, their personal and social awareness, their ability to contribute to a world that "cares" for them— cares not in the custodial sense of the word, but in the rationally loving sense of concern.

In an article on sex education and the mentally retarded, I once wrote:

Is it possible that we can learn to rise above the negativism of the past and present, pluck sexuality from its traditional entropic state, and move into a new era in which its potentially constructive energy can be available as a major personality resource, rather than as a grim liability?[2]

I think that put what is still my basic question rather well. Knowledge, technology, and social change point in new directions. Are educators of the mentally retarded up to the new challenge?

REFERENCES

1. FUJITA, B., WAGNER, N. N., & PION, R. J.: Sexuality, Contraception, and Mental Retardation. *Social Medicine,* 47:193-197, May 1970.
2. JOHNSON, W. R.: Sex Education and the Mentally Retarded. *J. Sex Research,* 5:179-186, August 1969.
3. KEMPTON, W., BASS, M., & GORDON, S.: *Love, Sex, and Birth Control for the Mentally Retarded: A Guide for Parents.* Planned Parenthood Association of Southeastern Pa., (1402 Spruce St., Phila.), 1971.
4. JOHNSON, W. R. & SCHUTT, M.: Sex Education Attitudes of School Administrators and School Board Members. *J. of Sch. Health,* June 1966.
5. KAVANAUGH, J.: *A Modern Priest Looks at His Outdated Church.* New York, Simon and Schuster, 1967.

4

A Response to Warren Johnson

SOL GORDON
College for Human Development
Syracuse University

IN HIS PAPER, DR. JOHNSON has served the field of mental deficiency well by forcing professional persons to recognize what almost everybody knows—that the so-called mentally retarded are not exceptional in their sexual impulses. In the past, we in the professions have joined everybody else in a crusade against the sexual impulses of the retarded. Dr. Johnson, a pioneer in sex education, is saying to all of us that the mentally retarded as human beings are as entitled to expression of impulses as anybody else. Like the rest of us, they are entitled to the kind of sex education that is not based on the presumption that sexual impulse must be contained at all costs.

Dr. Johnson conveys well the idea that in all likelihood what we (the so-called normal) have most in common with the mentally retarded are hang-ups, guilt feelings, and fantasies about sexual expression or the desire for it. He validly points out that the very vulnerability of the retarded makes the case for sex education even more compelling for them than for most people.

My main area of disagreement with him concerns some of his points about what it takes to be a sex educator and what it is that we must communicate.

Everybody has to be so well qualified these days to do anything that it is difficult to get anything going. Yet some of the best education is done by formally unqualified people. I have not noticed that teachers, nurses and doctors are, in general, especially good sex educators. We have overstated the importance of expertise when what counts is attitude and good will.

The problem is with a society, a school, or an institution that permits its employees to function in terms of their own prejudice or ignorance. For example, in several hospitals in New York State, nurses are wearing buttons that read, "Abortion is Murder" and are harassing women who come to the hospitals for abortions. Clearly, hospital administration is responsible for permitting such behavior.

In an institution for the mentally retarded where I recently addressed the staff on sex education, I invited the aides and nurses to submit questions before I made my presentation. The majority of the questions could be summed up as one: *How can we stop masturbation?* In this institution, a great deal of the staff's energy was obviously being devoted to catching or curbing the masturbators.

At a time when the residents of this institution consisted only of males, much of the available staff energy was spent in punishing or curbing homosexual behavior, but now with females included, the staff's main thrust is against any expression of heterosexuality.

Administrators of institutions and schools blame their staffs for such anti-sex attitudes. Staff is "expected" to be conservative. Yet the administrators are the ones to blame, for they have provided their institutions and schools with irresponsible leadership.

Confirming this point are numerous examples of staff members who have been fired because they have not maintained the conservatism that staff members traditionally are supposed to hold.

Actually, the retarded (and perhaps also normal people) do not need to know many facts about sex. The information that needs to be imparted to them can be given in a few minutes, though it must be repeated many times and for different levels of understanding.

Let me suggest the points that sex educators need to communicate:

1. Masturbation is a normal sexual expression no matter how frequently it is done and at what age. It becomes a compulsive, punitive, self-destructive form of behavior largely as a result of suppression, punishment, and resulting feelings of guilt.

2. All direct sexual behavior involving the genitals should take place only in privacy. However, since institutions for the retarded are not designed or operated to ensure privacy, the definition of what constitutes privacy in an institution must be very liberal. Bathrooms, one's own bed, the bushes, and basements are private domains.

3. Any time a girl and a boy who are physically mature have sexual relations, they risk pregnancy.

4. Unless both members of a heterosexual couple clearly want to have a baby and understand the responsibilities involved in child-rearing, they should use an effective method of birth control.

5. Until a person is about 18 years old, society holds that he or she should not have intercourse. After that age, the person can decide for himself.

6. Adults should not be permitted to use children sexually.

7. The only way to discourage homosexual expression is to risk heterosexual expression.

8. In the final analysis, sexual behavior between consenting adults (regardless of their mental age and of whether their behavior is homo or hetero) should be no one else's business—providing there is little risk of bringing an unwanted child into this world.

Consideration should also be given to achieving greater acceptance of 1) abortion as a safe, legal, and moral alternative to bringing an unwanted child into this world, and 2) voluntary sterilization as a protection for those retarded persons who could function well in a marriage if they did not have children.

People who work with the retarded must begin to show some honesty, courage, and integrity in facing the issues of human sexuality. Right now we should spread the word—

1) that girls of any age should not be conditioned to believe that every normal woman wants and must have babies;

2) that masturbation is all right;

3) that sex is enjoyable but use birth control.

If we did these things, we would be doing almost all the sex educating that is needed.

Psychosocial Development and Sex Education

(SESSION TWO)

GENERAL DISCUSSION

ROBERT W. DEISHER, *Presiding*

In responding to Dr. Gordon, Dr. Johnson agreed that the simpler the information presented to the retarded person, the better, but he insisted that the teacher must have enough knowledge of the subject to have confidence in what she or he teaches and to be prepared to answer completely unexpected questions. He supported Dr. Gordon's statement that the emphasis on expertise can be overdone, however, and cited the success of the Children's Physical Developmental Clinic at the University of Maryland in training and using 120 college students as volunteer clinicians each semester.

The question of values in sex education was introduced by Dr. Reiss who said that while he believed in the liberal ideas about sexual activity expressed in Dr. Gordon's approach to sex education, he agreed with Dr. Money that the sex education, particularly in a public school, should be nonjudgmental and should not espouse values on controversial moral areas. Young people, he said, should be given enough background to make their own choices, without being told, for example, that masturbation or abortion is "good" or "bad."

Disagreeing with Dr. Reiss, Dr. Gordon called the issue between them as one of the crucial ones in sex education today. Saying that a neutral, "antiseptic" approach just "turns kids off," he maintained that there is no way to teach sex without being controversial. The young people who want to know more about the mechanics of sex, he said, can find out on their own; what sex education should deal with are the things young people want to know to help them make decisions. Out of 5000 questions high school students asked about sex, he reported, none had to do with "plumbing"; they were concerned about such things as the importance of penis size and whether oral or anal sex is healthy or unhealthy. Sex, Dr. Gordon said, should be discussed as a subject having controversial aspects about which people have different values, and these differences in values should be presented. He maintained that there is nothing wrong with telling teenagers that it is medically undesirable for them to give birth or with suggesting that if they are going to engage in sexual activity they should use birth control. Any sex education that does not deal with values is a waste of time, he maintained.

Protesting that he was not arguing for teaching "plumbing," Dr. Reiss agreed that various values must be presented, but added that this should be done without taking sides.

Dr. Gordon said his remarks were prompted by the failure of institutions to liberalize their policies toward sexual activities and marriage or even to provide enough sex education so that the mentally retarded person who has not connected sex with pregnancy can have a basis for making a choice.

Dr. Athanasiou called the idea that controversy could be introduced into the public schools—"which haven't gotten past the monkey trials"—absurd. Public institutions, he said, function on the basis of values held by the majority of the people. He suggested that the best hope of having meaningful sex education programs in the future is to get at the parents. Dr. Deisher said that education on the importance of sex in people's lives is also needed by physicians, who are in a position to provide leadership, but may be no different than the rest of the public in their attitudes.

Expressing the opinion that, in general, attitudes toward sex are becoming more liberal, Dr. Johnson pointed out that because of the variety of cultural groups in this country, the word "moral" means different things to different people. He suggested that in discussing any type of behavior the question should be raised not of whether it is moral but of whether it is damaging to the individual or to society.

Dr. Gordon maintained that the real problem lies with administrators who purport to represent people's feelings but do not recognize recent changes. Agreeing with Dr. Athanasiou about the need to get to parents, he said he had found that if there is an opportunity to speak first about sex education to the parents of the retarded, even once, virtually all opposition declines.

Saying that she, too, has found parents of the retarded eager for help with the sexual problems of their children, Mrs. Bass told about a group of parents in Philadelphia that has formed, in cooperation with Planned Parenthood Association, a council on human sexuality and mental retardation. She also reported that she has found the subject to be less controversial in the schools than the alternative of "letting a girl drop out pregnant at 11 or 12 because she doesn't know how to control her own fertility." On the other hand, Mrs. Bass said, institutions and halfway houses were releasing girls into the community with no knowledge about how to protect themselves from sexual exploitation, until the local Planned Parenthood Association obtained permission to run some programs for the girls before release.

The question of who is entitled to make a decision about surgical or chemical contraception for the retarded was brought up by Dr. Athanasiou. He said he would not want alone to take the responsibility of deciding that a young girl had to have her tubes tied just because she had a low IQ. Dr. Gordon suggested that perhaps the decision should be made by "advocates" representing a group of people known for their humanistic views. While granting that such a decision is difficult to make, he pointed out that making no decision might lead to a birth that is tragic for the parents, the grandparents, and the child.

Dr. Gingrich commented that, with today's emphasis on environmental problems, the day might be arriving when society will have to take serious and major initiating responsibility in the area of "people planning."

Dr. Money said that many retarded young people can make their own decisions about contraception or sterilization in individual discussions with a physician or another responsible party. He identified a more difficult problem as getting parents to help make a decision for a person obviously too retarded ever to be able to take care of a baby and perhaps carrying a retardation-producing genetic defect. He suggested that different cases may require different ways of reaching a decision: sometimes a decision may be reached in counseling discussions with the individuals or their parents, and sometimes it may require a special jury of outside advisers.

Dr. Morgenstern, however, expressed doubt about the validity of relying on a decision-making body that would inevitably involve difficult problems of organization, structure and composition.

Dr. Reiss suggested that perhaps the questions of whether or not any voluntary sterilization program is launched ought to depend on how great the likelihood is of a mentally retarded person's producing a defective child. Dr. Gordon pointed out that there is another issue involved: whether a retarded person can take care of even a normal child. A lot of children become retarded, he maintained, because of the type of care they get. To these issues Dr. Reiss added still another: whether a retarded child is of less value than a non-retarded child and should therefore be prevented from being born. When Dr. Johnson said the answer may lie in the definition of morality as having something to do with what is good for society, Dr. Reiss replied that this does not clarify the issue because there would be a multiplicity of pluses and minuses no matter what value system were used. Dr. Johnson agreed that any complicated question involves a balancing out of plus and minus factors.

The question of what intelligent parents of the retarded would choose should also be considered, suggested Dr. Boggs. She asserted that anybody who lives with a seriously mentally retarded person has to think of what being retarded means to that person. Consideration for the individual whose defect is so great that his suffering and frustration far outweigh any satisfaction he may derive from life, she maintained, may lead to the conclusion that the birth of children so handicapped ought to be prevented.

PHYSICAL AND BIOLOGICAL ASPECTS
ASPECTS
(Session One)

5

Family Planning Programs for the Mentally Retarded in Institutions and Community

RUSSELL GOODMAN
Family Life Development Specialist
Minnesota Department of Public Welfare

IN MY FUNCTION AS FAMILY life development specialist in the Minnesota State Department of Public Welfare, I work with rather broadly representative community agencies—ministerial associations, school systems, and colleges—that offer family life education, including information about family planning and contraception. My discussions of contraception are therefore nearly always presented within a broader context of family life education. I work closely with the Department's family planning specialist, whose function is to increase the staff's knowledge of family planning and the Department's responsibilities in this regard. Our positions were both created in 1969.

While there are some very good family planning programs in Minnesota, they do not by any means cover the state. There are some wide gaps in service and some real areas of resistance. However, our department and the welfare departments of the other 49 states do have a legal framework—in fact a legal mandate—for extending such programs. This lies in the public welfare provisions of the Social Security Act as amended in 1967.[1] According to Federal guidelines issued by the Department of Health, Education and Welfare, to receive reimbursement for services rendered under these provisions the states must make contraceptive service available on a voluntary basis to any person of child-bearing age asking for it, regardless of age or marital status.

In Minnesota we have a State policy to match the Federal guidelines, so that all county welfare departments are theoretically operating under a mandate to provide contraceptive devices and prescriptions where these are not otherwise available.

That policy, however, has been rather loosely interpreted, with the result that, in many instances, it has been construed as not necessarily including the mentally retarded, particularly those living in institutions. In fact, a characteristic of contraceptive programs is that information does not always get translated from a policy level to the operational level.

I think this is going to change because of a step-up in the Federal monitoring of services. When a program is mandated, the state is expected to set up some performance criteria, which can be used in applying for Federal reimbursement, to demonstrate that the program has in fact been provided throughout the state and the nature of the services it has provided. Currently, however, there is a great unevenness in the availability and quality of contraceptive services in counties throughout the state.

Another characteristic of contraceptive educational programs in Minnesota is the participation in their operation of persons from a wide variety of professions and occupations. In my opinion, it is not possible to make a general statement about who is the most likely provider of contraceptive information in a community or in an institution. It can as well be the agency's janitor or switchboard operator as the person to whom the responsibility has been officially assigned. Therefore, in training the staffs of agencies and institutions, primarily on an invitational basis, our department has included the janitors, secretaries, switchboard operators, ward attendants, and social workers—the whole broad range of persons who have some contact with the residents—in the particular institution or community facility with which we have been dealing.

There are some people who work in these institutions or agencies whose jobs have not in the past had any connection with contraceptive education, but who, because they have become experts in dealing with people in their communities, have provided a new channel for the flow of this type of information.

Another factor we have found important is parent involvement. A great many parents want to know how to provide contraceptive information to their sexually developed retarded child. The possibility of their child's becoming pregnant is one of the major worries of the parents with whom I have worked. It is second only to the issue of how to handle masturbation.

I sometimes feel it necessary to say some things to parents' groups that they find very hard to take. I tell them that the sex drive is something that will come out in behavior in some way; that sublimation—channeling the sex drive to other pursuits—once regarded as contructive, has never worked very well. Even so, I get invited back and when I ask the parents "why," since I have not solved their problem, they generally answer that it is because I describe the world as it is, not as it should be or as I imagine it to be. Many parents in these groups have become advocates of sex education—including contraceptive education—for the retarded.

Once, when I was talking about human sexuality and contraception to the staff of a small institution, some of the staff members spoke up angrily against the things I had said and a controversy ensued. The institution's advisory committee, however, remained very supportive of our program and expressed the opinion that the staff needed to face in frank discussion the issues arising from their charges' sexuality.

No program of this nature will work without the cooperation of physicians. When we began this program in Minnesota, we found that some of the physicians serving institutions would not prescribe contraceptive pills or devices for anybody under any circumstances. The program stopped with them. That attitudinal obstacle seems to have disappeared. But physicians who will prescribe pills are not always willing to insert intrauterine devices and some who are willing are not as skillful in doing so as others.

All methods of contraception should be available in a good family planning program, particularly one serving the mentally retarded. There is an excellent family planning program in St. Paul, for example, where physicians skilled in IUD insertion prescribe pills or IUDs on an individualized basis. Girls as young as 12 have been fitted with IUDs as a protective measure at their parents' request, if it has become evident that they are physically mature and are participating in sexual intercourse.

While some ingredients are necessary to all family planning or birth control programs, successful programs have various forms, which depend largely on the character of the setting in which they are located. Let me give four examples from our state.

One program is in a sheltered workshop in a rural area. It is not a formal program, and its administrative sanctions are weak. Its major ingredients are a well-trained social worker on the workshop's staff and a helpful physician in the community. The social worker, who is in touch with all the workshop's employees, is well-informed about contraception and believes she has a responsibility to talk to individuals about their sexual patterns and sexual lives and to refer girls and women who are sexually active to the physician for contraceptive devices. The girls have been able and willing to talk about their sex lives and their sexual plans. In general, their plans do not include having an unwanted child.

The second example is a program run under the auspices of a public school system by a mental health clinic for educable mentally retarded students and their parents. The mental health clinic provides the educational aspects and refers both students and their parents to a nearby family planning center for contraceptive prescriptions and devices.

The third example is a program in a state hospital. I would like to digress a bit here to point out that Minnesota has recently shifted from having separate state hospitals for the mentally retarded and the mentally ill to establishing combination state hospitals, which serve both groups, although separately. This means that some hospitals have had a large turnover in staff. I have noticed that among the state hospitals I have visited those that have done the best job in providing both sex education and contraceptive aid to the mentally retarded are those with the newest staffs; and that the state hospitals with the oldest, most experienced staffs have been very unresponsive in this regard. Attitudes do not seem to be so strongly based in stereotypes in a newer facility as in an older one. In referring to "younger" or "older" staffs, I am not speaking of the age of the staff members but of the length of time they have been working in the institution.

The state hospital in our example is one of the newer state hospitals and has a special education emphasis. The entire staff, rather than just the "experts," is involved in a broad-range program of family life education. However, professional people from the Planned Parenthood Association, the State Health Department, the State Department of Public Welfare (including myself) and perhaps other departments of state government are called upon when needed for consultation, training, or service. The residents have been very, very responsive to both the educational content of the program and the idea that they could do something to avoid having children they did not want. For example, one day when I was at the hospital a woman with Down's syndrome said to me, "My mother said I cannot have children."

I said, "Your mother may be wrong. If you have sexual intercourse, you may be able to have children."

She then said, "I shouldn't have children. I am a mongoloid, you know, and that is not good."

The staff members who heard that comment were amazed. Here was a woman they regarded as too retarded to have good judgment who was clearly aware in her own mind that she should not have children; that there were better ways to live than to be a mongoloid; that she would not wish to bring a mongoloid child into the world.

I do not know what the average level of mental retardation is in that particular hospital. I was working directly with about 30 mentally retarded women and girls ranging in verbal ability from completely non-verbal to fairly capable. To test the effectiveness of my training, I asked them to repeat to me what they had learned so that I would have an idea of whether they had absorbed the information enough to be able to act on it—in other words, whether they could choose to use contraception or not. After about five hours of training, about six of the 30 were able to give me the kind of feedback that indicated to me that they had in fact learned what I had tried to teach them about the possibility of using an intrauterine device or contraceptive pills.

I later learned that a fair number of patients in that particular hospital were using contraception and were able to follow the medical regime required. Nobody ever learned to say "intrauterine device," but several learned to say "little plastic thing." Thus, language barriers did not prove to be a problem.

The fourth example is a referral program in an urban day activity center for the mentally retarded. After receiving training in the availability of contraceptive services and the right of the retarded to have contraceptive information, the center's staff prevailed upon a reluctant county welfare department to provide contraceptive information and devices to the mentally retarded on request. The issue first arose over the question of whether an adolescent girl, who was having sexual intercourse, should be fitted with a contraceptive device or placed in an institution as a mode of contraception. The county department opted for institutionalization; the day care center for a contraceptive device. Because the administrator of the center knew about the county's responsibility, the center could insist. Consequently, the department relented and the girl, provided with contraceptive information and fitted with a device, remained in the community.

In summary, we have found the key ingredients of successful programs to be the following:

1. A clear understanding of the welfare department's responsibility for providing contraceptive service to all who want it.

2. The availability of a wide variety of trained professional persons.

3. The involvement of the parents of the mentally retarded.

4. The cooperation of physicians.

5. Administrative clarity on what constitutes delivery of the service. This is, perhaps, the most important ingredient of all.

We have studied several counties in our state and have found a great deal of difference in the adequacy of their services. Where administrators clearly announced that the provision of contraceptive service is part of their responsibility and that the service will be given without regard to age, race, or marital status and where they allow their staff the time for following through on this responsibility, respectable programs exist.

I see no major problems in the utilization of this kind of service. I do see a major problem in getting the information to the people who need it.

REFERENCE

1. Social Security Act, Title IV, as amended 1967.

6

Physical and Biological Aspects

DONALD W. HELBIG
*International Institute for the Study
of Human Reproduction
Columbia University*

FIRST, WHAT IS THE FUNDAMENTAL question that we must ask? I would put it this way: how does reproductive capacity—meaning both fecundity (the physical capacity to reproduce) and the social capacity to bear and raise children—differ between normal persons and mentally retarded persons of varying degrees of severity and various diagnoses?

There are several possible approaches to studying the question of what the reproductive capacity of mentally retarded persons actually is. The first approach is to study, for example, the development of secondary sex characteristics, bone age, onset of menstruation, and incidence of ovulatory cycles in a representative retarded population.

There is another approach to the question of the reproductive capacity of the mentally retarded. That is through retrospective surveys of accomplished fertility in variously defined populations. However, the reports of such studies present contradictory evidence regarding fertility in the retarded—some indicating that it is higher, some lower, and some the same as in a normal population. Most of this evidence, I think, represents beliefs and myths rather than any solid research findings.

I cannot claim to have done an exhaustive search of the literature, by any means, but I have found interesting examples to illustrate the kind of evidence that now exists.

J. A. Böök, professor and chairman of the Department of Medical Genetics, the University of Uppsala in Sweden, reported in the *Eugenics Quarterly*, 1959, on some data he had collected.[1] He started out by citing data Dahlberg had collected in 1951 in Sweden,[2] indicating a very low fertility among persons registered as mentally retarded.

Dahlberg's data included 1,258 unmarried and 18 married retardates. The mean number of children per person for the unmarried was 0.06, for the married 3.60. He actually cited the mean fertility as 0.11 and used this as evidence that fertility of retarded people is very low. And there was no statement as to the age of the people studied or what proportion of them were in institutions.

Böök took issue with this conclusion, but I take issue with Böök because in reporting the following data I think he made essentially the same mistake: he looked at the extramatrimonial fertility and intramatrimonial fertility of 54 retardates to arrive at a mean fertility rate for retardates as a group.

I'm not sure I understand why, but he used the figure 54 for the unmarried and 7 for the married, though the total was 54. I think he was looking at the fertility before marriage and after. The 7 ultimately got married. He did not explain that, however. There were eight children among the unmarried and 32 children among the married. Thus, with an average of 0.15 children per unmarried individual and of 4.60 per married individual, Böök arrived at a mean fertility of 0.7 for the group as a whole.

He did the same for 108 controls. Again, he had 108 unmarried and 85 (of the same 108) married. There were 16 extramarital children, 384 marital children. The rates were 0.15 and 4.50 respectively, with a mean fertility of 3.7. He, therefore, issued a statement that the fertility of the mentally retarded is 0.7 and of normal persons 3.7. I think it is clear, if you allow for the difference in marital status, the fertility is exactly the same.

Böök also noted a study made by Juda[3] in 1934 in Germany.

The data on 97 persons who were classified as intellectually inferior on the basis of school records were compared with data on 85 normal persons, apparently also selected on the basis of school records. Net fertility was 2.5 and 2.3 children per person respectively, obviously not significantly different. Since Böök made no comment about age or whether this was completed fertility, I am not sure this evidence is of any value whatsoever. Moreover, the use of school records as a basis for population selection means the study group itself is composed of individuals who are almost normal.

Böök went on to discuss the apparent high fertility of persons carrying a gene for Huntington's chorea. There are some lessons to be learned from this evidence also.

First, he cited data by Reed and Palm reported in *Science* in 1951 suggesting that persons with Huntington's chorea have a higher than normal fertility.[4] Reed and Palm cited the historical case of two brothers who migrated to Minnesota in the mid-1800s. The two brothers each produced 10 children.

Brother A, who himself later developed Huntington's chorea, had a number of descendants who also developed Huntington's chorea. Brother B did not develop the disease himself, and none of his descendants did. Brother A with the Huntington's chorea ended up with 787 descendants, of whom 716 were still living in 1951. Brother B had 186 descendants, of whom 167 were still living.

The investigators concluded that the fertility of choreics before they developed the disease was much higher than that of persons without the gene.

They cited as further evidence for this conclusion that among the children of Brother A's descendants the mean number of children from affected sibs was 6.07 and from unaffected sibs 3.33. The difference in means is statistically significant.

Böök criticized these conclusions on the basis that a bias might exist in the data in favor of older families with relatively long marriage duration and a larger number of children. In reading the article by Reed and Palm, it *is* difficult to see whether in fact what was measured was completed fertility or partial fertility.

Furthermore, there may have been socioeconomic differences between the two groups of affected and non-affected people. Böök was interested in this and decided to test the hypothesis further on some data collected in Sweden by Sjögren in 1955.[5] He showed that the fertility of families where the father was affected by Huntington's chorea and families where the mother was affected was the same as in the general population at that time. All but one of the wives that he studied were age 45 or over and that one was 42. Essentially, these were completed families.

He matched his data with normal controls with regard to time, location, social class, duration of marriage, age of wife at marriage and so forth. So Böök's conclusion was that Sjögren's data did not indicate an increased fertility in persons with Huntington's chorea, at least in Sweden.

This example illustrates the many intricate problems involved in analyzing fertility.

Some other Swedish data relate Friedreich's ataxia, in which the age of onset is around 13 years, with low fertility: 83 patients had only 9 children. Persons with cerebellar ataxia had a higher fertility rate: 53 patients had 53 children, but they all belonged to 9 families. I do not know what conclusion can be drawn from those findings.[6]

Of more recent origin and perhaps more difficult to quarrel with are the findings of Shaw and Wright on a follow-up study of married retardates in Sheffield, England.[7] They were interested in following a population of 120 retarded men and 122 retarded women who had married. Ten of the subjects had married each other, so actually only 237 marriages were involved. The investigators were not able to find 45 of the subjects, but they did trace 197, that is, 81 percent.

The mean age of marriage in this group was 22.2 years for men and 25.2 years for women, the reverse of the pattern in England as a whole, where generally men marry three years later than women.

Shaw and Wright noted that in their study group there were 50 percent more live births per individual than for women in the general population married at the same age and for the same length of time. They did not actually give the details on their controls by age and marriage length, but they maintained that they did control for these variables. They also reported that the birth rate in their group was appreciably above that in families of unskilled workers.

It should be clear from the foregoing examples that any study of fertility of mentally retarded persons requires very careful analysis and control. The following important factors should always be taken into consideration:

1. The etiology of the retardation.
2. The degree of severity, measured either by appropriate IQ tests or tests for social maturity, or both.
3. The ages of the persons in the sample population.
4. Their marital status or the existence of any other type of union.
5. Time elapsed since sexual activity began, regardless of when marriage took place.
6. Frequency of sexual activity, including non-marital activity, and the use of contraception.
7. Socio-economic status.

Ideally, a study for the measure of reproductive capacity in the retarded should be both longitudinal and prospective. An ideal sample of retardates would be representative both of those who are institutionalized, either full- or part-time, and those in the general community. It would, of course, also have to take into account the seven foregoing factors.

Perhaps such a study should begin with essentially prepubertal individuals and follow them through life, recording the appearance of their maturational milestones and pertinent observations about their marital history, their sexual history, and their fertility.

Obviously, such a study would be expensive in time and money. I am not sure whether it would be warranted. Do we need such a study? Do we need to know the kind of information it would yield? Does it matter what the statistical physiologic reproductive capacity of mental retardates is? Do such data help us in dealing with the individual needs of an individual person who is retarded?

I submit that such detailed data would be of great academic interest, and I think all knowledge is of value. But what we are going to have to do, obviously, is to compromise since we won't have the resources for such an ideal study. We must do the best study we can with the reasonable resources available.

I would like to return to the fundamental question: How does reproductive capacity, meaning both fecundity and the social capacity to bear and raise children, differ from the normal among mentally retarded persons of varying degrees of severity and representing various etiologies?

As a kind of bridge to discussing Mr. Goodman's paper, I would like to point out that, in considering reproductive capacity, it is very difficult to separate physiologic capacity from social capacity. We must consider two intersecting axes. The first axis consists of the entire spectrum of retardation ranging from the near normal to the severe.

The second axis, obviously very closely related to the first, presents another spectrum: the broad range among retardates of capacity to function in the community as social beings—to marry, or at least to encounter other persons of the opposite sex, and to engage in sexual relationships. We institutionalize individuals at the lower end of this spectrum, segregating them by sex or otherwise limiting their ability to exercise any residual social capacity they might have. Such individuals might be physiologically capable of reproduction, but, either by social incapacity or imposed segregation, their opportunity to reproduce is sharply curtailed.

Obviously, those retardates whose capacity for reproduction interests us are those who are comparatively less severely retarded and comparatively more socially capable of approaching normal interpersonal relationships, including sexual relationships. Any comprehensive and definitive study of the reproductive capacity of the mentally retarded has to take these two intersecting axes into account. When we are dealing with individuals, we must obviously also concern ourselves with these two aspects.

In regard to Mr. Goodman's paper, I was very pleased to learn of the various family planning programs he described. It might be useful to look at the parallels and differences between family planning programs for people of normal intelligence and those for the retarded. There must certainly be tremendous similarities in such programs. Both kinds need to provide a full range of contraceptive services with technically trained staff and to concentrate, more than most of them do, on dealing with their patients on a warm, human, personal level. In actual practice, both kinds of programs have to cope with conflicts in staff and community attitudes toward premarital sexual activity.

The main differences in a program dealing primarily with the mentally retarded are in emphasis. First, such programs become far more concerned with the question of what the rights of a mentally retarded person are to engage in sexual expression, to marry, and to reproduce. They more generally involve the patient's parents, or if not the parents, at least the responsible members of the patient's family. They also have a much greater overlay of attitudinal problems—hostile attitudes toward mental retardation in addition to hostile attitudes toward sexual expression. They especially have to deal with the fears of people who think eugenically. Such people are apparently common in our society. The question of whether a mentally retarded person has any business trying to live a normal life is still an unsettled one.

Certainly, when we are instructing mentally retarded persons we have to be far more intense, far more careful, far more repetitious than with others. We need to look for more feedback in order to know whether the individual has understood what it is we are attempting to communicate to him.

Finally, we need far more careful follow-up—not only follow-up when asked by the patients, but going after them without being asked to see whether they have understood us and are practicing what we were trying to teach or whether there is anything else we can do for them.

I strongly second Mr. Goodman's suggestion that a family planning service in an institution should not be a separate function confined to Wednesday afternoons and a visiting doctor, but a function involving the entire staff working daily within the institution's normal patterns of instruction. Clinical services may or may not be provided on a scheduled basis, but if an institution's family planning program consists only of what happens during the clinic, it is an inadequate program.

On the other hand, I think it is fallacious to provide separate family planning services in the community for mentally retarded persons. It is more logical to open already existing community facilities and services to the mentally retarded and to train the staff of such facilities in ways of working with the mentally retarded. In serving the retarded, however, such programs would need to put greater emphasis than they do now on involving parents.

REFERENCES

1. Böök, J. A.: Fertility Trends in Some Types of Mental Defectives. *Eugen. Q.*, 6:113-116, June 1959.
2. Dahlberg, G.: Mental Deficiency. *Acta Genet.*, 2:15-29, 1951.
3. Juda, A.: Über Anzahl und Psychische Beschaffenheit der Nachkommen von Schwachsinnigen und Normalen Schülern. *Z. Neurol.*, 151:244-313, 1934.
4. Reed, S. C. & Palm, J. D.: Social Fitness versus Reproductive Fitness. *Science*, 113:294-296, 1951.
5. Sjögren, T.: Vererbungsmedizinische Untersuchungen über Huntington's Chorea in einer Schwedischen Bauernpopulation. *Z. KonstLehre*, 19:131-165, 1935.
6. Sjögren, T.: Klinische und Erbbiologische Untersuchungen über die Heredoataxien. *Acta Psychiat. Neurol. Suppl.*, 27:1-200, 1943.
7. Shaw, C. H. & Wright, C.: The Married Mental Defective. *Lancet*, 1:273-274, January 10, 1960.

7

Contraception for the Mentally Retarded: Current Methods and Future Prospects

GERALD D. LaVECK
and
FELIX F. DE LA CRUZ
*National Institute of Child
Health and Human Development
National Institutes of Health*

THE MANAGEMENT OF MENTAL RETARDATION is undergoing rapid change. The trend in institutions is to focus on the care and training of the profoundly and severely retarded, some of whom also have chronic disabilities such as epilepsy and motor dysfunction. On the other hand, more retarded children and adults, especially those mildly affected, are receiving special services in their own communities. Currently, many workers in the field advocate managing the retarded child as much like the normal child as possible.

One likely consequence of normalization is a greater opportunity for mentally retarded adolescents and adults to develop human interactions, including sexual experiences. Some segments of our society will find it abhorrent for mentally retarded individuals to engage in sexual activities. These may be the same individuals who espouse the idea that the mentally retarded have the right to education and enriching life experiences, except sexual expression. The central issue then is: should we, the so-called normal, regard sex among the mentally retarded as a right or as a privilege? If we regard it as a privilege, who decides which individual deserves such a privilege? On the other hand, if we consider sex as a basic human right, it behooves us to guide and inform the mentally retarded about the potential consequences of sexual expression, including pregnancy. For this reason, it is important for physicians and other professionals who are engaged in counseling the retarded to be aware of current and prospective contraceptive methods. Several excellent reviews pertaining to fertility regulation have been published recently.[1-4] Therefore, no attempt will be made to be comprehensive in this review. Instead, methods will be identified that now or in the future may have application for use by retarded men and women.

CURRENT METHODS

No completely new contraceptive drugs or devices have been made available in this country during the past decade. Of course, new formulations of the combined progestin-estrogen oral contraceptive and different types of intrauterine devices (IUDs) have improved these antifertility agents. The high cost of research probably has limited to some extent the development by industry of new technology in this field, but recent increases in federal support of research should accelerate product-oriented advances. Choices among all of the current contraceptive methods require judgment between risks to health and risk of pregnancy.

The Oral Contraceptives: Combined steroids taken orally are the most effective method of reversible contraception. When used as prescribed, they are close to 100% effective.[5] Tablets containing one of several synthetic progestins and a synthetic estrogen are generally administered for three weeks and then discontinued for one week.

These combined steroids produce many metabolic effects.[1-2] Morbidity and mortality from thromboembolic disease, including pulmonary embolism, occur with significantly greater frequency in oral contraceptive users than in non-users.[6,7] Oral contraceptives containing less than 50 micrograms of estrogen are preferred since thromboembolic disease reportedly occurs more often in women taking larger amounts of estrogen.[8]

Recent preliminary findings indicate that in "pill" users there is a greater risk of stroke; the incidence of breast cancer is not increased; the course of dysplasia of the cervix is unaffected; blood pressure is modestly elevated; and depression does not seem related to use of these drugs.

Some minor side effects that have been reported include migraine, breakthrough bleeding, nausea, vomiting, amenorrhea, chloasma, and change in libido.[1]

It is apparent that major and minor side effects limit the acceptability of this highly effective method of regulating fertility.

Omission of one or more tablets during the period when medication is to be taken daily can result in lack of protection against pregnancy. Because of the precise regimen that must be followed and the need for careful medical assessment of signs and symptoms of adverse effects, the oral contraceptives should be prescribed only for mentally retarded women who receive supervision from someone, such as a normal parent or spouse, or who are highly motivated and have mild intellectual impairment.

Intrauterine Devices: These devices usually are made of polyethylene and come in a variety of shapes. Recent new models include a plastic shield and a T-shaped plastic device wound with copper wire. The IUD is a very effective contraceptive as failure rates are about three pregnancies per 100 women during the first year of use, with lower rates with longer use.[9]

The most common side effects are vaginal bleeding, pain, cramps, backache, pelvic inflammatory disease, and perforation of the uterus. Spontaneous expulsion of the device occurs in about 10 percent of women during the first year after insertion. Another 10 percent are removed because of the users' complaints. Second generation IUDs appear to be more effective, are expelled less often, and cause fewer side effects.

Since contraceptive effectiveness is not dependent on sustained motivation or on any special intellectual skills, the IUD is particularly suitable for use by the sexually active retarded woman. Improvement of the IUD by the addition of metals or drugs will make this method even more effective and acceptable for the mentally retarded.

Other Methods: The vaginal diaphragm, condom, and temperature rhythm methods are also highly effective techniques. Less effective methods include vaginal spermacides, coitus interruptus, and calendar rhythm. The temperature rhythm method requires a high level of motivation, precise periodic observations, and prolonged abstinence, and is unsuitable for most retarded couples. The condom and diaphragm can be used by the mentally retarded, although they both suffer from low acceptability because of inconvenience.

Still another method, even though its use as a contraceptive is not approved by the Food and Drug Administration, is an injectable progestin, medroxyprogesterone acetate. The indicated uses are the treatment of certain cancers and endometriosis, but some physicians have administered this drug for contraception. They do so because of the simplicity of administration—the drug need be given only once every three or six months, depending on the dose—and because of the drug's effectiveness. Despite these attractive and unique features, this drug is not likely to receive wide use because the FDA is not expected to approve it for general use because of toxicologic considerations.

FUTURE PROSPECTS

About 50 percent of married women in this country who practiced contraception in 1970 reported that they used either oral contraceptives or IUDs. Still, neither of these nor any of the current methods is entirely satisfactory. Except for oral steroids, there is a significant risk of pregnancy with other methods and, with oral contraceptives, a concern about safety limits their acceptability.

There is a need to develop an array of contraceptives that meet the requirements of various population groups, including the mentally retarded. New agents must be safe and effective. Since mentally retarded men and women may have limited funds, new methods should be inexpensive. Other desirable features of new agents include reversibility and simplicity. Complicated surgical procedures and periodic professional intervention also will reduce acceptability. It is best if drugs have a local rather than a systemic effect. Unfortunately, we are not on the threshold of developing an ideal contraceptive, but exciting new leads are now being explored.

Improvements in Existing Methods: A variety of new ways to administer steroids will improve their acceptability. Progestins in small doses taken daily without estrogen have been investigated but have not been approved for general use in the United States. This method of hormonal contraception, unlike the combined steroids, does not suppress ovulation. Preliminary evidence indicates that it is less effective in preventing pregnancy than conventional oral contraceptives. The "minipill" also has been associated with irregular bleeding. One particular progestin that was available abroad has been withdrawn from use in the United States because it produced breast tumors in beagles. However, other progestins are likely to become available soon.

Clinical studies are now under way to evaluate systems and materials for uninterrupted administration of drugs and their slow and constant release. These include subcutaneous and subdermal progestin implants and progestin-releasing intrauterine devices, as well as injectables.[1] If new technology for releasing steroids leads to safe and effective regulation of fertility, retarded women would be potential users.

Development of Sterilization Techniques: Surgical sterilization is an effective antifertility procedure. However, the surgical techniques that are available at the present time—tubal ligation in the female and vasectomy in the male—usually result in permanent loss of fertility. Reversibility requires surgery and is less than 50 percent successful.[4,10] Efforts are under way to develop reversible means of tubal and vas occlusion by using implanted devices.

During recent years the estimated number of vasectomies performed in the United States has risen dramatically, reaching a total of over 300,000 in 1970. The operation in which the vas deferens is severed is relatively simple to perform and is believed to be safe. A major factor which limits the usefulness of the present procedure is the difficulty of surgically rejoining the cut ends of the vas and restoring fertility to men who request it. Attempts are under way to develop prototype devices which can be surgically inserted in the vas and produce a reversible occlusion. For example, ball valve devices are being evaluated. By turning the stem of the valve, it is possible to either block or permit passage of sperm through the vas deferens. If the approach proves safe and effective in animals, human trials would probably follow.

The development of reversible sterilization in the female is more complex. Still, several methods are being pursued in which sterilization would be carried out by transcervical instrumentation obviating the need for abdominal surgery.

The development of simple, reversible methods of sterilization would result in a particularly appealing way for mentally retarded persons to control family size. But, by providing them the opportunity to have children, are we not taking the risk that these children might be mentally retarded? Will they, as parents, be able to provide the physical and emotional nurturing that their children need?

A number of investigators have demonstrated that some mentally retarded individuals have the ability to support themselves and their families.[11, 12, 13] Among the 93 surviving children of 73 mentally retarded women with a mean IQ of 73.5, Brandon[11] observed that "being brought up by a discharged mental defective does not appear to depress the children's level of intelligence." In this study, the average intelligence of all the children who received psychological evaluations was found to be 91.3; those who were brought up by their own mother had a mean IQ of 98.7.

Prostaglandins: In pregnant women, the corpus luteum is probably indispensable for the maintenance of pregnancy during the first seven weeks. This suggests that termination of pregnancy would occur if corpus luteum function were disrupted early. The search for a luteolytic agent has considerable relevance since this type of drug could be taken by the woman at the time of her expected period. It would physiologically inhibit the function of the corpus luteum and bring about menstruation.

The influence of prostaglandins in reproductive function has been of recent interest. Prostaglandins are biological substances that have a remarkably wide-range of effects. They are distributed in many mammalian tissues in very small amounts. Although in lower animals prostaglandins may be luteolytic, in women the abortifacient activity attributed to prostaglandins is probably based on the initiation of myometrial contractions.[1] Recent studies tend to support the thesis that, in the monkey and human, the pregnancy-terminating effect of prostaglandins is not related to their effect on the corpus luteum.[10]

Studies have been carried out with prostaglandins for the purpose of inducing labor, abortion, and menses, but more time is needed to assess these effects. The study of prostaglandin analogues and antagonists now being synthesized may shed further light on prostaglandins' role in fertility regulation.[10] What place prostaglandins will have as antifertility agents remains to be seen. Regardless of the outcome of these studies, the development of a menses inducer would be particularly adaptable for use as a contraceptive by retarded women.

Prediction, Detection, and Control of Ovulation: The oral contraceptives inhibit ovulation by acting on the hypothalamus. Hormonal substances from the brain with LH and/or FSH releasing properties in turn act on the pituitary. These hypothalamic releasing factors are relatively simple decapeptides. At least one such factor has been identified and synthesized.[14, 15] Research is now under way to determine if these substances can be used to induce ovulation, making the rhythm method more precise. Also research is being carried out to produce inhibitors of hypothalamic releasing factors that selectively inhibit ovulation or induce the menses.[1] Finally, the possibility of producing analogues that would act as competitive antagonists holds promise as a method of fertility regulation. Unfortunately, many years of research and development are needed before such products become available.

Obviously, natural methods of family planning would be greatly improved by the development of a predictor of impending ovulation. A useful predictor would have to be simple, cheap, reliable, and become positive about 72 hours before ovulation. Many studies have documented changes in hormone and steroid levels in blood and urine around the time of ovulation. However, the detection of these changes is complicated and not of practical use.

A husband and wife team from Australia has trained large numbers of women to recognize the quantity and quality of cervical mucus secreted during the cycle as an indicator of fertile or infertile days. Women do this by noting the degree of dryness or moisture in the genital area. A number of dry days occur after the menstrual period and are followed by a gradual change to a wet or sticky sensation.[16] This method, even if it proves to be effective, would be too complex for the retarded woman.

Post-Coital Estrogens: The post-coital administration of large doses of estrogen interferes with pregnancy in animals and women, presumably by increasing the tubal transport of ova or zygotes.[17] However, once the ovum is implanted in humans, large doses of estrogen are ineffective.

The recommended dosage is 5 milligrams of ethinyl estradiol or 50 milligrams of diethylstilbestrol for five consecutive days. Preferably, the drug is given within 24 hours of exposure.[18] Although the Food and Drug Administration has not approved the use of estrogens as a post-coital contraceptive, they have been used for rape victims, women who have engaged in unexpected intercourse, and when more conventional methods of contraception fail.

More research is needed, but estrogens as a "morning-after-pill" would appear to be useful in avoiding unwanted pregnancies in mentally retarded women after unprotected intercourse. This method is not intended for regular use because of side effects, including nausea, vomiting, and bleeding.

Oral Contraceptives for Men: Modern male methods of fertility regulation are essential to family planning programs which would offer a variety of means for couples to control their fertility. However, there are fewer scientific opportunities to develop products for men because there are fewer steps in which to interfere with the male reproductive cycle. Opportunities to intervene are essentially limited to sperm production, sperm maturation, and sperm transport.

Important considerations in developing male methods of contraception are safety, effectiveness, and maintenance of libido. At least one study is under way in men which investigates the merits of combining an orally active weak androgen, which inhibits pituitary release of gonadotropins, with an orally active potent androgen, methyltestosterone. Gonadotropins regulate the production of sperm by the testes. Inhibiting gonadotropins with androgens results in progressive disappearance of sperm from the ejaculate. Preliminary studies indicate that after the androgens were discontinued, sperm production returned to normal levels. One cannot be optimistic that in the near future there will be a safe and effective modern method of contraception for males.

SUMMARY

The development of fertility regulating methods has not moved swiftly. In fact, since the advent of the IUD and oral contraceptives, no new methods have been introduced in this country. Increased fundamental and directed research during the past five years has resulted in a number of leads that eventually could result in new drugs, devices, and methods of contraception.

Mentally retarded men and women generally will be able to use the same contraceptives as normal couples. To avoid unwanted pregnancies, the intrauterine device appears to be the agent of choice for retarded women and the condom for retarded men at this time. The future prospect of voluntary reversible sterilization for men and women would appear to be especially suitable for the mentally retarded.

REFERENCES

1. SEGAL, S. & TIETZE, C.: Contraceptive Technology: Current and Prospective Methods. *Reports on Population/Family Planning,* Population Council, New York, July 1971.
2. SEGAL, S., CROZIER, P., CONDLIFFE, P. & CORFMAN, P.: *Control of Mammalian Reproduction.* Springfield, Charles C. Thomas, 1972, pp. 500.
3. ODELL, W. & MOYER, D.: *Physiology of Reproduction.* St. Louis, Mosby, 1971, pp. 152.
4. HELLMAN, L., CORFMAN, P., & BECKLES, F.: A Five-Year Plan for Population Research and Family Planning Services. *Family Planning Perspectives,* 3:33, 1971.
5. TIETZE, C.: Effectiveness of Contraceptive Methods. In Diczfalusy, D. and Borell, U. (Eds.): *Control of Human Fertility: Proceedings of the Fifteenth Nobel Symposium, Sodergarn, Lidingo, Sweden.* New York, John Wiley and Sons, 1971, pp. 303-314.
6. SARTWELL, P. E., MASI, A. T., ARTHES, F. G., GREENE, G. R., & SMITH, H. E.: Thromboembolism and Oral Contraceptives: an Epidemiological Case-Control Study. *Amer. Jour. of Epidemiology,* 90:365-380, 1969.
7. INMAN, W. H. W. & VESSEY, M. P.: Investigations of Deaths from Pulmonary, Coronary, and Cerebral Thrombosis and Embolism in Women of Childbearing Age. *Br. Med. J.,* 2:193-199, 1968.
8. INMAN, W. H. W., VESSEY, M. P., WESTERHOLM, B., & ENGELUND, A.: Thromboembolic Disease and the Steroidal Content of Oral Contraceptives: A Report to the Committee on Safety of Drugs. *Br. Med. J.,* 2:203-209, 1970.
9. TIETZE, C. & LEWIT, S.: Evaluation of Intrauterine Devices: Ninth Progress Report of the Cooperative Statistical Program. *Studies in Family Planning,* 1:1-40, 1970.
10. Progress Report on the Five-Year Plan for Family Planning Services and Population Research Programs prepared for the Special Sub-committee on Human Resources of the Committee on Labor and Public Welfare, United States Senate: United States Government Printing Office, Washington, D.C., January, 1972, pp. 157.
11. BRANDON, M. W. G.: The Intellectual and Social Status of Children of Mental Defectives. *J. Ment. Sci.,* 103:710-738, 1957.
12. MATTINSON, J.: *Marriage and Mental Handicap: A Study of Subnormality in Marriage.* Pittsburgh, University of Pittsburgh Press, 1970, pp. 231.
13. SHAW, C. H. & WRIGHT, C. H.: The Married Mental Defective: A Follow-Up Study. *Lancet,* 1:273-274, January 30, 1960.
14. SCHALLY, A. V., ARIMURA, A., KASTIN, A. J., MATSUO, H., BABA, Y., REDDING, T. W., NAIR, R. M. G., DEBELJUK, L., & WHITE, W. F.: Gonadotropin-releasing Hormone: One polypeptide regulates secretion of luteinizing and follicle-stimulating hormone. *Science,* 173:1036-1038, 1971.
15. GUILLEMIN, R.: Physiology and Chemistry of the Hypothalamic Releasing Factors in Gonadotropins: A New Approach to Fertility Control. *Contraception,* 5:1-19, 1972.

16. BILLINGS, E. L., BILLINGS, J. J., BROWN, J. B., & BURGER, H. G.: Symptoms and Hormonal Changes Accompanying Ovulation. *Lancet*, 1:282-284, February 5, 1972.

17. MORRIS, J. M. & VAN WAGENEN, G.: Compounds Interfering with Ovum Implantation and Development III. Role of Estrogens. *Am. J. of Obs. and Gynec.*, 96:804-815, 1966.

18. HASPELS, A. A.: Post-Coital Estrogen in Large Doses. *International Planned Parenthood Federation Medical Bulletin*, 6:3-4, April, 1972.

Physical and Biological Aspects
(SESSION ONE)

GENERAL DISCUSSION
W. ROY BREG, *Presiding*

Mr. Goodman agreed with Dr. Helbig's emphasis on the need for follow-up of contraceptive services provided the retarded. He told of an institution with a good contraceptive service where, after the Congressional hearings on the contraceptive pill, the staff found pills under pillows and dishes and "everywhere." Advocating a kind of continuing process of contraceptive education, he said that such education should include "emotional inputs." In regard to the provision of contraceptives to retardates living in the community, Mr. Goodman pointed out that none of those served by the St. Paul Planned Parenthood Association had indicated that the service had made any difference in their level of sexual activity, although it had obviously allowed them, and their parents, a greater feeling of safety. An increasing number of parents have indicated that they do not want their offspring to be deprived of the elements of a full life, including sexual activity, he maintained.

Asked whether there were any difficulties in getting retarded people to use contraception, Mr. Goodman said that the key to an effective program lay in the attitudes of the staff. Among retardates with verbal ability, receptiveness to contraceptive advice is about the same as in a normal population, he said. Dr. Breg stressed the importance of recognizing the heterogeneity of the mentally retarded, especially with regard to intellectual capacities when considering their various behavioral characteristics. Because of this heterogeneity, generalizing from one group of retarded may be unwarranted. The findings in one study group may well not be applicable to another group of retarded individuals.

When the discussion turned to the relative reliability of the pill and the IUD as contraceptive prescriptions for the retarded, differing points of view emerged. Dr. Athanasiou expressed distrust in the ability of the retarded to take pills regularly or to recognize the expulsion of an IUD. Mr. Hellmuth and Mr. Goodman, on the other hand, expressed confidence that even persons with very low IQs could be trained to take pills regularly. Mr. Hellmuth pointed out that retardates are used to taking medicine regularly for all kinds of conditions. Mr. Goodman pointed out that women with very low IQs have been trained to use sanitary napkins, a more complicated procedure than taking a pill or recognizing the expulsion of an IUD. Mr. Goodman also suggested that the supervision provided in institutions can deal with resident's problems in pill-taking or IUD expulsion. He suggested, however, that specific investigations are needed on the reliability of the residents taking the pill.

Some doubts were also expressed about the pill as a safe medication. Dr. Salerno commented that he would hesitate to prescribe it to teenagers because of its possible effect on endocrine function, and Mr. Goodman said that this was a point of view apparently shared by many physicians who, in spite of the problems of IUD retention, prefer fitting teenagers with IUDs to prescribing the pill for them.

Dr. Salerno asserted, however, that although the pill is more reliable as a contraceptive method, it must be taken without fail on a regular schedule. Although there has been a reduction in the expulsion rate of IUDs, pregnancies do occur with IUDs in place, as well as due to expulsion. Dr. Gordon, on the other hand, suggested that the IUD holds more promise for effecting contraception for the mentally retarded in the future. He pointed out that most of the data on IUD reliability available today relate to the loop, which is now being superseded by the superior Dalkon shield and a newer copper-tipped device that experimental data suggest is even superior to the Dalkon shield.

Asked whether the institutional birth control program he described is voluntary or compulsory, Mr. Goodman replied that the institution's decision to establish the program was voluntary, but that for some sexually overactive residents contraception is prescribed for protection and "not necessarily" on a voluntary basis. Others have asked for contraceptive service, he said, but have not subsequently changed their life style. He added that his work with retardates has given him the impression that they have a far greater amount of sexual experience than he had once thought possible. One of the commonest forms of contraception among those who are institutionalized, he said, is homosexuality.

PHYSICAL AND BIOLOGICAL ASPECTS
ASPECTS
(Session Two)

8

Effects of Changing Sexuality on the Gene Pool

SHELDON C. REED
and
V. ELVING ANDERSON
Dight Institute for Human Genetics
University of Minnesota

IN OUR RESEARCH, we have attempted to understand the factors that have been maintaining the frequency of mental retardation in the general population at a relatively constant level for at least several generations. Such an understanding would seem to be important to any consideration of policies that might bring about any major change in the sexual behavior of the mentally retarded.

While our definition of mental retardation (IQ 69 or below) is arbitrary, it is a satisfactory convention for our research. The major problem in such research is an inability to distinguish between the interacting genetic and environmental factors in the etiology of the various types of mental retardation. In most cases of mental retardation, it is still not clear whether a strong or weak genetic component is involved. This is true largely because no specific diagnosis exists for the majority of cases; they are merely labeled "idiopathic" or "undifferentiated." Therefore, in considering the effects of retardation on the "gene pool," we cannot make calculations based on knowledge about specific types of genes but must consider the genotype as a whole and the environmental components as well.

There are two major variables in any equation describing the population dynamics of the mentally retarded:

1) the relative reproductive rates of retarded and of non-retarded persons, and

2) the relative risks of retardation among the offspring of the two groups.

We would expect appreciable differences in retardation (and presumably in the gene pool) of the next generation depending upon whether all of the retarded persons in the present generation reproduce or none of them do.

In the years following the acceptance of Mendel's laws, there was a widespread belief that practically all mental retardation was caused by a few recessive genes. Investigations into the causes of retardation generally neglected the environmental components of the various kinds of retardation. Even today, attempts to elucidate the specific environmental insults contributing to mental retardation have met with only modest success.

Appalled at the very large families produced by some retarded parents, early investigators had an honest fear that eugenic disaster was just around the corner. Their fear would have been justified if *all* mentally retarded persons had gigantic families. The retarded who produced no children were omitted from their calculations.

Work with population dynamics should include two or more consecutive generations if the calculations are to be tested by what actually takes place.

Between 1911 and 1918, a project was begun at the State colony for the mentally retarded at Faribault, Minnesota, which has made it possible for us to do just that. IQ scores were obtained not only on a selected group of patients, but also on the members of their families, including, whenever possible, their parents, their siblings, and their grandparents. At the Dight Institute for Human Genetics we began our studies of mental retardation with data from these investigations, selecting as our probands 289 white persons with IQ scores of 69 or less who were institutional-

TABLE 1

Average Number of Offspring Per Individual in Relation to IQ

(Both married and unmarried siblings included.)

IQ range	Number of siblings in parental generation	Average number of offspring
70 and below	106	2.09
71 - 85	283	2.30
86 - 100	1010	2.22
101 - 115	1122	2.20
116 - 130	376	2.49
131 and above	48	2.98
Total combined sample	2945	2.26

ized at Faribault during this period. We have traced the descendants of the grandparents of these probands forward to 1961. The resulting data cover up to 7 generations and include more than 80,000 persons.[1]

In analyzing some of these data, Higgins, Reed and Reed,[2] and then Bajema,[3] have shown very clearly that there is no correlation between measured intelligence and family size when the childless persons in the parental generation are included in the data. Childless persons are not only significant members of their generation, but they include disproportionately larger numbers of people having low IQs. Omission of the childless members of the parental generation from the data results in unacceptably biased statistics that relate family size and intelligence. Unfortunately, the groundless fears that the mentally retarded will outbreed the more intelligent are still very much alive.

A further analysis of the data shows very clearly that when the childless members of the parental generation are all included, the mentally retarded have the lowest average number of children and the group with the highest IQs have the highest.

Table 1 shows that when the childless members of the parental generation are included, the group with IQs 70 and below pro-

duced the lowest average number of children (2.09 per retardate),
while the group with IQs 131 and above averaged the highest
number of offspring (2.98 per person).

Similarly, Higgins, Reed, and Reed divided their data into
three IQ groups: individuals in the parental generation with
IQs 70 and below; with IQs between 101-110; and with IQs of
131 and above.[2] Nearly a third (31 percent) of the individuals
with low IQs had had no children, in contrast to only 10 percent
in the middle range of intelligence, and 4 percent of those in the
highest range. The three groups came nearer together in percentages of those who had only one child (20, 19, and 17 percent
respectively). Far fewer of the retardates had 2 to 5 children than
either of the other groups, among whom 2 and 3 children were
the most common size of family. Among all individuals having 6
to 10 children, the retardates were again in the ascendancy, but
here the percentages of the total number of retardates were small,
adding up to less than 15 percent of all.

In the 1965 sample of 1,450 unselected retardates descended
from our probands' grandparents, 43.4 percent had never reproduced and for various reasons (death, institutionalization, sterilization, age) would probably never reproduce; 35 percent had
reproduced at least once; 17.4 had not reproduced but were
judged capable of doing so, and the reproductive status of 4.2
percent was unknown. Of the 867 men in the total sample (59.8
percent), only 247 had reproduced, but of the 583 women (only
40.2 percent of the total sample), 260 had reproduced.[1]

Another analysis compared the IQs of 7,778 children descended
from the probands' grandparents according to whether one, both
or neither parent was retarded.[1] The results show that nearly 40
percent of the 89 children both of whose parents were retarded
had IQs below 70, and only 20 percent had IQs above 90. The
mean IQ of these 89 children was 74. Of the 654 children with
only one retarded parent, 15 percent were retarded, and 54 percent
had IQs above 90; their mean IQ was 90. Of the 7,035 children
with neither parent retarded, only one percent were retarded and

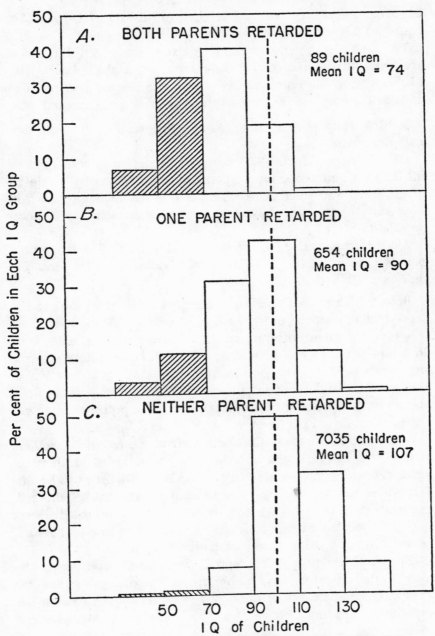

IQ Ranges of 7778 Children with Both, One, or Neither Parent Retarded.

91 percent had IQs above 90; their mean IQ was 107. (See figure 1.)

We have just shown that the reproductive rates of the retarded are lower than those of the non-retarded, but the relative risks of retardation are *much* higher among the offspring of retarded persons than among the normals. Let us ask two more questions:

1. *What proportion of retarded offspring have one or both parents retarded?*

Slightly over a third (33.4 percent) of the parents of the 289 institutionalized probands were retarded, as shown in Table 20 of the Reed and Reed book.[1] This is a much higher proportion than can be expected for parents of retardates in the general population.

2. *Does the risk of retardation for children of one retarded parent depend partly on whether that retarded parent was the mother or father?*

Before attempting to answer these questions, let us look at the reproductive histories of our probands' siblings. Along with their offspring, on whom information was obtained at the same time or in follow up, they represent completed families. Table 2 presents the numbers of retarded and non-retarded siblings in relation to the numbers and mental status of their offspring and Table 3 translates these numbers into proportions. The probands were not included in these calculations.

These tables show us that there were more retarded brothers than sisters, but less than one-fourth of the retarded brothers reproduced as against nearly half of the retarded sisters. The difference is statistically highly significant. Furthermore, the risk of retardation was higher for the children of retarded sisters (about 1 in 6) than for children of retarded brothers (about 1 in 10). Here the difference is statistically significant.

Thus both the proportion reproducing and the risk of retardation in the offspring were higher for retarded females than for males. The joint effect of these two variables can be seen in the net number of retarded children per individual. As variable 6

TABLE 2

REPRODUCTION BY SIBLINGS OF RETARDED PROBANDS, AND MENTAL RETARDATION IN OFFSPRING

	Sisters of Probands		Brothers of Probands	
	Mentally Retarded	Not Retarded	Mentally Retarded	Not Retarded
Number of individuals	144	365	186	352
Those who reproduced	68	268	44	212
No. of children	275	966	189	780
Children surviving two or more years	238	899	166	739
Mentally retarded children	45	19	18	22

TABLE 3

COMBINED EFFECT OF SEX DIFFERENCE IN REPRODUCTIVE RATES AND RISK OF MENTAL RETARDATION IN OFFSPRING

	Sisters of Probands		Brothers of Probands	
	Mentally Retarded	Not Retarded	Mentally Retarded	Not Retarded
1. Proportion ever reproducing	0.47	0.73	0.24	0.60
2. Children per reproducing individual	4.04	3.60	4.30	3.68
3. Proportion of children surviving	0.87	0.93	0.88	0.95
4. Net number of surviving children per individual	1.65	2.44	0.91	2.10
5. Risk of retardation per child	.189	.021	.108	.030
6. Net number of retarded children per individual	0.31	0.05	0.10	0.06
7. Net number of non-retarded children	1.34	2.39	0.81	2.04

in Table 3 shows, this was 3 times greater for retarded females than for retarded males.

Table 3 also shows clearly that the proportions of retarded sisters and brothers who reproduced was much lower than the proportion of the non-retarded siblings who did so and that the normal siblings produced on the average almost twice as many children as their retarded siblings.

However, those retardates who did reproduce had more children than their normal siblings. The difference, though slight, was statistically significant.

Let us leave our institutionalized probands and their relatives to see what is going on in the general population. It is necessary to construct models because data from the general population are still lacking. Consequently, we have built a model with a hypothetical population of 100,000 persons with equal numbers of females and males. Such a model requires a percentage of mental retardation in the general population to be arbitrarily set; we have selected 2 percent as a reasonable proportion. We have also assumed that the proportion of females among retardates in the population is close to the proportion in Table 2, that is, 144 out of 330, or 43.6 percent. This assumption gives us 872 retarded females and 1,128 retarded males in our hypothetical population of 100,000 persons, as shown in the first line of Table 4.

The proportion of each type of person reproducing, including the normal siblings, is obtainable from Table 3, as is the number of surviving children per pair of reproducing parents. The risk of retardation per child is also obtained from Table 3.

The most important outcome of this hypothetical model is that 12 percent of the retarded children in the population would have a retarded mother and only 5 percent a retarded father, making a total of 17 percent with at least one retarded parent. Almost half the excess of retarded children having a retarded mother over those having a retarded father results from the fact that twice as many retarded females reproduce as do retarded males. The other half of the excess results mostly from the greater risk of retardation for children of retarded mothers. The model also indicates that

TABLE 4

HYPOTHETICAL POPULATION OF 100,000 PERSONS ILLUSTRATING
EFFECT OF SEX DIFFERENCE IN REPRODUCTIVE RATES AND
RISK OF MENTAL RETARDATION IN THE OFFSPRING

	Retarded		Not Retarded Both Sexes	Total
	Females	Males		
Initial numbers*	872	1128	98,000	100,000
Proportion reproducing	0.47	0.24	0.67	
Individuals reproducing	410	271	65,660	66,341
Pairs reproducing	410	271	32,490	33,171
Surviving children per pair	3.51	3.78	3.42	
Number surviving children	1439	1024	111,116	113,579
Risk of retardation per child	0.189	0.108	0.017*	0.020
Number retarded children	272	111	1,889*	2,272*
Distribution of retarded children	12%	5%	83%	100%
		17%		

* Arbitrarily set to result in 2.0 percent retardation for both generations.

neither parent of 83 percent of the retarded children in the population is retarded. Very similar findings were observed in our current study of families with psychotic disorders.[5]

The next question is: Are there any data with which to test the model? The only large study that would permit us to challenge the model is the one done by Reed and Reed in 1965, as it is the only one having IQ values on more than two consecutive generations of relatives. Measures of intelligence for many thousands of persons are shown in the pedigree charts of that report, and when all are combined, as they are on page 54 of their book, an essentially normal curve for the distribution of intelligence results.[1] In the entire study population of about 80,000 persons, only 2.6 percent were retarded, including the 289 retarded probands.

If the probands and all their first, second, and third degree relatives are removed from the 80,000, the remaining population consists of many thousands of distant relatives of the probands who have very few genetic or environmental similarities to the probands and their close relatives. In fact, this group of fourth and fifth degree relatives should have a *lower* frequency of retardation than that of the general public. This expectation derives from the fact that the general public includes some clusters of retardation surrounding a proband, while the removal of probands and close relatives removes these clusters from the study group.

The Reed and Reed book[1] provides the detailed pedigrees from which we made the following analysis after removing all descendants of the parents of the probands, including the probands. All remaining persons shown in generation IV of each pedigree are the first cousins once removed from the proband. These first cousins once removed, who share only one-sixteenth of their genes with the proband, are the parental generation in the analysis and the offspring are the "children." Most of these "children" were actually adults at the time of the study and appear in generation V in the pedigree charts. They are first cousins twice removed from the probands and share only one-thirty-second of their genes with the probands. The offspring for whom we had no information regarding intelligence have been omitted from the table, but the percentages of retarded persons among them probably would not be significantly different than among those for whom information was available.

Table 5 shows that among 10,403 children of these first cousins once removed, there were only 163 retarded persons, or 1.6 percent of the total. This is a lower proportion than would be expected in the general population, for the reasons already mentioned. For the same reasons, the proportion found to be retarded children of two normal parents—1.3 percent—is also lower than would be expected in the general population.

It seems reasonable to assume, on the basis of this analysis of a sample biased by selection toward a lower incidence of retardation than in the general population, that the frequency of mental

TABLE 5

Children of First Cousins Once Removed of 289 Institutionalized Retarded Probands

Children grouped according to parents' status	Total number of children	Number retarded	Number normal	Percent retarded
Both parents retarded	21	13	8	62%
One parent retarded, one normal	163	16	147	10%
Both parents normal	10,219	134	10,085	1.3%
All groups of parents	10,403	163	10,240	1.6%

retardation in the white population of the upper Middle West is about 2 percent and that the percentage of retardates with both parents normal is just about the 1.7 percent predicted by the model in Table 4. Thus, observations from the data and expectations from the model are in good agreement.

Moreover, the model predicts that both parents of 83 percent of the retarded persons of any generation have normal intelligence. In our analysis of the offspring of our probands' first cousins once removed, we found that both parents of 134 of the 163 retardates, or 82.2 percent, had normal intelligence, as Table 5 shows. This finding is in excellent agreement with the model's prediction.

This confirmation of the model allows us to proceed with more model building as a way of finding out what might happen if the reproduction of all retardates increased to the level of that of their normal siblings. Such an increase, of course, is not a realistic expectation, as many retardates, including those with Down's syndrome, Tay-Sachs disease, and all the most profound types of mental retardation, often fail to survive to reproductive age. Consequently, our second model, which gives the same proportion of persons reproducing among retarded persons as among their normal siblings, presents as an absolute maximum the percentage of retarded children in the general population that retarded parents would produce. The calculations are presented in Table 6.

In our first hypothetical model (Table 4), retarded parents

TABLE 6

REPRODUCTIVE EXPECTATIONS OF HYPOTHETICAL POPULATION OF 100,000 PERSONS, ASSUMING THAT THE RETARDATES WOULD REPRODUCE AT THE SAME RATE AS THEIR SIBLINGS

	Retarded Females	Males	Not Retarded Both Sexes	Total
Initial numbers*	872	1,128	98,000	100,000
Proportion reproducing	0.67	0.67	0.67	
Individuals reproducing	584	756	65,660	67,000
Pairs reproducing	584	756	32,160	33,500
Surviving children per pair	3.42	3.42	3.42	
Number surviving children	1,997	2,586	109,987	114,570
Risk of retardation per child	0.189	0.108	0.017	0.022**
Number retarded children	377	279	1,870	2,526
Distribution of retarded children	14.9%	11.1%	74.0%	100%

26%

* Arbitrarily set to result in 2% retardation.
** Total number of retarded children divided by total number of surviving children.

produced 17 percent of the retarded. Therefore, if none of the retarded parents had reproduced, there would have been 17 percent fewer retarded children born. The benefits of contraceptive action on the part of these retarded parents would have been even greater than the statistics indicate because their own retardation would probably have made them less than satisfactory parents for both their normal and retarded children.

In other words, there would have been a drop in the percentage of mental retardation in the general population from 2 percent to 1.7 percent if all the retardates in the parental generation had refrained from reproducing. A 0.3 percent reduction in mental retardation may not seem to be a very large economy, but it is extremely significant in terms of the reduction of human misery. While such a reduction is unlikely to be achieved, even a smaller reduction could be of tremendous importance to the families at high risk of producing retarded children and to society as a whole.

On the other hand, if all the retarded persons in our model reproduced at the same rate as their siblings, their share in the production of mentally retarded children would increase from 17 percent of the total to 26 percent—a 53 percent increase in the number of mentally retarded children produced by retarded parents. This large increment would increase the frequency of retardation in the general population from 2 percent to 2.2 percent—only a 0.2 percent increase, but a considerable one if viewed in terms of the human beings involved.

As Table 4 shows, if none of the retarded in a population of 100,000 persons of the same generation had any children, the generation would still produce 111,116 children who would survive beyond the age of 2 years and of these 1,889 would be retarded. However, as can be seen in Table 6, if all the retarded reproduced at the same rate as their normal siblings, the generation would produce a total of 114,570 surviving children of whom 2,526 would be retarded—an increase of 637 retarded children. It is highly unlikely that an increase of this size would ever occur. However, the model indicates the importance of accompanying any encouragement of increased heterosexual activity for retarded persons with effective contraceptive methods.

What effect would increased reproduction of the retardates have on the gene pool? This question cannot be answered with precision because of our inability to distinguish clearly between the genetic and environmental factors in retardation. However, it is reasonable to assume that any change in the reproductive rate of the retarded will be echoed by a change in the frequency of the genes related to mental retardation, though not necessarily in exactly the same proportion.

In principle, society should never encourage the reproduction of persons with gross defects. It may encourage reproduction for specific individuals as exceptions to the general rule. However, exceptions should be most rare for couples in which both members are retarded, for they are at highest risk of producing a retarded child. In such instances, therapeutic abortions may be justified.

The group carrying the second greatest risk of retardation to their prospective offspring consists of retarded women, and next comes retarded men.

SUMMARY

1. Higgins, Reed and Reed[2] first demonstrated that there is approximately a zero correlation between measured intelligence and family size when the childless persons in the parental generation are included in the data.

2. Some retarded persons have very large families, but more than half of them do not have any children. As a result, the average number of children per individual produced by the retarded segment of the population is a little smaller than the average produced by the non-retarded.

3. It is possible to construct models to demonstrate what could be expected if more retarded persons were reproducing. Our model shows that, at present, retarded parents produce about 17 percent of all retarded children. Consequently, if no retarded persons had any offspring, there would be a 17 percent decrease in the proportion of mentally retarded persons in the next generation.

4. Another model shows what would happen if all retardates reproduced at the same rate as their normal siblings—an assumption unlikely to be realized, for many retardates do not survive to reproductive age. However, if this rate of reproduction were possible for the retarded, the proportion of the retarded children produced by retarded parents would increase from 17 to 26 percent. Such a large increase would be undesirable from almost every point of view, even though it would only increase the percentage of retarded children born to all persons in the population from 2.0 percent to 2.2 percent.

Changes in the reproductive rates of retarded persons should be echoed by changes in the gene pool. At present, however, retarded parents produce 17 percent of all retarded children, and it is improbable that there will be any large deviation in this proportion in the immediate future.

REFERENCES

1. REED, E. W. & REED, S. C.: *Mental Retardation: a Family Study.* Philadelphia, W. B. Saunders Co., 1965, 719 pp.
2. HIGGINS, J. V., REED, E. W., & REED, S. C.: Intelligence and Family Size: a Paradox Resolved. *Eugen. Q.*, 9:84-90, 1962.
3. BAJEMA, C. J.: Estimation of the Direction and Intensity of Natural Selection in Relation to Human Intelligence by Means of the Intrinsic Rate of Natural Increase. *Eugen. Q.*, 10:175-187, 1963.
4. REED, S. C.: The Evolution of Human Intelligence: Some Reasons Why It Should Be a Continuing Process. *Amer. Sci.*, 53:317-326, 1965.
5. REED, S. C., HARTLEY, C., ANDERSON, V. E., PHILLIPS, V. P., & JOHNSON, N. A.: *The Psychoses: Family Studies,* (in Press).

9

Effects of Changing Sexuality on the Gene Pool

A Response to Sheldon Reed

EDMOND A. MURPHY

Division of Medical Genetics
Johns Hopkins University School of Medicine
Department of Medicine

PEOPLE WHO HAVE SPECULATED about the earthly fate of man have been divided between the optimists who believe that we progress quickly and the pessimists who believe we have reached our peak and there is no future but decay. But optimism and pessimism are attitudes. Chemists do not rejoice in the fact that the atomic weight of carbon is 12; mathematicians do not regard it as a scandal that pi cannot be expressed as the quotient of two integers. Optimism and pessimism are hardly matters for scientists whose business is truth. It seems to me we should not be concerned with attitude but with perspective, theory, and fact.

The first order of business is to decide what our hopes might be for the future of the race. Doubtless we would wish to achieve two objectives: survival and excellence. Of these, survival is a question of hard objective fact to which, at some time in the future, there will be a definite answer; excellence now, and perhaps permanently, involves value judgments which are incurably personal.

From one viewpoint, the objectives are the same: what conduces to survival is excellent, and to pursue the one is to pursue the other. Such are value judgments, however, that there may be some conflict between the two objectives, and this conflict must be resolved if any coherent policy is to result.

If we believe that

> *One crowded hour of glorious life*
> *Is worth an age without a name**

then it is clear enough we should cultivate only the excellent. There might however, be fierce dispute as to who are excellent. The judges are part of the judged, and we have reasons, mathematical, philosophical, and psychological, for believing that an epistemology for a system cannot be constructed entirely from inside that system. Thus, the ultimate practical criterion of excellence would perhaps be reduced to identification of people who succeed in killing off the rest, a criterion which would again imply that excellence is the capacity to survive.

A more successful approach to the future would seem to be the one that optimizes the chance of survival for the species. Since history seems to suggest that the ill-equipped do not survive, such a policy would guarantee some kind of excellence, though to the visionary and the poet it might seem somewhat drab. At least in a sense, the reference point would be something outside the system. While to find a common denominator we might have to settle for rather materialistic standards, there would at least be a firm criterion of excellence to which we might appeal.

This point of view is open to the old criticism that "survival of the fittest" really means "survival of the survivors." Furthermore, to argue the security of the future from the events of the past is to take a somewhat precarious position, since survival might not have been achieved through effective mechanisms, but might only be the realization of a very unlikely event; had the scheme failed, we would not be here to discuss it. Thus, we cannot

---

* Sir Walter Scott: *Old Mortality.*

really project with certainty the future of the race; the whole system might break down at the next challenge.

Nevertheless, we must pay some attention to the mechanisms that have maintained an unbroken thread of life for perhaps two billion years. To discard them out of pessimism after a few hasty speculations seems, to put the best face on it, a trifle arrogant.

The firmest fact known about the dynamics of genetic mechanisms is that they are conservative. An organism as it grows acquires all manner of insights, techniques, and useful habits. Nevertheless, in the offspring, all this acquired wisdom is erased. The offspring's endowment at birth is little different from that of his parents at their birth. The discrepancy between the quality of the adult at the height of his powers and the quality of the newborn is slight in insects and seems to increase steadily with ascent in the evolutionary scale.

Many years ago, the psychologist William McDougall, who was the formulator of most of our ideas about instinct, suggested that it is precisely because so little of human behavior is programmed through instinct that, while the young child is so helpless, the adult has such freedom of decision and such flexibility in adapting to strange circumstances.[1] Thus, what at first sight may look like a very clumsy mechanism may in fact be essential to the fullness of humanity.

The lesson from McDougall's observation seems to be that pursuing objectives implies accepting the means to these objectives. Superficial judgments about what in the human genome is desirable and what is not may lead to confident, but nonetheless disastrous, policies.

It is desirable that babies should be far from perfect human beings because their very incompleteness allows the development of a more subtle and adaptable final product. It is desirable that a gene pool be far from perfect because its variability makes possible a more subtle and adaptable species. The force of the former argument is easier to see, but the latter may be just as important. We do not perform drastic operations on babies because of the insouciant behavior of their bowels; perhaps we should beware of tampering with the genetic structure of the population until we are all satisfied that we know what the consequences may be.

I was struck by this sentence in the Reed and Anderson paper: "Appalled at the very large families produced by some retarded parents, early investigators had an honest fear that eugenic disaster was just around the corner." Even trying to match the authors' courtesy to other investigators, I find it difficult to recapture this primordial state of ignorance. Did these people believe that mental deficiency was a recent phenomenon? Or did they believe that there had been some tremendous disruption of the pressure of genetic selection by the therapeutic efficacy of medicine (which at that time was trivial)?

Today, geneticists are convinced that, because of the profound conservatism of the reproductive process, the gene pool has long been in a state of near equilibrium, perturbed only by an imperceptibly slow trend toward improvement of the genetic stock. Of course, the eugenicists in the early days may have believed that the majority of mankind was free of genetic taint. Now we believe differently. A very conservative estimate would be that 95 percent of all people carry harmful genes; a more reasonable estimate would be more like 99.9 percent. The majority of these genes, of course, are genes for recessive traits and for the most part difficult to detect. Thus, if the human race is to reproduce from unsullied stock only, a minute fraction of the population is going to be very busy indeed.

Before I get down to particulars, I must comment on the relevance of intelligence tests. An honest critic must recognize how difficult a task the psychologists have had to face in constructing these tests. They do not lend themselves to any of the classical statistical techniques, such as discriminant analysis or multiple regression, because there is no agreed outcome variable against which they can be validated; if there were, we could use the outcome variable and not the intelligence test.

If there is nothing to appeal to for validation, then inevitably the construction, the weighting, and the interpretation of the tests must be colored by the standards of the psychologists, for the most part middle-class males of European stock and academic cast. If the birds constructed such tests, we would all doubtless get low marks in building nests, hatching eggs, flying, and catching worms. We would be labeled hopeless imbeciles and perhaps be compulsorily sterilized by our well-meaning rulers.

So much for perspective. What does theory say would happen if we intervene? It will be profitable to consider the problem in the abstract and then to deal with concrete cases.

The capacity of a genotype to survive and produce viable offspring I shall refer to as its fitness. I employ the term in this genetic sense only; nothing that I say from now on must be construed as a value judgment on the *quality* of the life involved.

There is a solid mass of deterministic, and a growing body of stochastic, theory to support the so-called Haldane principle that the number of deaths attributable to a genetic mutation is independent of the fitness of the associated phenotype.[2, 3] For example, in a population of stable size, the inability to taste phenylthiocarbamide, recessive deafness, albinism and Tay-Sachs disease exact, on average, a toll of 1 death per 2 new mutations. If we wish to reduce this number of genetic deaths, we cannot do so by *genetic* manipulation; we must reduce the number of mutations, which I presume implies *environmental* manipulation. So from this standpoint, our deliberations do not deal with reducing the load, merely with how it is to be distributed.[4] Obviously, sickle-cell disease could be eliminated in one generation by sterilizing all the carriers. But those sterilized might well feel that they were being called upon to pay more than their fair share of the levy.

There are various methods by which we may regulate the distribution of payment for disorders stemming from a single locus on a chromosome: by forbidding or discouraging marriages between heterozygotes; by family limitation; by selective abortion; and by the early diagnosis and efficient treatment of cases. To discuss these methods adequately would take a long time. They have been dealt with elsewhere.[4-7] Almost any of these strategies will take the load off the few and distribute it among the many, with little, if any, change in the total burden and without giving rise to any uncontainable increases in the dimension of the problem. To err on the side of compassion is not only compassionate, but also not much in error.

However, a discussion of these single locus disorders may be somewhat beside the point. There are undoubtedly several well-known single locus disorders that cause mental defect;[8] at least some of these disorders are apparently treatable if there is prompt diagnosis. However, the whole structure of the discussion in the paper by Drs. Reed and Anderson implies a multilocal etiology. If I linger with single locus disorders just a little longer, it is not so much because I happen to be particularly interested in them as because I want to make an important contrast.

Most new mutations are harmful because most random changes in a complicated mechanism are for the worse. Only occasionally does a new mutation represent an improvement. Such a mutant may replace the established gene, but this result does not necessarily occur.

There is, however, a kind of intermediate condition in which a gene that is relatively harmful in the homozygous state is beneficial in the heterozygous state. We then speak of a balanced polymorphism.[9] The sickle cell hemoglobin gene which protects against malaria is a classic example of a balanced polymorphism in man. The abnormal and normal genes in combination, as in the carrier (or heterozygous) state, have this protective effect, while the homozygous sickle state produces sickle cell disease and the homozygous normal state is vulnerable to malaria. Thus, a system of balanced polymorphism tends to maintain both the ordinary and mutant lines by selecting for both in combination.

I have heard rumors of evidence indicating that the carrier state of Tay-Sachs disease is associated with a lower-than-average risk of tuberculosis. If this claim is substantiated and the protective effect proves to be striking, any policy of eliminating the Tay-Sachs gene in a population which is prey to tuberculosis might be open to serious question.

However, since a disorder such as Tay-Sachs disease involves a single locus (i.e. point on a chromosome) only, there is a choice of only three phenotypes: the two homozygous states (homozygous normal and homozygous abnormal) and the heterozygous. The choices are uncompromising: deaths from Tay-Sachs disease must be balanced against deaths from tuberculosis. One might wonder, however, if it is possible to have a genetic system which would combine the increased resistance against tuberculosis with a smaller price to pay in the severity or the risk of genetic disease. If it is true, as some hold, that multiple alleles at a locus are the rule rather than the exception,[10] a variable impairment of the corresponding function might occur, and, therefore, a variable severity of the disease. Thus, for any specified population, compromise might be obtained; but such a result would not enhance the elasticity of the gene pool.

An argument along these lines leads us to the idea that there are many adaptive advantages to the multilocal system.[11] Instead of producing only three states from the two alleles possible at a locus, there may be many combinations for the many loci and, therefore, a finer gradation in the phenotype.

Minor changes in the force of selection would lead to corresponding changes in gene frequencies and so to change in the usual phenotype, but without loss of the sources of variability. Furthermore, if the phenotype is to be determined by more or less equal contributions from all the participating loci, the more loci the greater the concentration of phenotypes about the mean (which must be presumed to represent an optimal value). For such a system to have any elasticity of fitness, however, there must be a high frequency of heterozygosity at the loci concerned; in other words, there must be heterosis, or hybrid strength. A completely stable system could be attained if there were homozygosity for genes tending t produce one extreme of the phenotype at some loci and for g nes tending to produce the other at the rest; but such a sys em would have no power of adaptability to new selection pressu

Thus, the price for adap ability is heterozygosity, and the price for heterozygosity is th   in the same pool there will be a bell-shaped curve of a measurable phenotype. Hence, there will be extreme forms of the phenotype which are less fit in the genetic sense, and this commonly, though not necessarily, implies less fit in a clinical or social sense also. There will be people whom, because of the conventional processes of thought, we would label "sick" or "abnormal" or "mentally retarded." Such people are, it seems, an inevitable concomitant of the multilocal system so long as the zygote represents a *random* assortment of genes.

There is, I think, nothing much we can do about the system without imperiling adaptability. A more drastic selection against the tails of the curve might drive the gene pool into homozygosity and the result would be somewhat like eliminating a balanced polymorphism. It would, of course, take a great deal of meddling with the gene pool to produce this effect; but then it would take a great deal of meddling to shrink the tails of the curve.

There are two other facets of the problem which we should keep in mind:

1. By shrinking the tails of the curve we would reduce not merely the number of the mentally retarded, but also the number of geniuses.
2. No amount of manipulation would make less than 2½ percent of the population fall below the 2½ percentile. If we insist on defining mental deficiency in these arbitrary terms, it will be quite impossible to eliminate it by any means whatever.

Finally, the facts. About the admirable analysis of Drs. Reed and Anderson, I have minor comments only. Two aspects of the method of ascertainment of the sample call for comment. The metrical assessment of mental deficiency is subject to experimental error. As is well known, retesting of persons who have been given extremely high or extremely low scores on first assessment will result in scores that, on the average, are closer to the mean for the population. The bell-shaped nature of the distribution of intelligence has a bearing on this probability. An IQ score of 65 might be an unusually low reading for a person whose true level is 70 or it might be an unusually high reading for a person whose true level is 60. But the former example is the more likely explanation because there are many more people at IQ levels of 70 than 60. Thus, among persons selected because they have low IQs, scores on repeated assessments will, in general, be nearer the mean.

In the study described by Drs. Reed and Anderson, the probands were selected on the basis of IQ scores. It is far from obvious what the impact of this bias might be on the ratio of affected to unaffected sibs and hence on the estimates used in the final analysis. To make my criticism any more precise, I would need to know what the reproducibility of IQ tests may be.

A second source of bias is that these pedigrees discussed were ascertained through an affected child and traced back. Such a method would distort the segregation ratios in sibs and ancestors, and this would be true whether or not the genetic traits were of a Mendelian type. I have done some preliminary analysis on the effect of ascertainment bias, in a system where the probability of a girl being the proband is different from that for a boy. My impression is that this bias may exaggerate the discrepancy between the proportions of the two sexes labeled mentally defective. Robinson has the matter under exploration.[12]

There is the further question of why the ratios are so strange. In the sample of 1450 unselected retardates whose reproductive histories were analyzed [see p. 114], retarded males outnumber retarded females in the ratio of about 4 to 3. No genetic reason for this inequality is forthcoming. The differences in the genomes in males and females are small: merely that the males have a Y chromosome which is not known to have any specific genetic content, and one X chromosome less. Since the extra X contains perhaps 2.5 percent of the genetic material and most of it is quiescent in the female, no striking result could be easily explained from this source.

It is tempting to suppose that this strange ratio—similar to the kind of ratio found in congenital defects believed to be multilocal—is some kind of artifact of scaling. It might be that the variance of intelligence is greater in men than in women and that, therefore, in intellectual level a larger proportion of men lie beyond some arbitrary threshold. But this explanation is, of course, not an explanation. Why should there be greater variance in men? Perhaps the difference is a cultural matter. For a woman to be recognized as mentally retarded, she would have to have a much poorer genetic endowment than a man would, and this poor endowment should be reflected on average in her male relatives, especially those of first degree. As we would predict from this hypothesis, in Table 2 [see page 117] we see that of 238 children born to mentally retarded sisters of probands, 19 percent are mentally retarded, while of the 166 children born to mentally retarded brothers of probands, about 11 percent are retarded.

It is a pity that the data are not classified by the sex of the offspring and by the sex of the proband. Such a classification would allow a more cogent test of whether or not variance is the true explanation.

It is perhaps not very surprising that the fertility of mentally retarded females is greater than that of mentally retarded males. A larger proportion of such females marry and a smaller proportion are committed to institutions. Competition to run a household may be less severe than competition for paid jobs.

Of the predictions made by these authors I have little to say. Adjustments of the data for bias of ascertainment, regression to the mean (which may differ in the two sexes) and variance might lead to refinements; but I think their overall argument would stand. I have much greater misgivings about the eugenic aspects of the problem and their concluding suggestions regarding restrictions on reproduction.

Conclusions

From a eugenic standpoint, we are in a difficult position. Wisdom demands much better scientific data and insights into the dynamics of this whole problem before we formulate any course of action. In particular, we need to know much more about the relative importances of cultural and genetic factors in the transmission of intelligence from parent to child. There will, however, be political pressures from those who want a bolder and more active course, and these pressures may be difficult to resist because of the ease with which public opinion is swayed in this delicate area.

Drs. Reed and Anderson recommend that the mentally retarded be discouraged or even perhaps prevented from reproducing. Such a course would involve arbitrary cut-off points, which would create problems in borderline cases. Moreover, it is somewhat drastic. I imagine that most people would defend the general right to reproduce, the one possible proviso being that the prospective parents must have sufficient insight into the nature of sexuality to be capable of deliberate and responsible consent. If we are in doubt as to whether this proviso is fulfilled and also about the eugenic impact of such a prohibition, we might take the less drastic step of allowing mentally retarded persons to reproduce unfettered and to place their offspring in foster care at birth. Perhaps even a few hours of mental stimulation a day would be sufficient to compensate for the child's environmental deficit. Such a scheme would have the following advantages:

1. While it would be an interference with the rights of the parents, it would be a less drastic one than denying them parenthood altogether.

2. It would avoid an over-hasty interference with the dynamics of the gene pool.

3. It would provide a direct measure of the importance of the genetic and cultural components in retardation, through observation of the similarity of intelligence levels between parent and child after elimination of the effects of a common environment. A more drastic policy would impede, and perhaps prevent indefinitely, the solution to this fundamental problem.

REFERENCES

1. McDougall, W.: *Outline of Psychology.* New York, Scribner, 1924, p. 130 et seq.
2. Crow, J. F. & Kimura, M.: *An Introduction to Population Genetics Theory.* New York, Harper and Row, 1970.

3. NEI, M.: a. Extinction time of deleterious mutant genes in large populations. *Theor. Population Biol.*, 2:419-423, 1971. b. Total number of individuals affected by a single deleterious mutation in large populations. *Ibid.*

4. MURPHY, E. A.: *Why Monitor?* In Hook, E. B., Janerich, D. T., and Porter, I. A. (Eds.). *Monitoring, Birth Defects and Environment*. New York, Academic Press, 1971.

5. MURPHY, E. A. & GUZMAN, R.: *Algunos aspectos téoricos del consejo genético*. In press.

6. MOTULSKY, A. G., FRASER, G. R., & FELSENSTEIN, J.: Public health and long-term genetic implications of intrauterine diagnosis and selective abortion. In Bergsma, D. (Ed.): Birth Defects: Original Article Series. *Intrauterine Diagnosis*, 7:22, April 1971.

7. STEVENSON, R. E. & HOWELL, R. R.: Some medical and social aspects of the treatment for genetic-metabolic diseases. *Ann. Amer. Acad. Polit. Soc. Sc.*, 399: 30-37, 1972.

8. MCKUSICK, V. A.: *Mendelian Inheritance in Man* (ed. 3). Baltimore, The Johns Hopkins Press, 1971.

9. DOBZHANSKY, T.: *Mankind Evolving*, esp. pp. 295 et seq. New Haven, Yale University Press, 1962.

10. CHILDS, B. & DER KALOUSTIAN, V. M.: Genetic heterogeneity. *New Eng. J. Med.*, 279:1205-12 and 1267-74, 1968.

11. MURPHY, E. A.: A scientific viewpoint on normalcy. *Perspect. Biol. Med.*, 9: 333-348, 1966.

12. ROBINSON, H.: Personal communication. (Text to be published in *Human Biology*, 1972.)

Physical and Biological Aspects
(SESSION TWO)

GENERAL DISCUSSION
PARK S. GERALD, *Presiding*

Some differences of opinion on the incidence of genetically caused retardation and possible methods of improving the gene pool emerged in the general discussion of the Reed and Anderson and Murphy papers.

Dr. Tarjan commented that Dr. Murphy's presentation was exceedingly important in calling attention to the great difficulties of measuring any kind of eugenic improvement in a normal distribution based on some cut-off point. He then asked Dr. Murphy whether the same problem of a cut-off point would not arise even if a test could be developed that would measure the capacity to add positively to the gene pool for the benefit of mankind rather than just intelligence. Dr. Murphy replied that he could find no statistical justification for the prevalent idea that the normal range on any distribution curve is that including 95 percent of the population. He said he regarded cut-off points as "an evasion of the need to make a responsible, if uncertain, judgment." If a eugenic policy is to be set, he maintained, all the value judgments should be brought out in the open.

Dr. Tarjan expressed concern over the data presented by Dr. Reed because of the bias introduced not only by institutionalization but also by the sociological phenomena that contribute to institutionalization. He maintained that the small proportion of the retarded that ends up in institutions arrives there not solely because of their IQs, but because of sociological forces that segregate them out for institutional admission, such as a lack of community services, and that, therefore, it is difficult to extrapolate from the institutionalized to any non-institutional population. He also suggested that the preponderance of males over females among the retarded in the Reed and Anderson data may only be a reflection of the fact that a woman needs less intelligence to "get by" than does a man.

Replying that he would not have used an institutional population as the basis of his studies if any other had been available, Dr. Reed suggested that it would be a good idea for someone to do the same kind of study beginning with the population of a county or of some other specific geographical area. He pointed out, however, that only 10 percent of the retardates followed in his 5-generation study were institutionalized, and the original institutionalized index case was not included in the models. Agreeing with Dr. Murphy that IQ tests are "highly unsatisfactory," he argued that they are better than subjective tests for defining retardation. He explained that many of the individuals in his studies had been tested several times and that when this was so, the middle score was selected for the data.

Dr. Reed denied that the preponderance of male retardates was unreal and suggested that part of the reason there are more retarded males than females may lie in the unprotected nature of the male sex chromosome, a phenomenon that he said may also be behind the greater mortality rate among males in early life. Granting that cultural and environmental factors may also be involved in the male-female ratio, he stressed the point that retardation is not the simple matter of a recessive gene that geneticists once thought it to be, but stems from complicated social, genetic, biological, and environmental forces. Nevertheless, he expressed the opinion that the percentage of the retarded that is produced by the retarded is not likely to vary more than 4 percent either way in the near future from his figure of 17 percent. Pointing out that the two percent used in his projections as the proportion of retardation in the total population was for an upper middle class white population, he said that in the center of New York city, where there is probably a higher frequency of environmental retardation, the figures would be different.

Dr. Li pointed out that the genetic equilibrium in natural populations could be changed drastically in the future by the introduction of human intervention in the process of natural selection. He pointed out that recent developments in our ability to diagnose prenatally an increasing number of hereditary abnormalities, liberalization of abortion laws in several states, and society's gradual acceptance of these laws may lead to a new genetic equilibrium. Dr. Li also commented on the concept of "lethal equivalent." This mathematical formulation may or may not have equivalent effects in a human society. One hundred persons, each with a one percent detrimental effect, is not equivalent to one person with 100 percent detrimental effect.

Dr. Salerno questioned the value of lumping together all retardation regardless of etiology, as Drs. Reed and Anderson had done. Obstetricians, he said, have observed that the major causes of mental retardation are not genetic, but environmental, and include birth trauma, prematurity, and other non-genetic causes.

There ensued a discussion of what percentage of retardation might have a genetic base. Dr. Salerno put the figure as low as one percent, but Dr. Reed argued for a much higher but unknown figure, that would include not only the diagnosable chromosomal and metabolic disorders but also a large proportion of the "undifferentiated" retardation which, he said, is caused by multi-genetic action at the lower end of the normal distribution curve. About 60 percent of the variation in intelligence at the two ends of the distribution curve is caused by genetic factors, he maintained. In closing the discussion, Dr. Gerald remarked that while the percentage is probably greater than Dr. Salerno assumed, major chromosomal abnormalities alone apparently occur in 0.5 percent of all births, he, nevertheless, felt certain that genetic factors were not the primary cause of retardation. Whatever the proportion is, he said, the figure is not available.

INSTITUTIONAL AND COMMUNITY ATTITUDES, PRACTICES, AND POLICIES

(Session One)

10

Sexual Behavior of Retarded in Institutions

ROBERT W. DEISHER
Department of Pediatrics
University of Washington (Seattle)

IT WAS ALMOST TWENTY-FIVE years ago that Dr. Alfred Kinsey first published his book "Sexual Behavior in the Human Male." [1] This work was the beginning of an increasing public awareness of the importance of sex in people's lives. Public attitudes and the knowledge and interest of the scientific community in this field have not grown rapidly, however. New journals, such as *Medical Aspects of Human Sexuality* and *Archives of Sexual Behavior* indicate the growth of contributions to the field. We are now at a point where we can talk and think about sexuality as something which is a normal part of human behavior, and which perhaps deserves the same study and research as many other types of human behavior.

Likewise, it was about fifteen years ago that public attitudes began to change regarding the needs of the mentally retarded. The first federal money specifically for educating the mentally retarded became available in the 1958 Education for the Mentally Retarded Act. Prior to that time in the vast majority of cases, the retarded individual was either tucked away in an institution to be forgotten, or kept at home surrounded by secrecy and shame. For the past twenty years, parents particularly have increasingly demanded that the retarded individual be treated as any other person, and that he be given the same rights and freedoms that the normal person enjoys. Particularly during the past ten years, we have increasingly recognized the rights of the retarded to be educated, to work and to fit into society in a way commensurate with their abilities. Although these are fairly recent concepts, they are concepts that are more or less being accepted. One area, however, that has almost entirely been neglected is the right of the retarded to be a sexual individual, to enjoy sexual pleasure and to experience feelings that are of a sexual nature.

It is not strange to see why we have been so slow to even consider the rights of the retarded individual to have a sexual life when we realize how slow we have been to consider sex as an integral part of human behavior. We still have a long way to go in allowing much freedom for the normal person, let alone a person who deviates in some way from what society considers "normal." It is actually not so much a matter of society's allowing sexual behavior; it is usually a matter of individuals demanding it, and sometimes ignoring society in order to have a sexual life.

For that individual whose life or a significant part of his life is spent in an institution, what opportunity does he have to enjoy any sort of sexual life? Individuals at most institutions are very carefully supervised and residents are not able to control this aspect of their life any more than they are able to control what happens to them in many other areas. Yet, it is well known that mildly and moderately retarded persons have sexual feelings, and if we are willing to allow them to have rights in other areas, they cannot justifiably be denied their right to express their own sexual feelings and lead a sexual life inasmuch as they are capable in the same way as any other individual. Institutions traditionally have had one overriding fear in regard to sexual behavior. This is the fear of pregnancy occurring in one of their residents. This fear is manifest on the part of all the staff, usually, from the superintendent down to the most junior staff member. It is usually manifest by the limiting of any sort of behavior that might be considered sexual and that might conceivably result in pregnancy.

Due to a lack of factual information regarding attitudes on the part of staff members, and actual practices in institutions in regard to sexual behavior, it was decided this past summer to do a survey of two of the larger institutions on the west coast. One institution was in southern California, the other in the State of Washington. Both are large, well-recognized institutions, and probably should be considered somewhat more advanced than the average institution for the retarded throughout the country.

We were interested primarily in two things. First, what did go on in an institution in the way of sexual behavior among the residents, and secondly, what were the attitudes of the people who were primarily responsible for controlling the activities and behaviors of the residents? What would they allow, and what were their own personal views and thoughts regarding sex, and particularly sexual activity among the people for whom they were responsible?

We attempted, through the use of a questionnaire, to reach a representative sample of the personnel assigned to wards who have responsibility for the direct supervision of the residents. Those attendants who were interviewed via the questionnaire were selected from wards in which the residents were considered to be either mildly or moderately retarded. In other words, those responsible for the more severely retarded and bed-ridden persons were not included in the study. The age range of the residents supervised by attendants in the survey was 8 to 60 at one institution and 7 to 71 at the other. The youngest resident in halls supervised by survey attendants was in the 16-20 age group in 53.5 percent of the supervised residents, averaging for both institutions.

Twenty-five persons from each institution responded to the questionnaire. They were selected from the morning and afternoon shifts and were therefore responsible for residents betwen 7:00 a.m. and 11:00 p.m. Twenty-one males and 29 females were interviewed. Ages of those interviewed ranged from 21 to 65, with the largest number, 17 (34%), falling in the age range 25 to 30. The mean educational attainment of attendants at one institution was 12.7 years and at the other 12.8 years. The mean duration of employment of attendants at one institution was 8.1 years and at the other institution 8.6 years.

In answer to a general question as to whether they felt that residents should be allowed to express sexual feelings, approximately one-quarter of the respondents indicated that the residents should be allowed to do this quite freely. Another 25 percent indicated that they should not be able to do this at all. Approximately 50 percent felt that the expression of limited sexual feelings was permissible. The question was asked, *"How do you feel about masturbation?"* Ninety-four percent of the 48 who responded indicated that they felt this was normal or that they were indifferent to it. Only three persons indicated that this was bad and should not be allowed. Another question asked was, *"What action do you take if you find a resident masturbating?"* Thirty-seven percent of those interviewed said they would stop it. The remainder felt that they would ignore it, if it were done privately. Only 12 percent indicated that they would punish an individual for masturbation. In reply to the question as to whether masturbation bothered them, 14 percent said that it made them very uncomfortable, while the remainder indicated that they were not bothered by it.

At the present time in most institutions it is common to have mixed social events, such as dances of one or two hours duration. These dances are well chaperoned, and residents are not allowed to be alone. Dating is not encouraged. In fact, dating is usually explicitly forbidden. Essentially, the chaperoned mixed social events are the extent of the heterosexual activity which is approved by the institution. The question was asked whether heterosexual contact should be allowed. Eighty-eight percent indicated that it should, while 12 percent felt that there should be no such contact. An additional question asked what this contact should be limited to, and 65 percent of the 28 respondents believed that it should be of a social nature only; 21 percent (6 respondents) felt that any kind of heterosexual contact excluding sexual activity was permissible, while 14 percent (4 respondents) indicated that there should be no limit.

The question was asked as to what would the attendant do if he saw two residents, male and female, kissing or petting. There was close to an equal division of opinion on this with approximately half in favor of stopping it, and the other half ignoring it. However, the persons at the two institutions revealed differences of opinion as to what they would do about heterosexual kissing or petting. At the Washington institution, 72 percent said they would stop it, 24 percent said they would ignore it, 4 percent said it was all right if done in public, and none said it was all right if done in private. Persons at the southern California institution responded 32 percent they would stop it, 60 percent ignore it and 8 percent felt it was all right if done in private.

Another question was asked about homosexual activity. What action would be taken if two male residents were found kissing or petting. Eighty-six percent of those interviewed said they would stop it and 14 percent said they would ignore it. In answering this question, persons at the two institutions continued to differ in their views, but not so markedly as on the questions on heterosexual kissing or petting. In Washington, 96 percent said they would stop such homosexual activity, while 76 percent in southern California said so. Four percent in Washington replied they would ignore homosexual kissing and petting, while 24 percent in southern California replied similarly. For the same question regarding two female residents, the percentages were almost the same.

To the question, *"What are your attitudes regarding homosexual behavior among residents"* (including orgasm), 75 percent of the Washington responses were to prohibit it, versus 56 percent of the southern California responses. Regarding limited homosexual activity, 17 percent of the Washington respondents replied it was all right, while 44 percent at the California institution felt so. Those favoring the option that homosexual activity should be allowed without special restriction were 8 percent in Washington and none in California.

Regarding the matter of sex education, or what residents should be told about sexuality or sexual feeling, only two persons of the total believed that this subject should be entirely avoided, that nothing should be said. Approximately 90 percent felt that the residents should be told what they were capable of understanding, and 6 percent believed that they should have as much information as anyone else, even though they might not be able to fully understand all of it.

The question was asked whether the ward personnel felt that his attitude toward sexual behavior on the part of the residents was more permissive, less permissive, or approximately the same as the other attendants. Sixty-seven percent believed that their attitude was more or less the same as that of the others; 25 percent felt that they were more permissive than the average; and only 8 percent felt that they were less permissive and more restrictive than the majority of the institutional personnel.

The survey asked the question as to whether the attendants felt the institution had a policy regarding the sexual behavior of residents. Sixty-three percent of those responding felt the institution did have, and 37 said that they felt that it did not. In answer to the question whether they agreed with this policy or not, 70 percent said they did, and 30 percent said they did not.

Another question was whether they believed intercourse should be allowed for residents if pregnancy could be prevented. Forty percent said that it should, and sixty percent said it should not. Eighty percent felt, however, that some contraceptive information should be made available to residents, while approximately 20 percent felt that this was not appropriate. Almost all believed that this information should be given by a trained person, usually the physician or a nurse. We asked them whether they believed that most of the girls whom they had had under their care at one time or another in their institutional work were capable of parenthood if discharged from the institution. Eighty-eight percent felt that they were not, and 12 percent felt that some of them might be.

There was one general question in the survey that did not relate at all to the institutions' residents, but was an attempt to get at attendants' own attitudes regarding sexual behavior in general. The question was whether normal people should be allowed intercourse outside marriage. Sixty-two and one-half percent of the 48 persons who responded believed that they should; 37.5 percent of the 48 felt that they should not. A breakdown of these figures by institutional location revealed those who thought intercourse should be allowed outside marriage were 54 percent of the 24 Washington respondents and 71 percent of the 24 who responded at the California institution. If we look at the total males responding from both institutions, we find 86 percent in favor of allowing this intercourse for normal persons versus 44 percent of the total females. In examining the views on this question in regard to employee age, the number of men and women from both institutions who thought normal unmarried persons should be allowed intercourse was 74 percent of those under 40 versus 45 percent of those over 40.

The question was asked what would happen if a girl and boy were allowed to be together for an hour in private: whether nothing unusual would happen; whether there would be a moderate amount of sexual play; or whether actual intercourse would be attempted. Forty-two percent of the total respondents believed that intercourse would be attempted. Thirty-three percent believed that there would be some sexual play. Twenty-five percent believed that nothing would happen.

Regarding the question as to whether the less capable or the more intellectually capable residents were more sexually active, approximately half felt that the mental limitations made no difference. Of course, one must bear in mind that the most severely retarded are not included in the responses here. Twelve percent of the institution attendants felt the least capable residents were more sexually active, and 34 percent believed the more capable were more interested.

We also asked whether the attendants believed the boys were more interested in sexual activity than the girls. Here again, about half felt that it was about equal, and the remaining 50 percent were equally divided between males and females.

The question was asked how they would handle the sex problem if it came up on the ward, and the majority felt that they would have a friendly discussion with the resident and talk with him about it. Approximately one-fourth believed that discipline should be meted out immediately so that the individual would know he had done wrong. The remaining quarter were divided between ignoring it or reporting it to the supervisor.

As is apparent, this survey was not meant to do more than obtain some general information regarding what is going on in these institutions at present, and what are the attitudes of some of the attendants. Several things, however, seem apparent. One is that there is no clear-cut policy regarding what kind of activity should be allowed in the institutions, and that the attitudes of the staff are mainly a reflection of their own personal values and ideas. It appears there was a slightly more liberal attitude among the people working in the southern California institution than in Washington. However, this was not as marked as I thought it might be. It is also apparent at the present time that there is little opportunity for the residents of mental retardation institutions to lead a life that can be called a life of a sexual nature. The questions that exist regarding sex education for the retarded, what kind of freedoms should be allowed, and, perhaps even more importantly, how one might go about working with the attendants in changing their attitude if necessary, need to be faced. It is probably true that one of the reasons many moderately retarded adolescents are institutionalized is that their parents feel incapable of providing education regarding sexual aspects of their life and are overly concerned and anxious about this particular aspect. It is up to us, the professionals in the field, to see that more realistic sex education is provided to the retarded, both inside the institution and in the community; to the staff of institutions; and to the parents.

REFERENCE

1. KINSEY, A. C., POMEROY, W. B., MARTIN, C. E.: *Sexual Behavior in the Human Male.* Philadelphia, W. B. Saunders Company, 1948, pp. 804.

11

Human Sexuality in a
Halfway House

DAVID GORDON CARRUTH
University of Washington (Seattle)

IN RECENT DECADES the stress on individual liberties, the spread
of Freudian psychosexual theory, and a new openness in the media
of mass communication have resulted in people being more aware
of their sexuality and feeling freer to talk about sex and to practice it than they used to be in this country. However, for a significant minority of the population—the mentally and socially
retarded—the expression of human sexuality continues to be
actively suppressed.

Recently, I interviewed members of the professional staff of a
halfway house for the mentally and socially retarded. Their attitudes towards sexual behavior on the part of retardates can be
expressed simply: they are just beginning to think about it.

During my investigation I made a strong effort to interview
the residents themselves. However, I met with considerable resistance from the administrator of the house. I did, however, get
information from members of the professional staff about the
kind of sexual behavior they had observed among the residents
and how the staff handled it.

I conducted three, two-hour interviews at the halfway house—
one each with the administrator and two counselors.

This halfway house, a state-supported institution, had been in
operation a little over a year. It is situated about 10 miles from a

major metropolitan area in the Pacific Northwest, far enough from the downtown area to present a difficult transportation problem for the residents.

The house was originally designed to serve as an intermediary residence for persons on their way from a state institution for the mentally retarded to life in the community. However, the majority of persons admitted to the house have been referred to it by parents whose children have never been institutionalized, by public welfare caseworkers, and by other state institutions.

The house itself is a modern construction with three separate units, each with two wings—one for male and one for female residents. In the center of each unit is a common room that serves many purposes—as television room, game room, classroom, cooking and dining area. The common rooms are bright, warm, and well furnished and are available to the residents 24 hours a day.

The house is well staffed, having one counselor for every four residents. The general policy is to encourage behavior appropriate for independent living in the community. The residents are called tenants, and each tenant pays rent according to his ability to pay.

The whole facility holds 48 tenants. The population at the time of my visit was 38—20 women and 18 men. They ranged in age from 18 to 40 years, the median being 24. Intellectually, the tenants were described by the staff as high borderline retarded.

All of the tenants eat breakfast and dinner together and maintain full-time employment away from the house in sheltered workshops. Their social relationships are almost exclusively with one another.

The maximum allowable stay is one year. The average stay during the first year was 8 months.

The tenants are allowed to visit one another in their rooms up to 9:30 p.m., and to receive visitors up to 11:30 on weekends. However, they are required to inform their respective counselors of a visit and must leave their doors wide open. Most rooms hold three tenants, a few hold two, and two rooms in each unit are single rooms.

After one year of operation, only one incident of sexual behavior had been witnessed by the staff; a counselor had found two male tenants unclothed and lying on top of each other, with the door to their room wide open. The counselor told the men that their behavior was inappropriate in public and would upset the other tenants. Subsequently, the staff tried to keep these men apart.

The staff estimated that only about 10 to 15 percent of the total population date members of the opposite sex, but such dating occurs exclusively with other tenants.

One marriage took place between two tenants after a four-month courtship at the halfway house. The husband was described by one staff member as an "exhibitionist" and the wife as mentally retarded. On a follow-up visit, a staff member found the couple living happily together in the city with support from public assistance. Both husband and wife were unemployed.

One staff member speculated that during visits home some tenants of both sexes may occasionally have sexual contacts with members of their families—fathers, step-fathers, brothers, and mothers.

The major social activity in the common rooms is watching television. Some touching and pinching occurs between male and female tenants. The staff members call such behavior "necking" and tell the tenants that is is inappropriate in public.

The staff has attempted to provide some sex education for the tenants, in separate classes for males and females. The instruction usually consists of showing old anatomy films and the use of a few outdated books.

According to the staff, the female tenants seem more interested in the classes than do the males but their interest is primarily centered in contraceptive information. These classes revealed that while the tenants vary greatly in their knowledge of human sexuality, most of them are unaware of the basic structure of male and female anatomy.

The staff also reported that discussion of sex between tenants and staff members rarely occurs and that when a tenant does bring up the subject the discussion is very indirect and accompanied by a great deal of embarrassment.

The female tenants seem to have more opportunities for outside sexual contacts than the male. Several had told of being approached by men at work and at bus stops on their way to and from work.

Two staff members reported having attended a meeting of operators of state and private halfway houses to discuss the methods of dealing with sexuality in the residents. They both received the impression that the operators of private group homes were highly moralistic in their attitudes toward the subject.

Clearly, it seems, although the mentally and socially retarded persons in halfway houses have sexual drives as varied and intense as other people's, they are being denied both the opportunity to engage in sexual activity and adequate knowledge about human sexual behavior. It may be slightly encouraging that the staffs of these facilities are just beginning to think about the problem.

One step towards helping this minority group achieve more sexual freedom might be through the establishment of a series of sex education classes geared to three different groups: professional staff, parents of the retarded, and the retarded themselves.

Utilizing the multi-media approach to sex education, these classes would range in sophistication from a concentration on basic anatomical information to discussion of the full richness of human sexual and sensual experiences. But sex education is meaningless without opportunities for relationships between the sexes to begin.

Now is the time to stop theorizing about normalization as a goal for the mentally and socially retarded and to become advocates for the retardates' rights as human beings.

12

Community Attitudes Toward Sexuality of the Retarded

MURRY MORGENSTERN
New York Medical College

TO ADDRESS OURSELVES SUBSTANTIVELY to the complex factors involved in defining community attitudes toward sexuality in the mentally retarded, we need to develop criteria for assessing the validity of particular views or conclusions. Although studies of attitudes often produce perplexing incongruities, we could have greater confidence in them if the results were interpreted from a number of unexpressed, often unexamined and, even, contradictory assumptions.[1]

To obtain a significant cross-section of opinion, it may be necessary to develop a "man in the street approach" similar to the method used in the Harris and Gallup Polls. Even though the "popular poll" approach may not be considered scientifically valid by the professional community, these polls (with few exceptions) have an impressive record of accuracy and ability to predict. They have the important advantage of reaching a broad representative segment of the population in contrast to the more limited groups to whom most clinicians and behavioral scientists have access.

My own conclusions derive from three sources: 1) the literature (admittedly meager) ; 2) long years of direct clinical observation, and 3) information obtained in clinical interviews with people of different ages, occupations, and educational and economic backgrounds. One group interviewed, for example, consisted of "blue

collar" workers who attended a community health facility operated by a trade union.

I do not maintain that my findings can or should be considered
the results of a complete piece of work meeting all the criteria
of a sound research study. Definitive results must await further
investigation and refinement. The paucity of material on the
subject, however, impels me to present for consideration and discussion the material that I have thus far assembled.

Let me begin, therefore, by stating that my findings have led
me to the conclusion that community attitudes toward the sexuality of the mentally retarded reflect community attitudes toward the retarded in general.[2]

In good part, these attitudes represent the views of the majority of people in our society. In an open, democratic society,
however, the opinions of the majority often shift quickly and
radically under the influence of a strong minority. This is particularly true today as our rapidly changing society moves toward
greater acceptance of groups and individuals formerly viewed as
unacceptable and even dangerous social deviants.

Despite a growing relaxation of rigid moral standards, changes
in society's attitudes toward the mentally retarded continue to lag
behind the liberality increasingly shown towards other minorities,
including the homosexual. Perhaps this lag exists because the
retarded lack skill in verbal communication and, therefore, have
not been able to organize themselves into an articulate entity as
have other minority groups.

Sexual activity, with its long history of evoking taboos, anxiety,
and feelings of guilt among all levels of society, is understandably
the most difficult aspect of behavior for society to accept among
the retarded. Therefore, when we begin to probe, in depth, community attitudes towards the sexuality of the retarded, we un-
cover an entire spectrum of attitudes towards this segment of the
population. In the information I obtained, three main categories
of attitudes defined the retarded as 1) The Sub-Human, 2) The
Child-Innocent, and 3) The Developing Person. Within these
categories, there are, of course, variations in emotion, concept,

and overt action. Moreover, many individuals may entertain attitudes from more than one category. Nevertheless, it may be helpful to define what may be described as the elemental, classic attitudes.

The Sub-Human

The attitudes in this category may be described as the most primitive and, when translated to action, the most alien to our view of ourselves as an enlightened, compassionate people. Nevertheless, there are individuals in our society who look upon the mentally retarded as sub-human anomalies. They believe that the retarded are more akin to animals than humans and should, therefore, be segregated in closed institutions where they would have minimal rights and amenities.

Where such attitudes prevail, the existence of the retarded is ignored, and the question of their sexuality does not intrude upon the consciousness of the "normal" members of the community. Should the question of their sexuality be raised at all, the attitudes it evokes might be the same as those evoked by the observance of two dogs copulating. In some instances, particularly after a sex crime has been committed, members of the community may immediately regard all the mentally retarded with suspicion. Those who hold such attitudes often argue that abnormal characteristics are inherited and, consequently, society must be protected from those who suffer from intellectual deficiencies.

The Child-Innocent

Attitudes under this category reflect a view of the retarded as eternal children who are to be pitied and even cherished. Some religious people regard them as "holy innocents" or "chosen children of God," who should be treated benevolently and somewhat indulgently.

Essentially, these are paternalistic attitudes. Assistance to the retarded takes the form of charity, and, in return, the retarded are expected to be grateful and conforming. Self-sufficiency is neither expected nor encouraged. These attitudes also dehumanize the retarded, producing passivity and an "other world" quality in them.

If the retarded's sexuality comes to the attention of persons with these attitudes, its expression is diverted into expressions of other feelings. Innocence is expected to prevail; therefore, sexuality must be negated.

The Developing Person

Attitudes in this category emanate from the enlightened and progressive elements in our society, the same elements that have given impetus to the movement for civil rights for all minorities. They take an optimistic view of the retarded as "developing persons" with good potential for growth and inclusion within the mainstream of the community. In line with their beliefs, they advocate full rights for the retarded in all areas of living, including sex.

A few administrators of institutions and community facilities for the retarded attempt to put liberalized attitudes into practice by making available to the retarded programs in sex education, birth control, maternity and infant care, and individual counseling on sexual problems. These exceptional administrators recognize the retarded's need for sexual expression and believe that opportunities for love-making and mating should be provided within the institutional setting.

However, when closely examined, the practice of many professional persons or parents who express liberal attitudes often is not the same as what they preach, particularly in the area of sexuality. They become caught up in stereotypes of the retarded and in old moral persuasions against encouraging or even permitting sexuality between two intellectually deficient persons.

The greatest difficulty lies in the problem of separating sexual activity from marriage and procreation. The fear that sexual expression by the retarded will produce more retarded children leads even the enlightened community to limit the retarded person's right to experiment with or demonstrate competency in sexuality. Restrictions on the individual's right to direct his own sex life are set by assessments of his level of retardation and predictions of his ability or inability to be productive in work and social activities and to have a successful marriage. Such criteria are not applied to "normal" individuals before they are allowed to indulge in sex or to marry. They are, however, often advocated for the retarded by otherwise progressive groups who worry about a possible threat to the general intellectual level of the population and rationalize their restrictive attitudes toward the retarded on the basis of lofty social goals. When liberal groups in a community call for sterilization of the retarded and assurances that children, if they are born, will be raised properly, they often find themselves allied with those who view the retarded as "sub-human."

Even where the retarded can engage in sexuality, they are made to feel obligated to follow society's traditional mores and conventions. Thus, the sexual freedom allowed in society today is denied the retarded.

Summary of Observed Attitudes

Our findings to date indicate that the following factors strongly influence community attitudes towards sexual activity in the retarded:

1. Positive attitudes are more likely to be achieved when individuals and society as a whole have more precise knowledge about mental retardation.

2. There is, however, a definite distinction between attitudes towards mental retardation as a condition and toward people who are actually retarded. The condition is viewed more negatively because of deeply rooted stereotyped concepts. Negative attitudes toward the unpleasant, abnormal characteristics of retardation affect attitudes towards unimpaired characteristics and often result in a general rejection of retarded persons and restriction of their rights, particularly in the area of sexuality.

3. Attitudes vary among people according to how much education and how much experience with mentally retarded persons they have had. Availability of services to the retarded, i.e., recreation programs, walk-in clinics, to help resolve problems they may present to the community increase positive attitudes.

4. Ethnocentricism is strongly related to negative attitudes. A mixed socio-economic, racially integrated community is likely to be more accepting of the retarded and offer them more opportunities for self-expression.

5. Age, maturity, and sex are determinants in attitudes. For example, women tend to be more accepting of the retarded than men. This may be partly related to the fact that women themselves are more subject to social pressures (despite the growth of the Women's Liberation Movement) and so tend to identify with the "underdog." On the other hand, women are usually as disturbed as men if their normal sons and daughters start "dating" a retardate, although they do not object to socialization in school or in shared recreational activities, particularly before the children reach puberty.

6. Prejudgments of the attributes of the retarded are not exclusively negative. In fact, there is in some circles a growing tendency to exaggerate the positive qualities of the retarded, and in others a tendency to continue to stress the old stereotypes.

In conclusion, we can say that our knowledge of community attitudes towards the sexuality of the retarded is very limited. We all have some repressed fears and prejudices in regard to the sexual rights of the retarded that obstruct the accumulation of knowledge in this area.

Fortunately, increased interest is emerging in the sexuality of the retarded, and this interest will undoubtedly lead to investigation and research. There are healthy signs that our society is abandoning the tendency to stereotype the retarded. As this interest grows under progressive leadership, people will reexamine their attitudes towards the sexuality of the retarded. The fact that the subject is the focus of attention at this conference seems to confirm this optimistic view.

REFERENCES

1. TRIANDIS, H. C.: *Attitude and Attitude Change.* New York, Wiley, 1971, 232 pp.
2. MORGENSTERN, M.: *Attitudes Toward Sexuality of the Mentally Retarded,* Unpublished data.

Institutional and Community Attitudes, Practices and Policies

(SESSION ONE)

GENERAL DISCUSSION

MICHAEL J. BEGAB, *Presiding*

In opening this session, Dr. Begab reminded the participants that the retarded are not a homogeneous group with similar behavior, needs, and educational problems, but present a wide range of abilities and disabilities, reproductive capacity, and potential for marriage and parenthood. He also noted that the families of the retarded differ greatly in their attitudes toward the expression of sexuality and toward their retarded children. Nevertheless, he said, society for the most part does not differentiate among the retarded and looks askance at the prospect of sexual activity or parenthood on the part of any mentally retarded person.

After the presentations, Dr. Begab commented that the reports of Dr. Deisher and Mr. Carruth clearly indicated the need for change in administrative attitudes. He pointed out, however, that the superintendents of institutions were vested with legal, ethical, and social responsibilities that may impose certain constraints upon their readiness to change either their own policies or the practices of their staffs, and he called upon Mr. Stevens, Dr. Roos, and Dr. Clark as persons experienced in institutional administration to discuss the problems impeding change.

Mr. Stevens said that while administrative policies may be a generation behind current thinking, the ability to catch up may be hampered not only by a fear of public reaction and hence a loss of operational funds, but also by some very practical problems of operation. Some of these problems, he said, stem from the fact that the populations of public institutions consist of increasing proportions of profoundly and severely retarded persons, many of whom have severe physical and sensory handicaps, and of moderately and mildly retarded persons with severe emotional problems. Questioning whether meaningful heterosexual activity could occur among the profoundly or severely retarded, he said that such persons are much more likely to engage in masturbation or homosexuality, and that more discussion is needed on the conditions under which these forms of sexual activity occur and the types of control that might be imposed.

Mr. Stevens also questioned whether opportunity for normal heterosexual activity could be considered an "inalienable right" of persons unable to accept responsibility for their own actions. Suggesting that it might rather be considered a "privilege," he said that an institution would be inviting criticism by granting such a privilege to mildly retarded persons who are so emotionally disturbed that they cannot get along in the community. Because public institutions today are finding it difficult to provide all the necessary medical, educational, and rehabilitative services desperately needed by their residents, he expressed doubt that either their superintendents or the administrators of the state agencies would want to request funds to provide opportunities for heterosexual practices among any institutional residents. Moreover, he added, if such provisions *were* made, the superintendent might be faced with the problem of how to deter an unscrupulous employee from engaging in sexual activity with a resident under the ruse of giving a practical lesson in the proper methods of heterosexual intercourse. (Dr. Boggs cited a scandal of this nature that had occurred in a New Jersey institution.)

Dr. Roos asserted that superintendents who keep their jobs are those who realize early that dismissal results from sins of commission rather than sins of omission or who are able to gain support for their policies from their staff, the central office, or the parents and the community. Because the climate of an institution has usually been set by the first superintendent, he said, a newcomer may find that his staff has a philosophy at variance with his own. He told of his staff's dire predictions of uncontrolled sexual behavior when he introduced coeducational eating at an institution where he was once superintendent, predictions that were not realized. Observing that institutions with heterogeneous populations tend to focus their attention on their least capable residents, he predicted that as the principle of normalization is recognized in the construction of facilities, grouping of residents, and selection of staff members, administrators will favor sexual expression as part of the normalizing procedure.

Dr. Roos also called for more attention in sex education programs as protection against disease. He told of how syphilis had spread in one institution from the homosexual contacts of residents who had picked up the spirochete while out on leave.

Dr. Clark said that in the past 10 years at Elwyn Institute, which has a population of a thousand, he has found that changes can be effected if introduced slowly and unobtrusively. By proceeding quietly, he said, the Institute has been able to introduce sex education into its academic and training programs and to provide more and more coeducational activities, and even to assign boys and girls to rooms on the same floor in its halfway house. In its sex education program, it emphasizes the relationship, rather than the mechanical aspects of sex. While the Institute avoids situations that might lead to conflict, such as pushing or promoting birth control, its counseling staff discussed the possibilities of contraception with girls who are preparing to go out into the community and refers them to the local Planned Parenthood Association or a private gynecologist if they wish to receive such help.

Staff members, said Dr. Clark, sometimes want to move faster than the administration in allowing more sexual freedom, for the administration has a medical-legal responsibility for the resident's protection. If a female resident, particularly a minor, becomes pregnant by another resident or employee, the institution and/or the superintendent may be sued. In some instances, parents have sued and won, he reported.

Some policies, said Dr. Clark, can be encouraged but should not be put in writing since they may fall into the hands of emotionally involved parents or people in the community. He gave as an example discussions on masturbation. Dr. Clark advocated heeding an aphorism of Bertrand Russell's: "You can practice something if you don't preach it, and can preach something if you don't practice it. If you do both, you will come into considerable conflict with society." In the administration of a program, it is easier to make constructive changes if they are evolved progressively without fanfare.

Dr. Gordon spoke of the need to recognize "the politics of sexuality," and to devise "a strategy of implementation" for introducing changes in institutional policies having to do with sex. He suggested that today's high level of unemployment might be regarded as an opportunity to be more selective about attitudes toward both sexuality and mental retardation in employing staff members at all levels. Some of the healthiest influences emerging in institutions today, he said, stem from the conscientious objectors they employ. He also suggested that in some instances, as in providing contraceptives to minors, it may be necessary to break the law as a "calculated strategy" for meeting the needs of the mentally retarded.

Dr. Athanasiou commented that institutions for the mentally retarded today may be in the same developmental phase of emerging from the concept of "total institutional control" as were girls' college dormitories 10 years ago.

INSTITUTIONAL AND COMMUNITY ATTITUDES, PRACTICES, AND POLICIES

(Session Two)

13

Marriage and Mental Handicap

JANET MATTINSON
Institute of Marital Studies
Tavistock Institute of Human Relations
(London, England)

I AM GOING TO TALK about a few issues that emerged from a small, but intensive, follow-up study[1] that I did on 32[*] marriages in which both partners had at one time in their lives been designated subnormal, i.e. retarded. The marriages had been maintained for a varying number of years; the youngest marriage was one year old, the oldest was 15 years, and the average was seven years.

Apart from their low intelligence, there was one other factor all these people had in common. As a result of the designation of subnormality, they had all been admitted to a hospital for the subnormal in southwest England, and the majority of them had been committed there on a legal order and retained for many years. Only in 1960, when a new Mental Health Act came into force, were the majority of these legal orders rescinded and many of these patients discharged. Many had been institutionalized for ten years or more—some more than twenty. The majority of them were admitted between 1930 and 1959, and none were discharged before 1950.

The hospital, founded in 1864 with nine beds, was originally "devoted to the peculiar case of idiots." By 1960 this hospital had

---

[*] I started with 40 couples on my list. Four couples were not traced. Four marriages were not being maintained.

TABLE 1

NUMBER OF YEARS SPENT IN HOSPITAL

No. of years	No. of patients
3-5	13
6-10	20
11-15	16
16-20	16
21-25	8
26-30	4
31-35	2
36-40	0
41-42	1
	—
	80

over 1,800 beds. The large, main hospital building, Victorian in style and built in the local grey stone, stands just back from a main road to the coast, dwarfs the small village in which it is situated, and commands a spectacular view of the estuary in front of it. Behind the main building is a maze of more recently built wards and workshops. The brilliant geraniums in the formal front garden and the crude bright paint inside only alleviate its institutional character. Many of the people in my study did not think of it as a hospital: in their terms it was, "Put Away," which is the title of a recent sociological study of English institutions for the subnormal, published in 1969.[2] It has a catchment area covering two counties, one of these being the largest geographical administrative unit in England. The homes of some of the patients could be over 80 miles away, which, in England, is a long distance to have to go to the hospital, and metaphorically even further in this particular rural area, where any place other than the nearest market town can be considered by the locals to be foreign.

The care the patients in my study received in this hospital remained for a long time very Victorian in character. They were offered sanctuary and asylum from conditions and experiences that had hampered their intellectual, emotional, and social de-

TABLE 2

RECORDED IQ ON ADMISSION

IQ	No. of patients
20-29	0
30-39	1
40-49	11
50-59	23
60-69	21
70-79	10
80-89	4
90-99	2
100-110	0
Not recorded	8
	80

velopment. Some of them welcomed the nurture they received and remained very dependent. Some resented the authority and rebelled and absconded. Some of them just gave up trying. Only slowly did the legal "care, segregation and control" change to "special care and treatment," literacy, occupational and social training. And much of this training still has to remain geared to the inappropriate system rather than to the individual needs of individual patients.

Their measured IQs ranged from 38 to 93, the majority of them having scored in the fifties and sixties on a Stanford-Binet test. I put very little reliance on these scores; I think that many of them were inaccurate. In the earlier days they were done by people who had not had a full or detailed training in testing, and we now know that a Stanford-Binet is not a good test for adults on the lower end of the intelligence scale. And, even more important, they were done at a time when the patient was probably very frightened, placed in an overwhelmingly large and strange environment, perhaps just having committed an offense or been removed from his home, and probably very un-understanding of what was happening to him. But I do want to stress that they are important in the fact they were one of the determinants of their committal to the hospital.

The social factors were always considered to be as important as, or more important than, the IQs, which accounts for the 16 people with scores over 70.

Their deprivation was to me very overwhelming. Many of them had been orphaned, had a broken home, or had been seriously neglected or ill-treated. As one woman said to me, "My life history would make you laugh and cry in turn." When they told me about their backgrounds, the rejection, and circumstances they had experienced, I, a layman, found the subnormality receded in importance. It is not always easy to distinguish the interrelationship between mental disorder and mental deficiency, but this group of people suffered from many character disorders and gross emotional immaturity which, in view of their histories, was not surprising.

Courting. The majority of these couples did their courting in the hospital. When most of them were first admitted, the sexes were officially segregated. Then they used to do their courting behind the hedge. As one woman said, ". . . if we heard someone coming, I'd run one way and he'd go over the hedge." But increasingly they were allowed more contact, and much of their dating was done at the weekly hospital dance. But this took time, because initially they were allowed only one dance an evening with the same partner. A few of the couples met only after they were out on trial leave. Some of them escaped, and married before they were found.

The purpose of my inquiry into the lives of these people was to discover their viability in the community. It was essentially a follow-up study, and aimed specifically to ascertain two things: firstly, whether they were capable of maintaining life in the community, able to work, maintain and manage a home, and to bring up children in a manner acceptable to the community; and secondly, how much help and support they required from relatives, neighbors and friends, and the Social Services to be able to do this. One of the main interests was what were the social and personal consequences of having been labelled as intellectual failures.

THE RESULTS

I am going to go through the results very quickly and give you five main findings and four non-findings, and then spend the rest of my time not only on what I thought, but also on what they thought were the less classifiable reasons for their success or failure.

The Findings

The first main finding was that four marriages were not being maintained. Two couples had separated and two couples had been through the process of a divorce, which in England requires considerable initiative and, even with legal aid, costs money. I was able to find only one partner of these four broken marriages, and, as I was not prepared to rely on only a one-sided and retrospective account, I did not pursue the inquiry in detail. The study relates in detail to the 32 ongoing marriages, where I could observe with my own eyes the interaction that was occurring between the couple and between them and their children.

The second main finding concerns their practical achievements. I obtained information about the facts of and their attitude to seven categories of behavior: employment, financial management, accommodation, criminal activity, care of the children, receipt of social benefit, and receipt of a personal casework service. The results showed, not surprisingly, a great variation in the abilities and performance of these people once designated subnormal, and lent additional support to the optimistic view that many people whose recorded IQ scores suggest mental deficiency, and whose behavior was seen to be socially incompetent at a particular point in their lives, can mature and can develop into responsible citizens.

The following is an extract from one of my tape-recording transcripts. The two speakers' recorded IQs were 48 and 41 on

TABLE 3

MAINTAINED MARRIAGES

		Couples
Partnership broken		
by divorce	2	
by separation	2	
	—	
		4
Partnership maintained supportively and affectionately, and not regretted*	19	
affectionately but with symptoms of stress*	6	
with one partner depending heavily on the other*	4	
unsatisfactorily*	3	
	—	
	32	32
		—
		36

* For details of criteria, see pages 176, 177, and 178.

a Stanford-Binet. I do not think the man would be capable of holding down a job, but with his being home all day, the two of them make one apparently very adequate mother, and the Health Visitor* has no complaints about the care of the children of pre-school age. Fortunately, no social worker has become over-anxious to rehabilitate Mr. Scott back into employment. I would love to quote you many extracts from my recordings, but this is just one with two people, once designated as imbeciles, expressing their attempt to come to terms with living in the community. They are talking about the police. Mr. Scott said:

> "I think some of them try to cause trouble sometimes. But they're only human beings; it's only the uniforms make them different."

* In England all children under five years are visited by a Health Visitor, employed by the local authority.

"Some of them are helpful. When I lost me purse, he helped me find it."

"Yes, he's a good policeman; helps a lot. And if you're lost they give you the right road. It's a good job we've got police, 'cos they are the only ones you can depend on if anything gets stolen."

"I found someone's wallet and gave it to the police."

"If nobody claims it, we can have it."

The results overall are surprisingly even, and these couples seemed to divide themselves into thirds. About a third were well housed, and had been so for a number of years, in unfurnished houses or flats provided by the local council; there were very few rent arrears. About a third were in less stable accommodations, and a third were movers and shifters. In an area of high unemployment, 12 men had had regular employment and had been so employed for several years, 14 were in less regular employment, and six were permanently unemployed. A quarter were not known to any of the social workers, even the Mental Welfare officers; a quarter were receiving intensive help.

I graded their achievements on a four-point scale, and Table 4 shows their mean scores. Two of the five top scoring families would have scored a perfect 3 if they had not received a government sickness benefit for a period of less than six weeks in the previous two years. The hardness of the categories showing pressure on the social services deprives them of the mark of perfection, even though they were only exercising a "social right" normally considered to be justifiable.

The third main finding concerns their marital relationships. This was obviously much more difficult to assess and categorize, and I did not attempt to say that this was a good or a bad marriage by any objective criteria—that seemed too arrogant. But I did score their marriage, again on a four-point scale, according to whether *they* thought it was satisfactory and satisfying. These are the criteria of the scoring, and examples:

TABLE 4

Scores on Achievement Criteria

Mean Score	Families
3	0
2.5 - 2.9	5
2.0 - 2.4	6
1.5 - 1.9	13
1.0 - 1.4	4
0.5 - 0.9	3
0.0 - 0.4	1
	—
	32

Score of 3

Those in which the partnership was acknowledged by both partners to be supportive and affectionate, despite the minor ups and downs usually attendant when two people live in close proximity. The quarrels, disagreements, and external stresses are not seen to be destructive to either of them. They thought they had done better in life by being married to each other; neither of them regretted the union and both of them were proud of their joint achievements. No separations or physical violence were admitted.

Example:

"Well, it's had its ups and downs like everybody else's, but we've always pulled back together again. It's never gone that far that we couldn't sort of think back."

"I will say about her, she's always home when I come home from work. My meal's always on the table."

"Sometimes I might grumble when he goes out for a drink and I'm here alone and it's too late for me to go anywhere— nothing very big, just piffling things really."

Score of 2

Those in which the partnership was basically affectionate and caring and not regretted, but which was not mutually helpful enough to keep each other out of trouble, or to withstand the personality difficulties of one or both as displayed in the interaction between them. There had been temporary separations, or criminal activity committed by one partner.

Example:

"Here's our photographs. Look how I'm holding on to him. You'd think I runs away from him the way I was holding on there. I can't help it; I'm always on the worry all the time. The least little thing will upset me. Now, who could be more good to me than my husband? But, if I run away, he's the worst in the world. I say things about him sometimes that are not true. Then I might say something one day that's going to lead him to the Court, maybe prison. The only thing is I upset my husband and I runs away. God knows what I run for."

Score of 1

Those in which one partner depended heavily on the other and both partners expressed resentment about this type of relationship.

Example:

"I give him his credit, 'cos he's a good boy really."

"I'm not a boy."

"Well, he is to me. Well, he's not acting like a man, is he? He comes and gives me a hand if I'm busy. He never hits me, if we have a tiff—well, anybody do, don't they?"

"I've never laid a hand on her. I never will, either. It isn't in me to do it. If a man hits a woman, he's a proper coward. She treats me like as if I were her son at times. I did get annoyed the other day, because I went with her to fetch my shoes from the menders, and the woman behind the counter said, 'Here's your son's shoes.' I looked a right idiot. I won't go out with my missus, not very often."

The recorded IQ of this husband is 34 points higher than that of his wife.

Score of 0

Those in which the partnership was acknowledged to be unsatisfactory, but which was held on to strenuously. Although there had been many voluntary and enforced separations, no attempt had been made to part on a permanent basis; there appeared to be a strong negative tie.

Example:

"So he said to me, 'You will not do your washing' and I said to him, 'I will do my washing.' 'Oh, do what you bloody well like,' he said. So I said, 'That's all right.' I got me way, I did the washing. I made some buns whilst me boiler was boiling up. I whipped they in the oven. So I thought, 'That's that.' Then I did the cleaning. Then he went out and when he came in for dinner this barney was still going on, so I turned the key in the door and said, 'Now you're out, you stay out until I've finished, and I'll call you when it's teatime.' He came to the window and wanted a drink, and I said, 'No, I'm not having you in here.' He was flaming mad and he said, 'Open this door.' and I said, 'I'm not, not with the temper you're in.' And he said, 'Open this door,' so I said, 'Yes, I'll open the door and I'll run.' I ran out there and he kicked me in the face, cut me in the eye, kicked me down the leg here and bruised the spine up me back. I said, 'Right, you've cut a rod for your own back.' He took the buns I'd made and scrambled them up and threw them to the floor. I'd bought meat to make a pie with and he threw that about the floor and he threw the cake. I went up and phoned. I came back and he was coming up the road. I said, 'I shouldn't run away, because I've phoned the police for you.'"

(This scene was described to me a week later, when they were reconciled, and after he had been charged with assault. I was asked to admire the love bites on her neck and through part of the interview she sat on his lap.)

The fourth main finding. I then placed the achievement scores alongside the marital scores, and the table produced a very marked pattern. The two factors of marital happiness and achievement

TABLE 5

MARITAL RELATIONSHIP SCORES

	Score	No. of Couples
Supportive and affectionate partnership, not destructive, better married than single	3	19
Affectionate partnership, not regretted, considerable stress, but better married than single	2	6
One partner heavily dependent on the other, and this resented by both partners	1	4
Predominantly unsatisfactory partnership, strong negative tie, no attempt to separate permanently	0	3
		32

TABLE 6

ACHIEVEMENT SCORES AND MARITAL RELATIONSHIP SCORES

A.S.	M.R.S. Scored 3	Scored 2	Scored 1	Scored 0	Total
2.5 - 2.9	6				6
2.0 - 2.4	5				5
1.5 - 1.9	8	3	2		13
1.0 - 1.4		3	1		4
0.5 - 0.9			1	2	3
0.0 - 0.4				1	1
	19	6	4	3	32

co-existed. What I could not tell was whether either was causative of the other.

The fifth main finding was that there were not very many children. Thirty-two women had only 40 children between them. Fifteen couples, nine of whom were of child-bearing age when they married, had no children. The other 17 couples had an average of

TABLE 7

SIZE OF FAMILIES

No. of live children in family	No. of families	No. of children
5	1	5
4	1	4
3	5	15
2	6	12
1	4	4
	17	40

just over two each. When I excluded the couples who were not of child-bearing age, but included those who could have had children but did not, the average was 1.5, lower than the national average for the same age group.

The largest family of live children was five.

Two children had died, and neglect was queried at the inquest of one of them.

Six of these 40 children (from three families) had been removed from their parents' care, and 34 were still with their parents.

Three of these children were retarded in their development, and two of these were in special, non-residential training centers.

But it must be noted that these families are not necessarily completed, although many couples were using contraceptives.

The Non-Findings

As there was such a wide range of achievement amongst these people, I looked at four factors which might be seen to have predictive value.

First, I took their IQ scores, not because I relied on these, but because they had been an important factor in determining their committal. But I found there was only a very weak association, not significant, between their joint IQ scores and their joint achievements accomplished many years later. The exceptions were of more interest; some low achievers had IQ scores above the median, and some high achievers had scores well below the median. It seemed to make no difference whether there was or was not great disparity between the pair or whether the man or the woman was more intelligent.

I then took the length of time they had been in the hospital. But this was as fruitless. I only learned that the low achievers had a wider time span between them. Some of them may have been retained too long, and some not long enough.

Then I took their behavior in the hospital. My private guess had been that the more aggressive patients, who had refused to give in, might be those who would be able to use this same aggression more constructively in the outside world. But I was wrong. There was a very even distribution of type of behavior amongst both high and low achievers.

And then, and getting quite desperate, and having been analytically trained, I was sure I would find a relationship between the early histories and background of deprivation with the present performance. But the backgrounds of the high achievers and the low achievers were all remarkably similar. There was no correlation at all of shared or lack of shared experience in four categories of deprivation.

I was defeated. The old hospital files yielded up nothing else consistent enough for me to use with all the couples. I had to go back to my own observations of their current behavior and their own views of themselves.

And I will now mention six characteristics which, I think, related to many of these marriages being remarkably effective.

Firstly, the majority of these marriages worked on a complementary basis, the skill of one partner supplementing the inability of the other.

"He doos the reading, and I doos the writing."

The next quotation is of a man speaking:

"Cooked a chicken last Sunday, roast potatoes, batter pudding."

J.M. "You cook the dinner on Sundays, even though she's here?"

"Yes, 'cos I like roast dinner."

J.M. "Your wife doesn't cook the Sunday dinner and things like that?"

"No, she ain't too good for cooking. She never learned, I don't think."

At the time of doing this study I did not know of the work of Roman and Bauman[3,4] on the possible use of an Interaction Product Analysis using the Rorschach, Wechsler, and other tests to estimate how well people work together as opposed to working on their own. I had been very apologetic when I explained to a statistician that I had put the IQ scores together. In this respect this group of people was very "normal," and was obviously pooling their joint resources. Singly, these people had shown themselves defective in social living; paired, they were much less defective.

The second characteristic, which relates to the first, and partly explains why they were able to pool their resources, was that they were able to take help from each other, whereas in the hospital they had often not been able to use the help offered to them by the doctors and nurses. This presumably is something to do with the type of success that "Alcoholics Anonymous" sometimes achieves —that sometimes like can help like better than unlike. I think that this applied to this particular group of people because of the unfortunate experiences they had had under the authority of their parents; anyone else in authority was very suspect and probably damned before he opened his mouth. Just because of the authority of the doctors, accentuated by the compulsory orders of detention, I do not think the patients could listen to the doctors.

Mr. Turner explained to me:

"Doctor used to give me lectures, but I used to ignore them. Still, I realize now he was only telling me for my own good."

Mrs. Acton said:

"Well, we're both on the same level. I helps him and he helps me."

Another couple talking together said:

"He's a nice lad, beginning to spell better. He used to be a boozer once, but he ain't now."

"Used to drink like a fish."

"But not since he's married."

"Gived it up—just like that."

Thirdly, and again this is probably connected with the last characteristic of self-help, these couples seemed to be highly motivated to prove the hospital to have been wrong in containing them so long.

"I wanted to settle down. I wanted to prove that I could maintain a home and also rear children. I didn't see why I couldn't just because I'd been an in-patient."

And another said:

"This'll make you laugh. They knew right away. They thought, I can't see they two going very far. You see what I mean. Well, they were wrong, we did make it."

It seemed the hospital had served a very important function; it had proved a useful object for displacement of anger. It was a ready butt for much of the anger these people felt about their parents and home circumstances. And it must have made their anger very much safer, because however much they resented its authority and the compulsory orders, as many of them did, they could never destroy it. With its impregnable, granite, fortress-like aspect, it is very difficult to imagine how even a demolition contractor would set about it.

Fourthly, they were very unidealistic. They did not set their sights very high. The nearest to a trite comment I heard was, "True love never do run smooth, do it, dear?" Much more common was the sort of remark, "I choosed him and his needs. So I got to put up with them. Look at those potatoes over there." Or, as another woman said, "I'd probably be lonely without a man."

Fifthly, many of the marriages were very cocooned. They did not rely on relatives, friends, and neighbors as much as I had expected them to do. The concept of friendship was relatively unknown to them.

"Who are your friends?"

"Me and the wife. Can't grumble at all, can we?" And when asked the same question, another said:

> "Well, I dunno. I think Ern's my best friend, though he's more than that to me—more than a best friend."

They kept well away from their neighbors, afraid to admit that they had been in a "mental house" or "put away." "I keep meself to meself." This may have been very impoverishing, but it did protect them from attempting to compete and from reaching above themselves.

Sixthly, few of these people denied their subnormality. "I'm not no reader. I'm not no speller. I don't mind admitting it." They seemed to accept themselves as they were, but were afraid that their children inherited this disability. I eventually realized that the present functioning of these people was not directly related to the degree of deprivation or ill-treatment they had experienced as children. It seemed that it was more related to their feelings about what had happened to them, rather than the actuality. But, even more important was the type of defense they used against these painful feelings. Many of them were very good displacers, as I have illustrated, but they were not good deniers.

Denial is a much more primitive and less satisfactory defense than displacement. But, perhaps even more important than the actual defenses they were using was whether the defense most in operation was of value to, and valued by, the partner. If one partner was not threatened by the defense used by the other, and even admired him for it, and even found it useful for himself, there seemed to be less inappropriate projection and therefore less imbalance emotionally between the two of them.

Conclusion

My ultimate conclusion about these former patients of a hospital for the retarded was that, paired, many of them were able to reinforce each other's strengths and established marriages which, in the light of what had happened to them previously, were no more, no less, foolish than many others in the community, and which gave them considerable satisfaction.

REFERENCES

1. MATTINSON, M. J.: *Marriage and Mental Handicap.* Pittsburgh, Pa., University of Pittsburgh Press, 1971, 231 pp.
2. MORRIS, P.: *Put Away: a sociological study of institutions for the mentally retarded.* London, Routledge and Kegan Paul, 1969, 355 pp.
3. ROMAN, M. & BAUMAN, G.: Interaction Testing: a technique for the psychological evaluation of small groups. In Harrower, Molly; Roman, Melvin; Vorhaus, Pauline; and Bauman, Gerald (Eds.): *Creative Variations in the Projective Techniques.* Charles C Thomas, 1960, pp. 93-138.
4. BAUMAN, G. & ROMAN, M.: Interaction testing in the study of marital dominance. *Family Process*, 5:230-242, September 1966.

14

Marriage and Mental Handicap: Some Observations in Northern Ireland

BRIAN G. SCALLY
*Consultant Psychiatrist, Eastern Special
Care Management Committee
Northern Ireland*

INTRODUCTION

MISS MATTINSON GIVES an in-depth approach to the problem of marriage and mental handicap in her follow-up survey of 32 marriages in which both partners were at one time in their lives designated as subnormal. In my own survey of this problem in Northern Ireland, I came across many cases in which the responses were similar.[1]

In my survey I attempted to look at the records of all mentally retarded persons who were married, whether or not they had offspring, or who, although single, had given birth to live children or had had miscarriages or stillbirths. The total mentally retarded population at that time was 4,631, giving a prevalence rate of 3.2 per thousand of the general population. From these, a total of 342 (32 males and 310 females) met the stated criteria. The mean chronological age of these survey subjects was 36.7 years, with a range from 17 to 84 years. The difference between the chronological age of males and females was not significant. All of the males were married. Of the females 63.5 percent were single and of those who had married five percent were separated, six percent were widowed, and less than one percent were divorced.

The mean chronological age at marriage was the same for both males and females, 26.4 years. As would be expected, the ratio of married to unmarried mentally retarded persons was extremely small when compared with the ratio of married to unmarried in the general population.

The mean social quotient (SQ) of all the mentally retarded persons in the survey was 58, with a range from 21 to 90. The mean social quotient of their spouses was 88, considerably higher than that of the survey subjects. This finding supports the commonly held view that mentally retarded persons tend to marry persons of higher intellectual and social abilities than themselves. Only in one case was a retarded person married to a retardate. None of the males and only seven of the females had been sterilized, one of them married and six single. However, there is an increasing tendency in Northern Ireland for retardates to marry each other and an increasing tendency for sterilization to be carried out.

The question of whether retardates should marry is a controversial one. Tredgold in 1949 suggested that such marriages be prohibited by law because of a curious tendency for like to mate like.[2] That same year Penrose noted that the likeness between husband and wife with respect to intelligence level was very strong and might be represented by a coefficient of 0.5.[3] Gunzburg, however, expressed the opinion a decade later that the tolerance toward such marriages must be continued until it has been proved beyond a reasonable doubt that they do indeed produce children of low mentality or of lower mental ability than their parents.[4] He qualified this opinion by stating that there was much justification for making negative decisions in individual cases where it could be shown that marriage would be detrimental to the individual and to society.

A 1962 report[5] of a working party set up by the Pediatric Society of the South East Metropolitan region of England states that studies have shown that fertile marriage by individuals of subnormal intelligence produce children whose intelligence is, on the average, only a little below that of the general population.

There is, in other words, a "regression to the mean" and dull people, even very dull people, tend to have children who are rather more clever than themselves. Mentally retarded parents, however, do need considerably more support from social services than normal parents if their children are not to suffer from lack of stimulation. The report of the London Departmental Committee on Sterilization states on page 32: "We think that the marriage of a sterilized defective would be less likely to fail and, in the event of failure, would be less disastrous and far reaching if uncomplicated by children." [6] This view has been supported by various authors. [7-9] However, Milner has questioned the fairness of preventing marriage of unsterilized retardates by pointing out that many intelligent adults are unfit to rear their offspring. [10]

In the United States some States have enacted laws prohibiting the marriage of mentally retarded persons, but according to Wallin these laws have not been very effective and would not be 100 percent effective even with registration of the mentally retarded. [8]

In Great Britain the law has never been clearly defined in relation to marriage of the retarded. Under an old Act of 1811, dealing mainly with property, the marriage of mental patients could, in certain circumstances, be declared void. The Matrimonial Causes Act of Northern Ireland (1939) [11] also laid down certain circumstances where application could be made to have marriages declared void. Study of legislation on this subject shows that Parliament has never been inclined to lay down any definite principles prohibiting the marriage of persons with any kind of handicap, mental or physical.

In Northern Ireland, unless a retardate has been taken under the control of the Lord Chief Justice under a procedure laid down by the Lunacy Regulation (Ireland) Act of 1871, [12] it is doubtful whether there is any legal authority to prohibit marriage if the prospective couple has given proper notice to the appropriate marriage authority. However, the powers exercisable under the Mental Health Acts (Northern Ireland) [13] of 1948 and 1961 have been used to institutionalize a retardate known to be considering the contracting of an undesirable marriage.

Spouses and Offspring

There are two "common sense" views about the union or mating of retardates. The first holds that like mates with like. The second holds that retardates tend to mate with persons who are intellectually and functionally superior to themselves. Both these views are rather nebulous, the first the more so since its validity clearly hinges on the definition of what constitutes "like." It is not surprising, therefore, that the findings of my survey paradoxically seem to support both views. To be specific, the retardates who were married tended to have married persons more accomplished than themselves (thus supporting the second "common sense" assumption), but the difference between retardate and spouse was not so great that the mean social quotient of the spouses was normal. In other words, the retardates married a little above themselves, but the differences in social or intellectual levels between husband and wife tended to be small. Thus "like" married "like" if the term "like" is taken to mean broad similarities in intellectual and social accomplishments.

Another more cogent suggestion about the union of retardates concerns the effects of assortative and non-assortative mating, that is, between equals and non-equals in intellectual and social ability. The argument runs this way: the offspring of assortative mating are likely to be legitimate whereas the offspring of non-assortative mating are more likely to be illegitimate. The reasons underlying this view are not altogether clear, but one point frequently made is that when non-assortative mating takes place, it is likely to be a transient affair. The participants may be too widely different in character, temperament, general abilities, background, and the like to want to make the union permanent. Thus, the argument goes, the offspring tend to be illegitimate. On the other hand, when assortative mating takes place, the conditions for making the union permanent are more favorable.

It may be argued that the offspring of non-assortative mating will be brighter intellectually than the offspring of assortative mating, but such an argument is unwarranted even on *a priori* grounds. A more reasonable supposition is that the offspring of non-assortative mating will show greater variability in intellectual and social abilities than the offspring of assortative mating. However, the findings of my survey do not support this view. The data showed that the mean SQ of the legitimate and illegitimate offspring were very nearly equal and, more important, the variability within the two groups of offspring was equal.

Many authors writing in the early decades of this century claimed that the mentally retarded tend to propagate at an excessive rate.[14-17] Later authors did not agree, and maintained that the retarded were scarcely holding their own in the general population.[18-21] Penrose pointed out that the majority of mental retardates, particularly those of low IQ, were unable to propagate efficiently due to psychological causes.[18] Kemp stated that more retarded mothers were observed by the authorities than retarded fathers and that there was almost complete absence of effective fertility among the profoundly retarded,[19] while reproduction in the severely retarded was possible but rare.

In my survey, I found a total of 342 subjects who already were parents or were potential parents (married)—only 7.5 percent of the total mentally retarded population of Northern Ireland and 10 percent of the mentally retarded population over 16 years of age. The finding that only about 10 percent of these 342 persons were males agrees with Kemp's statement about the higher notification rates of retarded mothers. We can logically assume that a mentally retarded girl can be more attractive to a man than a mentally retarded male would be to a female. Opportunities for marriage and parenthood are probably greater for retarded females than for retarded males. Moreover, retarded females who are regarded as being in moral danger or who have already had children are more likely to be referred to the authorities for help and protection because of social inefficiency. Promiscuity in itself

—without retardation—is not, however, regarded as a sufficient cause for a person to be classified as socially inefficient.

Mentally retarded persons, whether male or female, do not appear to be more libidinous than their normal contemporaries. The so-called immorality of female retardates is caused more by their craving for attention and affection, coupled with lack of judgment and control, than by a strong sexual drive.[22] Milner has pointed out that female retardates are even more resentful than male retardates of the sexual frustration imposed upon them.

Many male retardates have demonstrated an inability to control the more perverted forms of sexual impulses such as indecent exposure, homosexual aggression, or assaults upon young children, and are thus as likely to come under the provisions of the Mental Health Acts as female retardates. The male subjects in my survey consisted of only 1.4 percent of all the known male retardates in Northern Ireland and the female subjects 14.4 percent of all the known female retardates. The survey's female subjects who were between 15 and 44 years of age consisted of only 17.9 percent of all the retarded females of the same age range in the population. My survey, therefore, does not support the popular supposition that as a whole the mentally retarded are exceptionally prolific.

I would like to make a few observations about the offspring of the mentally retarded. Among the survey's 342 subjects, sexual activity had resulted in a total of 887 pregnancies. Those pregnancies resulted in 791 births, of whom 71 were deceased at the time of the study, 55 having died before the age of two years. The average number of children born alive per individual in the total group was 2.3. This figure included the illegitimate children of the married and single females, but not of the males. In Northern Ireland in 1961 the mean family size for all children born alive to women in marriage, including any that died, was 2.97.

Among the 71 deceased children of the retardates, significantly more were born before 1948 than after 1948—a difference which may be due to the national decline in infant mortality and the improvements brought about by post-war social legislation, including the National Health Act of 1948. Of the 720 offspring still living at the time of the survey, 669 were examined. Their mean social quotient was 89.6 as compared with 58 for the mentally retarded parents and 88 for the spouses of the retarded parents.

Suitability as Parents

While the phenomenon of biological regression has been found to operate in this survey, it does not of itself provide sufficient grounds for condoning marriage among mentally retarded persons. It does, however, suggest that the old theories concerning the encroachment and final swamping of "normal" society by people of low intelligence are not tenable. Nowadays, these crude theories have been discarded by professional persons, but vestiges still remain, for example, the belief that a relationship exists between size of sibship and intelligence. Although most of the concern about the union of retardates seems to center on the hereditary effects on the progeny, other important issues should be taken into account. Among these issues are the related problems of the compatibility of husband and wife and their suitability as parents.

The first of these issues did not apply in all the cases in this survey, since more than half the female parents were single and most of these single mothers were looking after their children without the help of a male cohabitor. In the relevant cases, nearly 40 percent of the mentally retarded male parents and over half the mentally retarded female parents were rated, through the use of objective criteria, as having "poor" or "bad" relations with their spouses.

Over half the mentally retarded males and 90 percent of the mentally retarded females were rated as making less than adequate contributions to the running of the home and to the welfare of the children. This finding poses the question as to whether mentally retarded parents are capable of bringing up their own offspring or whether they should be allowed to do so. I doubt if poor husband-wife relationships and inadequacy in child-rearing among parents can be compensated for by the offspring's tendency to be more intellectually and functionally accomplished than their parents.

On the whole the survey showed that offspring reared in their own parents' or relatives' home reach a social quotient as high as or higher than offspring reared in other environments, such as adoptive or foster homes or institutions. However, this finding cannot lead to a dogmatic statement that the environment of the former was better for development of intellectual and social competence. The argument might be made that the children kept by their parents or relatives might have done even better in a different environment.

Northern Ireland, being an integral part of Great Britain, has in operation a comprehensive government health and social service that supervises to a degree all children, irrespective of parentage. If a parent is judged incapable of caring for his or her child, then action is taken to provide child care help in the home or alternative care for the child. My survey showed that only 30 percent of the offspring of retardates were being reared apparently satisfactorily in their own homes, whereas 62 percent had had to have other provisions made for them. It would seem, therefore, that the majority of retardates are incapable of caring for their children, and that this deficit in child care is more evident in single female retardates than in married female retardates. The married parents scored better in the rating scales than the single parents. This, in part, could be accounted for by the support a spouse gives in the home, particularly since spouses scored significantly higher than the retarded subjects on the same rating scales. In any consideration of the marriage of a mentally retarded person, it would appear to be important to assess the level of the intellectual or social competence of the intended spouse.

I believe, however, that the marriage of retardates should be discouraged rather than encouraged. In my own practice, when the possibility of the marriage of a mentally retarded person comes to my notice, I consider it from all aspects and even go so far as to interview the intended spouse. However, in many cases my advice is ignored or perhaps not even asked for. It is always my belief that if a mentally retarded person shows such initiative, the marriage, with adequate support, may well survive.

REFERENCES

1. SCALLY, B. G.: A clinical and epidemiological study of the offspring of mental defectives. *Ph.D. Thesis*, Dublin University, 1966.
2. TREDGOLD, A. F.: *A Textbook of Mental Deficiency*, (ed. 4). London, Bailliere, Tindall and Cox, 1949.
3. PENROSE, L. S.: *The Biology of Mental Defect*. London, Sidgwick and Jackson, 1954.
4. GUNZBURG, H. C.: *Social Rehabilitation of the Subnormal*. London, Bailliere, Tindall and Cox, 1960.
5. Report of a working party set up by the Paediatric Society of the South East Metropolitan Region, England: *The Needs of Mentally Handicapped Children*. London, Wellbrook Press Ltd., 1962.
6. Report of the Departmental Committee on Sterilization, London: HMSO, 1934.
7. GOSNEY, E. S. & POPENCE, P.: *Sterilization for Human Betterment*. New York, Macmillan, 1930.
8. WALLIN, J. E. W.: *Mental Deficiency*. Vermont, Brandon, 1956.
9. BUTLER, F. O.: A quarter of a century's experience in sterilization of mental defectives in California. *Amer. J. Ment. Defic.*, 50:508, 1945.
10. MILNER, K. O.: Delinquent types of mentally defective children. *J. Ment. Sci.*, 95:842, 1949.
11. Matrimonial Causes Act, Northern Ireland, 1939. Belfast: HMSO.
12. Lunacy Regulation Act, Northern Ireland, 1871. Belfast: HMSO.
13. Mental Health Acts (Northern Ireland), 1948, 1961. Belfast: HMSO.
14. LOMBROSO, C.: *Crime: Its Causes and Remedies*. London, Heinemann, 1911.
15. DAVIES, S. P.: *Social Control of the Mentally Deficient*. London, Constable, 1930.
16. BERRY, R. J. A. & GORDON, R. G.: *The Mental Defective*. London, Kegan Paul, 1931.
17. LIDBETTER, E. M.: *Heredity and the Social Problem Group*. London, Arnold and Co., 1933.
18. PENROSE, L. S.: Propagation of the unfit. *Lancet*, 259:425, 1950.
19. KEMP, T.: *Genetics and Disease*. London, Oliver and Boyd, 1951.
20. BURT, C.: *The Subnormal Mind*. London, Oxford University Press, 1955.
21. DAVIES, S. P.: *The Mentally Retarded in Society*. New York, Columbia University Press, 1959.
22. CLARKE, A. M. & CLARKE, A. D. B.: *Mental Deficiency: The Changing Outlook*. London, Methuen, 1958.

15

The Moral and Ethical Implications of Human Sexuality as They Relate to the Retarded

RABBI JOSEPH R. NAROT
Temple Israel (Miami)

WHEN I WAS FIRST INVITED to share in this conference, I held my breath in astonishment. If I had been asked to choose a subject for study and discussion, the sexuality of retardates would hardly have occurred to me as a primary moral and ethical question. Furthermore, what did I know of the general theme itself? With typical rabbinic fervor, however, I resolved not to let my ignorance stand in the way. I accepted this assignment, unprejudiced by facts, because I was challenged by the theme. I sensed in it a subject worthy of study and reflection.

As a rabbi, I must ponder the subject of the sexuality of retardates in the moral context of Judaism. As a Reform rabbi, I must relate that context to what is generally called the liberal Jewish religious attitudes and interpretations.

This means, first, that I regard sexuality generally as inherently neither wicked nor shameful, but as an instinct that can be gratified for itself alone. And it suggests, further, that the consequences of sexual activity must not add to the misery of persons already living or those yet unborn but likely to be born.

It is a universal experience that as soon as new vistas open before our eyes, we quickly are made to realize how common and familiar the problem is to others. No sooner had I accepted this assignment, than there came to my attention the plight of a family involving a retardate, the mother. The parents of this retarded woman literally bought her a husband—a man whose experiences in a Nazi concentration camp had left him with serious personality disturbances. I do not know into what category of retardation this woman fits. Perhaps it will mean something to you when I tell you that when the son that was born to this retarded woman and emotionally disturbed man was a little boy, the mother would fight with the child for the possession of his toys. Suffice it to say that the son, now a boy in his teens, is a psychological disaster and an emotional tragedy. This poses some hard questions concerning the sexual activity of the boy's parents, if not, indeed, ultimately of the boy himself. The thought of these questions intensified my desire to know more about the subject of this conference.

As a rabbi, I was led by both curiosity and a wish to link my thoughts to Jewish roots to find what ancient Hebrew literature might teach me on the subject of the retarded. I found that the Bible could shed but little light on the subject, but that rabbinic literature did consider what must have been retardation, although the term was not used. Ancient rabbinic law exempts three categories of persons from fulfilling the religious mandates, including foremost the mandate to be "fruitful and multiply."

The first exemption from the requirements of the law is the person unable to hear or speak the *cheresh*. Since moral instruction traditionally was given orally, the deaf were excluded, and since learning involved oral repetition, the dumb were also excluded. Another category exempted from the requirements consisted of young children, the *koton*. For example, if a child was too young to sit on the shoulders of his father, or too young to accompany his father by holding the father's hand, that child was not asked to do the bidding of the teachers.[1]

The third category of exempted persons consisted of those we call today the retarded. The Hebrew word is *shoteh*, which means in a sense the "fool" or "madman." The Talmud[2] defines the *shoteh* as follows: "He who goes out alone at night," who "sleeps in the cemetery at night," or who "tears his clothing." A Medieval commentator[3] adds, "He who destroys everything that is given him." And the 16th century code of law, the *Shulchan Aruch*, adds, "He who walks about naked, breaks dishes, and throws stones," and also "he who shows a generally deranged and confused intelligence." [4]

The crucial point is that a *shoteh* cannot be a witness, his word is not taken in the case of either selling or buying, he cannot legally obligate himself or another person, and he is not expected to fulfill the commandment to be fruitful and multiply. The Talmud[5] tells us that the *shoteh* may marry, but that there is no communal moral compulsion placed on him to marry. Such marriages and their consequences are not considered normal and are not subject to any other marital considerations.

Rabbi Immanuel Jakobovitz, the Chief Orthodox Rabbi of Great Britain, in his book, "Jewish Medical Ethics," [6] has made certain observations pertinent to our questions here. He reminds us that Judaism places special emphasis on the choice of a partner in marriage, that the partner must be equipped with the highest intellectual and moral virtues, and that when the Bible says, "Cursed be he that lieth with any manner of beast," [7] it should include the man who marries with the daughter of an ignoramus. In a society and culture in which learning was compulsory from the child's earliest years, the definition of ignoramus might easily have included the person who could not learn.

Jewish law, states Dr. Jakobovitz, was clearly motivated by a eugenic consideration for the moral excellence of the progeny. The character and health of the brothers of the bride, for example, had to be studied since it was believed that children take after their maternal uncles. Great stress was laid on physical compatibility in marriage, age, size, height, and so forth—with the physical structure of the offspring in mind. There was an injunction against marrying into a family suffering from epilepsy or leprosy, or any hereditary disease. Insane persons could not contract a valid marriage for they could not be happy or peaceful with each other and would probably produce "backward" children.

We come nearer to our specific interest when we study classic Jewish sources on the subject of abortion, especially in relation to instances in which a child is likely to be born with some kind of impairment. True, many rabbis and other Jewish leaders today take a very severe stand against abortion. Nevertheless, the main thrust of the authoritative Jewish sources leaves no doubt as to where Jewish law stands on abortion. Two facts make this clear. The first is that in Judaism a fetus is not considered an individual soul, but part of the mother. The second fact is that the literature and law in Judaism have always taught that the fetus, as part of the mother, may be sacrificed when the mother's mental and physical well-being is at stake.

Solomon B. Freehof, perhaps the foremost authority on Jewish law, in his book, "Recent Reform Response," [8] says of abortion: "Where there is a strong preponderance of medical opinion that the child will be born imperfect, physically or mentally, the mother may sacrifice that part of herself." Dr. Freehof cites the Orthodox scholars whose decisions have set the precedents for his statement.

The Roman Catholic View

In presenting the morality and ethics involved in our subject, it would be unfair to give only the Jewish point of view. I have, therefore, sought information from the Roman Catholic Archdiocese in Miami. In reply, The Reverend John Block of the Seminary of St. Vincent de Paul has written to me as follows:

"The Church's position is that mental retardation in itself would not deprive the person of such a basic right as the right to marry. If the retardation was such that it would not permit a person to give the requisite consent for marriage or it would not permit the married people to carry on a normal married life, then the person would not be capable of entering into a marriage due to natural causes."

"The question of children," Father Block continued, "depends upon the prior question of the marriage which is responsible for these children. Every married couple is privileged to be able to bring children into the world. If they are mentally capable of being married, they have the privilege to bring children into the world."

Father Block also sent me some very illuminating material, including a long article written by Ralph Brown, D.S.J. for an international Catholic periodical. In his article Dr. Brown maintains that Catholic laws need to be updated. "The time has come when we must expand our explanations to far wider horizons. For example, it is not enough to speak of the permanence and fidelity required for marriage and the right to children. It is also essential that a man should love his wife and she him, that a man can bring home his paycheck and not spend it before he gets home. It is vital that he should be able to discuss the upbringing of the children with his wife and generally for both persons to be able to cooperate in reaching and fulfilling the ultimate ends of marriage." [9]

Guidelines for Sexual Behavior

There still remains the phenomenon of sexuality, apart from marriage and child-bearing. It is generally understood, I believe, that Judaism accepts this sexuality as a gift of God and of nature. Not sexuality, therefore, but its misuse or abuse is to be condemned or shunned.

Judaism says little, if anything, about premarital intercourse or intercourse between free or unmarried persons. Perhaps this is so because, in ancient Jewish belief, cohabitation was another way of legally consummating a marriage. Sexual intercourse was as legally binding as any written marriage contract. Common law marriage was sacred in Judaism.

Clergymen of all faiths who do not wish to moralize unrealistically today need to formulate honest, constructive criteria for moral judgment in the area of human sexuality. We need to do this for students in colleges, where cohabitation of men and women in dormitories is a common occurrence. We need to do this also for high school students, among whom sexual experimentation is increasing. And we need to do this for the mentally retarded.

Now there is one premise that has been impressed on my mind by everyone I have consulted about the retarded: "There is no room for generalizations." I have been repeatedly told that every situation of retardation must be judged for itself alone, that any moral or ethical considerations must not take the form of absolutes.

"I have known certain retarded adults who have been reasonably good parents," a practicing psychologist has informed me.

"It is always possible to remove a child from the retarded parent and place him for adoption, or in the hands of legal guardians," another man has observed.

In a dissertation on retardation, Leon Cytryn and Reginald Lourie have described the complexity of the problem:

"Counseling the family about procreation of the mentally retarded themselves presents several legal, ethical, and scientific problems. The severely retarded are seldom fertile, and the proof of genetic inferiority of the majority of the mildly retarded is still lacking. Regional approaches to this problem are reflected in differing State laws affecting sterilization and abortion. An increased interest in this question can be anticipated with the present trend to keep the mentally retarded within the community. An appointed panel of medical specialists and lawyers acquainted with the intricacies of this problem would seem most suitable to examine each case on its own merit and to pay attention to possible hardships to the family, the community, and the patient himself. Judicial sterilizations and abortions may be very helpful in individual cases, but their influence on prevalence of mental retardation in the population is negligible." [10]

Warnings against ethical and moral absolutes and generalizations are familiar today with regard to physically and mentally healthy men and women. The new morality has been properly entitled "Situation Ethics." Its well known exponent, the Protestant theologian Joseph Fletcher, has pleaded that we judge each situation on its merits.[11] Some Catholic thinkers and certainly many Jewish teachers share this opinion. And young people today rationalize their sexual conduct with the phrase, *"If it is a meaningful relationship. . . ."*

This new morality offers us a new realism, a new honesty, a new individualization of ethical and moral precepts. Certainly the retardates and their sexuality deserve consideration in the same light.

Nevertheless, certain guidelines seem not only warranted but necessary. We may need to depart from them, now more and now less, but they must be there to point the way we must take, to serve as general criteria against which we can measure the possible solutions to serious human problems.

For example, when I was recently in Israel, with this coming conference on my mind, I consulted several specialists in law and medicine regarding the expression of sexuality in the retarded. There, too, I was warned that no strict rules can apply to all. Yet I learned from one therapist that in institutions for the retarded the authorities close their eyes to homosexual activities and, in settings where heterosexual contacts are possible, give contraceptive pills to retarded girls and women.

From what I have read, it seems to me that even geneticists do not counsel in a formless context. There are, I understand, several categories or degrees of retardation, each of which may call for different counsel. Yet there are apparently many retardates who fit into each of these categories. To that extent, perhaps, not absolutes but reasonably fixed relatives can be assumed.

For an example, Walter Fuhrmann and Friedrich Vogel in their book, "Genetic Counseling," say that in each counseling, "There is no such thing as being totally objective." They add: "That the parties involved must ultimately decide for themselves is self-evident; that the geneticist can disclaim all responsibility for influencing the decision is, in our opinion, not really justifiable. . . . It is in the nature of the doctor-patient relationship that the doctor assumes at least some responsibility for the patient, influences his decisions, and, therefore, must answer for them as well. . . . If a strong desire for children on the one hand is countered by an increased probability of a genetically ill or malformed child on the other, a compromise solution of one child only might be recommended . . . provided, of course, that the risk is not too high. . . . If one is going to recommend that a marriage remain childless, then one must be prepared to help with the problems of birth control as well. . . ."

Drs. Fuhrmann and Vogel discuss sterilization as the only sure method of birth control and point out the disadvantages, side effects, and uncertainties of contraceptives. "Because sterilization and its effects are absolute, there is no one proper attitude toward it," they conclude. "Sterilization, however, does remain a reasonable solution for those carriers who consciously and out of a sense of social and personal responsibility decide never to risk passing on their defect." [12]

These two physicians have obviously made moral and ethical decisions in their work. A similarly moral decision was made by Arno G. Motulsky and Frederick Hecht when, in writing on genetic prognosis, they made a plea "for a change of abortion laws to allow legal interruptions of pregnancy when serious and untreatable fetal disease may exist with a significant probability." [13]

Richard Warren, a physician at the Mailman Institute in Miami, has made an even more decisive statement. "I would be against any retardates having children," he said to me.

Robert Allen of the University of Miami, a physician who has worked with retardates in Florida and New Jersey, has told me of some of the practical problems that impinge on work with retardates who are faced with their sexuality. He spoke of the religious pressures that forbid sexual intercourse for the retarded or the dispensing of birth control information and materials among them and of the subterfuges that physicians must adopt to give out contraceptives to retardates. He told me how the girls in a home for retardates in New Jersey would repeatedly run away and return pregnant. The only preventive policy possible in that institution, he said, was to teach the girls how to masturbate.

Some Conclusions

As a rabbi, I believe I can now make a series of statements regarding the ethical and moral implications of the sexuality of retardates.

Insofar as sexual intercourse and masturbation are concerned, society cannot be more restrictive with retardates than with other people of all ages. In our time, in spite of a residue of restrictive laws and traditional pieties, freedom in sexual activities and relationships is becoming fully accepted. I am not the only clergyman today who has heard parents say to a son or daughter, "Live with him (her) for a while before you rush into marriage."

Ethically and morally, we cannot deny the retardates the elementary gratifications allowed others.

I share the opinion of those psychiatrists who regard homosexuality as an aberration or a sickness that should, at least, be studied with an eye to prevention, if not cure. Yet I would close my eyes to any homosexual activity on the part of retardates.

The question of whether retardates should have children is a more difficult one. It requires us to keep in mind not only the possibility and degree of genetic weakness, however slim, but also the kind of psychological, cultural, and emotional environment into which the child would be born. In weighing the ethical and moral factors involved, I would ask what economic sustenance the retardates could provide their offspring. I would consider the question of overpopulation in our society and the question of the effects on both the child and society when a child is born who cannot make the grade. In short, I would ask into what kind of world and home the child would be born.

Should we not strive to prevent the multiplication of tragedy by attempting to forestall the foisting of a miserable life on a helpless child? Must we not even take into account what happens to children born to parents of acquired retardation?

One day a woman in my congregation who has a retarded son said to me, "My husband and I had to decide about our son's future. We were told that he might very well have a normal child, but that the child would never have a normal father. We felt that the child would be cheated in life, and we had him undergo a vasectomy."

In this instance, the parents made the decision. I believe, however, that with the help of a physician with genetic knowledge, the family, the family's church or synagogue, and society, itself—through education and law—should share in such decisions whenever possible.

I am, of course, trying to put into words the question with which many of you live daily. With knowledge of religious support, not only from classic Judaism but other doctrines as well, I would encourage those who believe that retardates should be permitted to satisfy their sexual needs but that they should also be provided with contraceptive know-how or in some instances should even be sterilized. I would, in full awareness of moral and ethical teachings, allow retardates to gratify their instincts where such gratification does not do harm to themselves or others.

I share the view of those geneticists who believe in preventing the perpetuation of misery, even when the risk is mild or moderate, let alone when it is severe or profound. The ancient rabbis had a phrase for it. They said, *"dayah tzarah beshato,"* which means, *"sufficient unto the hour is the evil thereof."* On the superficial level, this suggests that we should not compound our worries. On the deeper level it means that we must not knowingly multiply the individual or collective griefs of humanity.

REFERENCES

1. *Mishneh Chagiga* (first paragraph).
2. Talmud to *Chagiga* 3a.
3. Bertinoro to *Chagiga*.
4. *Choshen Hamishpat*, 35.8.
5. Talmud to *Yevamot* 112b.
6. JAKOBOVITZ, I.: *Jewish Medical Ethics.* New York, Philosophical Library, 1959.
7. Deuteronomy 28:21.
8. FREEHOF, S. B.: *Recent Reform Responsa.* Cincinnati, Hebrew Union College Press, 1963.
9. BROWN, R., D.S.L.: *A Canonical Problem in Mental Incompetence in Marriage.* In *The Jurist,* Vol. 25, 1965.

10. CYTRYN, L. & LOURIE, R. S.: Mental Retardation. In Freedman, A. and Kaplan, H. (Eds.): *Comprehensive Textbook of Psychiatry*. Baltimore, William and Wilkins, 1967.

11. FLETCHER, J.: *Situation Ethics*. Philadelphia, Westminster Press, 1966.

12. FUHRMANN, W. & VOGEL, F.: *Genetic Counseling*. Heidelberg Science Library, New York, Springer-Verlag, 1969.

13. MOTULSKY, A. G. & HECHT, F.: Genetic Prognosis and Counseling. *Am. J. of Obs. and Gynec.*, 90:1227-1241, Dec. 1964.

16

Legal Restrictions on Sexual and Familial Relations of Mental Retardates —Old Laws, New Guises

ROBERT A. BURT
Professor of Law
The University of Michigan

SEVERAL KINDS OF STATE LAWS currently limit the freedom of those labeled "mentally retarded" to engage in sexual relations, to marry, and to rear children. In a significant number of states, persons found "mentally retarded" can be compulsorily sterilized, can be denied marriage licenses, or can lose custody of their children. In recent decades these laws apparently have been rarely invoked. This may be because the most likely targets for these laws are those "mental retardates" whom we have placed and forgotten in long-term custodial institutions. Greater efforts are now under way to avoid institutionalization of the retarded. This new emphasis demands that we scrutinize the existing state laws which threaten to curtail the freedoms that community placement for the retarded is intended to assure.

In 1966, twenty-three states had statutes providing for compulsory sterilization of mental retardates. In eight of these, the statutes permitted sterilization whether or not the person found retarded had been institutionalized on that ground. For the rest, sterilization laws applied only to institutionalized mental retardates.[1] As a general matter, however, these laws are rarely applied

206

today. It may be that little necessity for their application is seen, on the ground that life-long confinement in a single-sex unit of a residential institution is an even more effective means of constricting heterosexual relations than sterilization.

In practice, the prime targets for compulsory sterilization appear to be those retardates who are being released from institutions. Some state laws have in fact explicitly required sterilization as a condition for release.[2] Even where there is no state law authorizing compulsory sterilization, it apparently is often imposed as a condition for institutional release, usually with the pretense that sterilization is "voluntarily accepted." [1] (Similarly, state laws removing custody of children from the "mentally deficient" [3] or prohibiting the retarded from marrying—variously identified in state marriage licensing laws as "mental deficients," "idiots," "imbeciles," "feebleminded" and the like[3]—are most likely to be applied to those with prior histories of institutionalization.) There are no reliable statistics available on the frequency of application of any of these laws. The most recent report I have found regarding compulsory sterilization for mental deficiency in this country indicates a decline from 1,643 cases in 1943 to 643 in 1963.[1]

I believe the laws that single out "mental retardates"—or any stigmatized group, clearly identified as such—for special restrictions in sexual or family life violate the United States Constitution. The simple existence of laws that aim at vulnerable, stigmatized groups as such presents intolerable dangers of abuse and over-use.

The mentally retarded are not the only stigmatized group against whom special sexual and familial restrictions are directed. The retarded share this distinction with those whom we label "mentally ill" and "criminal." Virtually all state laws authorizing compulsory sterilization of mental retardates apply equally to the "mentally ill" [3] and about half of those laws also apply to "hereditary criminals." [3]

The stereotypes that are projected onto these deviant groups are remarkably similar in attributing dangerous sexual appetites. The Nebraska Supreme Court, in its 1968 opinion upholding the constitutionality of the state's compulsory sterilization law for institutionalized mental defectives, stated: "It is an established fact that mental deficiency accelerates sexual impulses and any tendencies toward crime to a harmful degree."[2] This statement has of course no empirical support. As an expression of popular prejudice, however, the statement could apply equally to those considered "mentally ill" or "criminals."

The prevalence of sexual imagery and fears regarding blacks in this country is a related phenomenon. The laws which forbade intermarriage among blacks and whites—rationalized by a potpourri of genetic and social arguments[4]—have a close kinship with the restrictive laws applied to the mentally retarded. Indeed, one important attribute of slave status in this country (but not, interestingly enough, in the Latin American countries where slavery also flourished) was that slaves were forbidden to marry, and that familial ties between parent and child were disregarded as a matter of course.[5] Mental retardates share with these other stigmatized groups the popular perception of "less-than-humanness" and they, like these other groups, become the target and repository of a cluster of fears that are felt to assault our "humanness" in general. Among these fears, unabated sexual appetite ranks high.

This special vulnerability of mental retardates as an irrationally feared and stigmatized group has important legal implications. It means that, as a group, they warrant particular protection, most notably against the operation of legislation aimed at their sexual and child-rearing behavior. Mental retardates are "a discrete and insular minority . . . [against whom prejudice] tends seriously to curtail the operation of those political processes ordinarily to be relied upon to protect minorities, and . . . [on whose behalf] a correspondingly more searching judicial inquiry [may be called for]."[6] For blacks—another such "discrete and insular minority"—the Supreme Court has increasingly done battle. In this pursuit, the Court has ruled unconstitutional the state laws prohibiting marriage between blacks and other races in a case appropriately denominated *Loving v. Virginia*.[7] This result was dictated by a prior series of Supreme Court holdings (beginning with the famed 1954 school segregation case) which invalidated any form of state action that singled out blacks as a group for special derogatory treatment.[8] Whether or not a similarly broad principle should be followed by the courts to protect mental retardates, their rights to sexual freedom should be judicially protected. The special status of family and sexual conduct in this society has been acknowledged in various Supreme Court cases as fundamental rights "to marry, establish a home and bring up children," [9] the right of "privacy surrounding the marriage relationship," [10] "the right to satisfy [one's] intellectual and emotional needs in the privacy of [one's] own home." [11] The Supreme Court has recently stated,

> If the right of privacy means anything, it is the right of the individual, married or single, to be free from unwarranted governmental intrusion into matters so fundamentally affecting a person as the decision whether to bear or beget a child.[12]

These familial and sexual freedoms, which the Court properly sees as the core of the right to privacy, are drastically and wrongfully infringed by such laws as sterilization and marriage prohibitions directed specifically against the mentally retarded.

Some state legislation imposes disabilities only on a specially designated class among mental retardates. The Utah Code, for example, provides for compulsory sterilization, among the retarded, only for those who are "probably incurable and unlikely to be able to perform properly the functions of parenthood." [13] This apparently more limited application does not, in my judgment, save the statute from the vice inherent in all of the restrictive legislation that singles out the mentally retarded as such. However uncertain our capacities to distinguish among good and bad parents generally, this society, and its officialdom, clearly is in the thralls of a strongly irrational attitude regarding the sexuality of the mentally retarded. Our officials share the incapacity of most people in this society to look at the retarded without inappropriate fear or pity, to look at them with sufficient clarity to permit sensible differentiation among them. Because the mentally retarded as a group are so readily victimized, because they are a vulnerable "discrete and insular minority," compulsory interventions in their child-bearing activities which might be tolerable for the general population are constitutionally intolerable if limited to the retardate group alone.

Justice Holmes' famous—indeed, notorious—opinion for the Supreme Court in 1927 upheld a state compulsory sterilization law with the aphorism "three generations of imbeciles are enough." [14] But Holmes' Court wrongly failed to appreciate their special role in protecting vulnerable minorities. A 1942 Supreme Court case, invalidating a state's compulsory sterilization law for habitual criminals on grounds that it made irrational distinctions between those criminals who should and those who should not be sterilized, reveals a different, and more enlightened, Court attitude.[15] The Court has not yet administered a *coup de grace* to these laws, though it appeared ready to do so when it took jurisdiction over the 1968 Nebraska Supreme Court's decision, noted earlier.[2] The Nebraska Legislature, perhaps reading between the lines of the Court's writ, repealed its compulsory sterilization law before the Court had an opportunity to rule on its constitutionality. When the Court is finally given the opportunity to rule on such laws, I have little doubt that it will overturn them.

But this Court action, when it comes, will remove only the easiest problem. Even if my argument here is accepted, and the courts strike down all sterilization, marriage prohibitory and child removal laws specifically limited to the mentally retarded, that will eliminate only the most obvious of legal impediments afflicting mental retardates. Most notably, such court action will not invalidate child abuse and neglect laws which generally authorize compulsory removal of children from their parents. Although these laws apply to the population at large, I believe that they will fall with particular harshness on parents who, by their residence in sheltered homes for the "mentally retarded" (often supported by public funds and thus highly visible to other public agencies), appear to flaunt their diagnostic label and thereby remain peculiarly vulnerable to community restrictions on sexual and child-rearing activities.

Child abuse and neglect laws of virtually every state are sufficiently broad-gauged to authorize compulsory removal of a child from a parent who is regarded as incapable of child-rearing merely because of mental deficiency. The Minnesota child neglect statute, for example, authorizes the state to take custody of any child "whose . . . condition, environment or associations are such as to be injurious or dangerous to himself." [16] Inevitably the fears and prejudices that stigmatize mental retardates will intrude on the judgment of court and social agency personnel who will apply these statutes.

But though these open-ended statutory invitations to state intervention bring this risk of abuse, these statutes cannot be overturned on this ground alone. Numerous procedural guarantees—such as right to counsel and opportunity to rebut all adverse evidence—should be provided to all parents, including the mentally retarded, who are subjects of child abuse or neglect proceedings. But the statutory standards for state intervention cannot be so narrowly defined as to eliminate the possibility of misuse without inappropriately withholding the possibility of state intervention to help children in serious jeopardy from inadequate parenting.[17] The opportunity for victimizing the mentally retarded in the application of child abuse and neglect laws must, regrettably, remain a reality.

This special vulnerability creates an obligation on the part of those planning new modes of introducing retardates into community life to defend their clientele—preferably, in my view, by appending special plans for intensive child-rearing services to any plans for sheltered community living in which normal heterosexual contacts are envisioned. Unless those who specially care for the mentally retarded can convincingly attest to the rest of the community that the children of retardates are being well-bred, it seems that these children will be lost, lost in many ways. The need for these special child-rearing programs seems to me even more urgent than the need for similar programs for those parents in the "normal" population who share the child-rearing disabilities of a portion of the mentally retarded population. The label of retardation threatens loss to all who bear it; it is to protect them, as much as to protect those among the retarded population who all "right-thinking people" would agree are incapable parents, that special protective programs are needed.

A second problem must also be faced. Statutes that authorize voluntary sterilization, abortions, or relinquishment of children present quite troublesome issues regarding mental retardates. The argument for compulsory sterilization of mental retardates founders in part on the uncertainty of genetic predictions. But new advances in intrauterine diagnosis—which permit wholly accurate detection of Down's syndrome and other kinds of developmental anomalies—change the context of the argument.

It seems unthinkable that the state would ever compel therapeutic abortions for the general population, even if developmental defects were detected *in utero*. But therapeutic abortions for mothers who so choose are increasingly accepted in state laws. Should maternal choice also govern if the mother herself is "retarded?" In what ways can the "retarded mother" be adequately helped to exercise choice? Should someone exercise choice for her? No matter how euphemistically we describe this last alternative, it is compulsory abortion limited to those whom we label "mentally retarded."

Legal authority to make such choices on behalf of mental retardates appears available in the guardianship laws in all states, which authorize the appointment of custodians for, among others, "mentally deficient" persons who are not institutionalized but are nonetheless regarded as incompetent to handle some portion or all of their affairs.[3] The potential for abuse of these guardianship laws is clear.

A case recently decided by the Kentucky Supreme Court should serve as a warning. In *Strunk v. Strunk*,[18] the court authorized the appointment of a 27-year-old institutionalized retardate's mother as his guardian in order to permit her to consent on his behalf to remove one of his kidneys to donate to his otherwise doomed, intellectually normal older brother. The court did not seem troubled by the mother's at best necessarily ambivalent role in making this decision for her retarded son.

But no matter who is given such power of choice over child-rearing for a retardate, similar conflicts—whether conscious or unconscious—are bound to be provoked. Can, for example, an administrator of a sheltered home for retardates address the question whether one of his charges should abort her genetically flawed child, or surrender her normal child, without being influenced by the impact of his decision on community approval of his enterprise generally and the implications of that approval for the welfare of all his charges?

I believe that a retardate who might require a guardian to make, or assist in, this choice is entitled at least to someone who is sufficiently trained and sufficiently detached to view the matter from the retardate's perspective, with other conflicting perspectives banished to as great a degree as possible. The laws and the judicial personnel involved in authorizing appointment of guardians for mental retardates are not sufficiently sensitive to these kinds of conflicts of interest that work against the deserved freedoms of mental retardates. If we intend to offer greater freedoms to those retardates whom we now institutionalize, we must assure that this problem is adequately addressed.

I have no easy answer to these questions. There is serious danger that generally applicable child neglect laws, for example, will be discriminatorily applied against the retarded. But I am unwilling to conclude that this danger is so great that we must leave the decision with the mother—no matter what her capacities—regarding, for example, whether to surrender her child for adoption. Reliance on parental choice in all child-rearing matters must be our primary goal. But I believe there will be cases in which such reliance would be misplaced, and detrimental to the child's interests.

We cannot blithely trust legal institutions to make wise and sensitive discriminations in applying authority to override parental choice. But in my judgment we cannot wholly deprive the state of this authority to protect against its abuse. We must instead maintain constant vigilance to protect the interests of those among us, including the mentally retarded, who are always vulnerable to excessive deprivations by those purporting to act for their benefit.

It is likely that courts can be persuaded to apply the Constitution in order to invalidate the injustices that previous generations of law-makers have imposed on the mentally retarded in their sexual and family lives. It is equally likely that, unless careful thought and planning is undertaken in conjunction with efforts to bring the retarded into community life, the same injustices will be imposed on the mentally retarded under new legal guises.

REFERENCES

1. FERSTER, E.: Eliminating the Unfit—Is Sterilization the Answer? 27 *Ohio State Law Journal* 591 (1966).
2. See *In re Cavitt*, 157 N.W. 2d 171 (Nebraska Supreme Court, 1968), *certiorari granted*, 393 U.S. 1078 (1969), *certiorari dismissed*, 369 U.S. 996 (1970).
3. LINDMAN & McINTYRE: *The Mentally Disabled and the Law* (American Bar Foundation, 1961).
4. See *Perez v. Lippold*, 198 P. 2d 17 (California Supreme Court, 1948).
5. TANNENBAUM: *Slave and Citizen* (1946).
6. *United States v. Carolene Products Co.*, 304 U.S. 144, 153 n. 4 (1938).
7. 388 U.S. 1 (1967).
8. *Brown v. Board of Education*, 347 U.S. 483 (1954).
9. *Meyer v. Nebraska*, 262 U.S. 390, 399 (1923).
10. *Griswold v. Connecticut*, 381 U.S. 479, 486 (1965).
11. *Stanley v. Georgia*, 394 U.S. 557, 565 (1969).
12. *Eisenstadt v. Baird*, 92 Sup. Ct. 1029, 1038 (1972).
13. Utah Code Ann. §64-10-7 (1968).
14. *Buck v. Bell*, 274 U.S. 200, 207 (1927).
15. *Skinner v. Oklahoma*, 316 U.S. 535 (1942).
16. Minn. Stat. Ann. §260.015 (Supp. 1965). See also PAULSEN, The Legal Framework for Child Protection, 66 *Columbia Law Review* 679, 693-94 (1964).
17. See BURT, Forcing Protection on Children and Their Parents, 69 *Michigan Law Review* 1259 (1971).
18. 445 S.W. 2d 145 (Kentucky Supreme Court, 1969).

Institutional and Community Attitudes, Practices, and Policies

(SESSION TWO)

GENERAL DISCUSSION

ELIZABETH M. BOGGS, *Presiding*

The shortcomings of the IQ in diagnostic assessment, the detrimental effects of labeling, the dangers of letting parents make crucial choices for their retarded children, the unfairness of judging the "parenting" ability of retarded persons on the basis of standards not applied to normal persons, all came under fire in the discussion following the Mattinson, Scally, Narot, and Burt papers.

Noting that Miss Mattinson's report shows that social intelligence is unpredictable from a standard IQ, Dr. Money spoke of the need for a social quotient (SQ) based on something better than the currently available social maturity scales. In any event, he said, IQs taken from case history files should never be used in decision-making, particularly if they are more than two years old, for studies have shown that IQs change. As an example, he cited a long-term study of children under treatment for cretinism, in which he found that IQs of 20 percent of the children had changed from 20 to 40 points in the direction of improvement.

Dr. Tarjan observed that the frequently noted lack of correlation between performance and IQ score has freed the clinician to make a clinical judgment of "total adaptation," but that any diagnosis is meaningless unless related to specific types of planning, such as school or vocational placement. While diagnostic

215

work-ups are getting more and more complicated, accurate, and predictive, he said, their components are predictive only for certain single aspects of life. There is no test, or combination of tests, he maintained, that would entitle the clinician to make a global prediction about a style of living.

Dr. Roos maintained that the very process of diagnosis can shape a person's entire destiny by giving him a label that will stigmatize him throughout life and significantly affect the way he perceives himself. Miss Mattinson pointed out the social assessments that had been made on all the subjects in her study had been based on standards that were shockingly middle class. She observed that another reason for not getting "stuck with a diagnosis" is that many retarded people have so much persistence that, if given good enough and long enough training, they can do really complicated jobs and retain what they have learned after interruptions.

Dr. Boggs said that a major problem lies in the fact that a label given for one reason, such as admission to a special class, is interpreted as relevant to an entirely different situation. She asked Dr. Burt whether the law did not require criteria for classification to be relevant to the purpose of the law. Dr. Burt replied that this is so but that a lot depends on how rigorously the courts scrutinize the standards for classification set by the legislatures. He pointed out that many states provide for commitment of "the feeble-minded" without any definition of the term.

Dr. Athanasiou asked whether a person committed or voluntarily admitted to an institution had any legal right to demand treatment or whether an institution could be legally required to stop interfering with the sexual life of its residents. Dr. Burt replied that an argument could be made that a person has a legal right to treatment, but that the argument would have to define the various components of treatment. He said that while the courts, if asked, might rule for a person's right to marry and set up a family within an institution, he did not think they would go against the dominant mores and rule for the right of persons within institutions to have extramarital intercourse. He agreed with a suggestion by Dr. Reiss that a more persuasive argument might be made for the right of the mentally retarded to choose their own life style, but he said he would rather see the principle applied to getting people out of large, remote institutions into sheltered settings where they could participate in community life.

Bringing up a "different legal problem which is not currently being addressed," Dr. Burt said he was troubled by Rabbi Narot's example of the mother who chose vasectomy for her son. Parents are often fighting their own battles in making choices for their retarded children, he said, and these cloud their judgment as to the best interest of their child.

In reply to a question from Dr. Burt about the sexual relations between the couples in her study, Miss Mattinson said she did not like to be specific because it is always difficult to know whether people are speaking the truth on such a subject. She added, however, that her impression was that the sex her subjects wanted and craved from each other was very "pregenital," and chiefly concerned mothering, cuddling, and loving each other. She suggested that before teaching sex education to mentally retarded people it is important to listen to them to find out where they are in their own psychosexual development and what they want emotionally.

Dr. Salerno asked whether Miss Mattinson had any evidence that the immaturity exhibited by her subjects in their sexual relations extended to other areas and influenced their children in any way. Miss Mattinson replied that there was enormous variation in the adjustment of the children who had remained with their parents; none had committed offenses or been officially declared as beyond control, but many showed signs of depression and mild maladjustment. The parents, she said, were very loving and determined to prove that the people who called them incapable of child-rearing were wrong, and not to do to their children what had been done to them. The chief lacks in their homes, she said, were probably stimulation and the presence of a true father figure, for the fathers, many of whom had had explicit homosexual experiences, were more like complementary mothers in the home.

Dr. Roos objected to applying such standards as quality of fathering, maturity of sexual relations, latent homosexuality, or degree of intellectual stimulation in judging the ability of the mentally retarded to raise children on the grounds that advantaged families are not subject to such judgments. Miss Mattinson said that she was not greatly concerned about potential deficits in the intellectual development of the children in her study, for she felt sure that because of the love they are receiving they will grow up to be loving adults—perhaps unstimulating and dull from the middle-class point of view, but not necessarily emotionally unhealthy or unhappy.

Dr. Roos commented that it was important to remember that many of the studies described in this conference were done in highly select samples of persons who had spent the formative years of their lives in institutions and that institutionalization, in addition to the diagnostic labeling, has a very significant impact on the development of personality.

NEW DIRECTIONS FOR RESEARCH
AND EXPERIMENTAL PROGRAMS

17

Sexual Behavior:
Research Perspectives

RICHARD E. WHALEN
Department of Psychobiology
and
CAROL K. WHALEN
Program in Social Ecology
University of California (Irvine)

IT HAS BEEN NOTED that some parents of moderately retarded children deny the existence of their child's sexuality.[1] Many people view retarded teenagers and adults as perennial children in the pre-Freudian sense, innocent and asexual. As with the nonretarded child, however, it is difficult to ignore the physical and behavioral changes accompanying puberty in children with IQs below 70. Retarded children do develop sexually; they become aware of their sexual desires as well as of the role prescriptions and restrictions of their societies. It is with this general issue of sexuality that we would like to deal today.

Before we raise theoretical and empirical issues about sexual development and expression, it might be of value to illustrate the existence of sexual concepts in retarded people. The following examples were taken from interviews with two young adults with reported IQs in the range of 50-70. At the time of these conversations, the informants resided in a state hospital. First, on a relatively elementary level, we might ask whether retardates understand gender differences. The following excerpt from an interview with 24-year-old Dawn is illustrative:

Q.: What would you have done if you were in her place?
A.: Well, I would have kicked him real hard where it hurts at.
Q.: Where's that?
A.: In the balls. (giggle)
Q.: Where did you learn that?
A.: Oh some people said that if you get in any trouble just kick your man in the balls.
Q.: What if he kicked you back in the balls?
A.: (Laughter) I ain't got no balls, I got a cat.
Q.: What's the difference?
A.: I don't know.
Q.: How come you don't have balls?
A.: Because I'm not a boy. I've got balls up here—my tits (giggle).
Q.: You say you have breasts and boys don't have breasts.
A.: Yeah—they have breasts up here—small ones though.
Q.: Why are your breasts larger?
A.: Because I'm a girl.

On a more complex level, we might ask about a retarded person's sexual motivation, his or her information about hetero-, homo- and autosexuality, and general responsiveness to social mores. The following excerpts were taken from an interview with another retarded inpatient, Connie, age 21.

Q.: How do people react when they know that you have a boyfriend?
A.: Well, I think they're happy for you.
Q.: Is there anything that they worry about?
A.: Well, they'll um they worry um they always worry about the fact that you could carry it too far, you know what I mean.
Q.: What do you mean?
A.: Well, I meant that parents or teachers or whoever also worry about the fact that of that getting pregnant, I mean, you know, the fact that maybe a boy will try to get funny with a girl.

Later . . .

Q.: What is getting fresh?

A.: Well, it's uh trying uh a boy uh wants an intercourse and um when he wants the intercourse he'll do anything in his power to get it, I mean like, well um um he'll um like he'll try to con you, I mean I wouldn't exactly say the word con but um um you know how a boy is um when he wants an intercourse, I mean like um he'll try to be real sweet to you, I mean like you know like he'll say "oh baby" and you know this and that and the other and that's a sign right there that he wants an intercourse very bad and you know.

Q.: Why does he want intercourse?

A.: Well, um, he, he wants an intercourse, um, for two reasons—one I'd say because well, of course it's nature, I mean everybody knows that, but. . . .

Later . . .

Q.: Are there names for people like that?

A.: Yes.

Q.: What kinds of names?

A.: Well like queers they call them.

Q.: A queer is what?

A.: A queer is when a girl and when a girl and um like when a girl goes with a girl and a boy goes with a boy, well, that's one way of putting it, and another way of putting it is, to me another way of putting it is when a girl and a boy have an intercourse before they even uh think about getting married.

Q.: I see. What other names do they call people like that?

A.: Uh, sexual maniacs or something like that.

Q.: What does that mean?

A.: It means that all they think about is getting an intercourse, I mean, you know.

Later . . .

Q.: Do people ever do it to themselves?

A.: Well, uh, yes, well, what I mean is when they're little. . . .

Q.: Does it feel a certain way? Does it feel good to do it?

A.: Um, maybe it uh maybe it does when you're little.

Q.: How about when you're big?

A.: Um, I wouldn't know about when you're older. . . .

Q.: How come?

A.: Well, because I've never tried it.

Q.: How come?

A.: Well, because it's, well because it's, well I mean it um, it's bad. Well I mean it could well I mean maybe it could cause something, you know what I mean, like if you play with yourself, you know I mean I'm not saying this for sure, but maybe it could cause an odor for instance, you know.

Q.: How does that work?

A.: Well, the stuff inside you, you know it's like usually, just like when you perspire you have an odor, right? I mean like, OK, and when you perspire, you feel wet, I mean you know, kind of damp like, and this is the reason we use deodorant to sorta control the odor or to get rid of the odor so we smell nice, and it's kinda that way with our uh with the front of us, you know what I'm talking, I mean with our um, with our private, more or less. If, for example, if we don't wash our private well when we bathe, or if we don't take care of it in the right way, then um there is an odor there just like there is an odor underneath our arms when we perspire and this odor is defenseless, I mean like when we um get next to someone, like if we talk to somebody or sit next to him or something he can smell the odor, and it offends them, I mean like they say you know, "Oh, I don't want to sit by her" or whatever.

Q.: So you mean they could tell that way if you've been playing with yourself?

A.: Yes, because it causes an odor.

A third important question concerns the amount of functional information mildly retarded people have about everyday life in the "real" world. Can they translate their global desires, e.g. to be a wife and mother, into the behavioral steps necessary to achieve these ends? Excerpts from another interview with Dawn are quite revealing:

Q.: What would you do? Say that you were walking out of the hospital today—today was the last day in the hospital and you were leaving this afternoon, what would be the first thing that you would do?

A.: I'll get a house first. I'd have to see about a house first. . . .

Q.: How do you do that?

A.: Well—you'd see "For Sale" and you'd ask how much it is—and pay for it, and if the furniture is OK, you just clean the house up, and you dust a little bit.

Later . . .

Q.: How will you find a husband?

A.: Well, I'll just—I'll just—(shrugged her shoulders) I don't know.

Q.: How do you do it?

A.: I'll just ask a boy. I'd probably just ask, "Would you like to take me for a date tonight?"

Q.: So, you'd ask him out?

A.: Yeah.

Q.: Where would you meet him?

A.: I'd probably meet a boy by the—I don't know. By the coffee shop, or something like that, or the dance hall, or something.

Q.: Then you ask him if he wants to take you out. What if he says, "yes?"

A.: "OK, I'll go with you."

Q.: Then, what would you do?

A.: Then, we'll start kissin'—

Q.: Yes.

A.: Then, we'll make love.

Q.: How do you do that?

A.: Put your arms around like this (she hugged herself). Then, we'll talk a little; and we'll go home and he'll give me a goodnight kiss. I'll give him a goodnight kiss —say "I'll see you tomorrow"—something—

Q.: Then what happens.

A.: And then we get married.

There are at least two ways in which the above excerpts can be viewed. On the one hand, they may help shatter the stereotype of the retarded as ignorant about sexual matters and mores and as being either asexual or totally "impulse ridden." Dawn and

Connie demonstrated knowledge about sexual functions and roles and concerns over appropriate sexual conduct. (See Edgerton & Dingman, 1964, for other intriguing examples of sexual behavior in retarded individuals.) [2]

On the other hand, this interview information may be viewed not in terms of society's stereotypes, but rather in terms of the minimum level of sexual knowledge and social competence needed to negotiate successfully the role demands of mate, spouse, and parent. Dawn and Connie did, of course, show incorrect labeling, false information and general confusion regarding many sexual matters. When they did not know the correct answer to a question they would make one up which was often quite logical, but incorrect. This lack of substantive knowledge may be due to a paucity of opportunities to discuss sex and receive corrective informational feedback. It is unlikely, however, that these informational deficiencies were due entirely to the fact that Dawn and Connie had spent many years in an institution. A recent survey by Goodman et al.[1] indicates that parents with retarded children living at home have limited knowledge of sexual functions and make only minimal efforts to give sex instruction.

We now have the knowledge and techniques to correct sexual misinformation and insure that retarded people learn the basic facts about sexual functioning. What appears to be a far more serious problem is the fact that retarded young adults often hold expectations for fulfilling the adult roles of wife, mother, etc., but lack the component skills necessary for interpersonal achievements. These disabilities are illustrated not only by Dawn's unrealistic explanations of how she would find a home and a husband, but also by studies of marriages of retarded people.[3]

Perhaps for these reasons, problems of developing sexuality often seem more consequential when they involve retarded than nonretarded persons, and there is a felt need to establish special controls over the sexuality of the retarded. Hospital personnel are particularly fearful of unwanted pregnancies or "homosexual" behaviors. In the community we express concern for the safety of the nonretarded neighborhood child as well as for the protection of the retardate's individual rights and the welfare of his offspring. When we talk of control we must consider two types, socio-educational and biological. Research needs are critical in both areas. We would like to focus first upon the biological systems which underlie sexuality.

Today, the biologist is concerning himself with two distinct facets of sexuality: the development of sexual systems and the expression of sexuality in the mature organism. Let us examine sexual development first. In a pioneering study Phoenix, Goy, Gerall and Young[4] demonstrated that the female offspring of guinea pigs which had received the synthetic male hormone, testosterone propionate (TP), during pregnancy were less likely to display female behavior and were more likely to display masculine behavior in adulthood. These workers suggested that the hormonal stimulation of the fetus caused a permanent masculinization of those neuronal systems which mediate sexual behavior. Since this germinal experiment, there have been a hundred studies directed toward understanding the nature of the hormonally controlled differentiation process. What have these studies revealed?

To answer this question we must first distinguish between three types of sexual differentiation. First, there is a sexual differentiation of the internal and external sexual organs. Second, there is a differentiation of those neuronal systems which control the secretion by the pituitary of the gonadotropins which activate the gonads. And third, there is a differentiation of those neurons which control masculine and feminine behavior.

Within each of these categories there appears to be a distinct critical period for differentiation. For example, in the rat, hormonal stimulation prior to birth controls to a large extent the later development of the external genitalia. If the female *fetus* is administered TP (or an androgenic progestin) just prior to birth, the external genitalia will develop in the masculine direction with a facilitation of phallic development and an inhibition of vaginal development. Similarly, if the male *fetus* is treated with an antiandrogen, such as cyproterone acetate, phallic development will be inhibited and the male will develop an external vaginal orifice. In spite of the massive effects such prenatal treatments have on the genitalia, they have no major effects upon the neuronal systems which control pituitary function or sexual behavior. If, however, the rat is hormonally stimulated or protected from hormonal stimulation by gonadectomy shortly *after birth,* there will be major changes in the neuronal systems, but only minor changes in the genitalia. Critical periods for differentiation, which appear similar in type if not in timing or duration (prenatal in guinea pig and monkey, postnatal in rat and hamster), have been found in a variety of mammalian species and presumably exist in man.

The sexual differentiation of the neurohypophyseal system is rather straightforward conceptually. Males of most mammalian species, including man, secrete their gonadotropins and gonadal steroids in a more or less constant or tonic fashion. Females of the polyestrous species secrete their pituitary and gonadal hormones in a cyclic fashion. If the male is prevented from responding to hormone during the critical period, he develops the female or cyclic pattern of hormone secretion. For example, if a male rat is castrated at birth and given an ovarian transplant in adulthood, that ovary will show cyclic secretion and cyclic ovulation in the female pattern. However, if the male is castrated ten days after birth, the ovary will not ovulate and there will be a tonic secretion of the ovarian hormones. Similarly, if the female rat is administered TP shortly after birth, she will be anovulatory, and therefore sterile, and she will secrete her ovarian hormones in an acyclic, tonic fashion in adulthood.

A great deal of evidence indicates that this difference between males and females in the pattern of hormonal secretion represents a difference in brain function. What is not yet clear is whether this *model* of differentiation, which is based primarily on research with rats, provides a realistic model for brain differentiation in the human. Some evidence suggests that it does not. For example, in humans with the adrenogenital syndrome, marked genital virilization is evident at birth as a result of a hypersecretion of androgenic substances from the hyperplastic adrenal gland.

In the untreated condition, the ovaries of these individuals do not function properly. Treatment with cortisol and the subsequent inhibition of adrenal secretion lead to reasonably normal ovarian function. Thus, these androgenized human females are similar to androgenized (TP-treated) rats in that their genitals are masculinized; they differ in that only the rat shows permanent anovulatory sterility.

The rhesus monkey appears to be like the human in this regard. There is some evidence to indicate that prenatal TP injections in the female monkey can masculinize the genitalia while having no permanent effects upon later ovarian function.

We do not wish to overly stress the apparent species differences in neural control of gonadal function. To date we know too little about the actions of hormones in developing primates. In particular, we know little about the relative timing of the critical periods for genital and neural differentiation in primate species. The differences which we see between rodents and primates may reflect no more than differences in critical periods of hormone action. We do need, however, to be alert to possible species differences in the development of sexuality. They may be extremely important. We would hope that during the coming decade we could direct a great deal more of our research efforts toward understanding neuroendocrine development and differentiation in primates, including man.

The sexual differentiation of neurobehavioral systems appears more complex than the differentiation of endocrine control. Hormone secretion occurs either in the male or in the female pattern. With behavior, however, there are no constraints which prohibit the organism from exhibiting a particular behavior in a male fashion at one point in time and in a female fashion shortly thereafter. Moreover, behavior has an almost infinite number of dimensions which are potentially characterized as sex-specific, and an individual could perform one behavior pattern in a "masculine" way and another in a "feminine" manner. Finally, behavior patterns have "intensity," a "more-or-less" quality which allows for wide individual differences in the degree with which a re-

TABLE 1

Relationships between Hormonal Conditions During Development and Sexual Responding of the Rat in Adulthood

Hormonal Condition During Critical Period of Development		Hormonal Condition During Adulthood		
		Androgen		Estrogen and Progesterone
	Mounts	Intromission Responses	Ejaculation Responses	Lordosis Responses
Male				
Testes Intact	+++	+++	+++	−
Castrated at Birth	+++	+	−	+++
Castration at Birth + TP	+++	+++	++	−
Female				
Ovaries Intact	+++	+	−	+++
Ovariectomized at Birth	+++	+	−	+++
TP at Birth	+++	++	+	−
TP Pre- and Post-natally	+++	+++	+++	−

See Whalen, R. E. 1971 for details.[13]

sponse pattern is exhibited. Because of this complexity, we must be cautious in our conceptualization of sexual differences in behavior.

Let me now present an animal model for the sexual differentiation of behavioral systems. Let us examine a simple study. Male and female rats are allowed to mature normally, or they are gonadectomized at birth, half of the gonadectomized animals being treated with testosterone propionate at the same time. When mature, the animals are administered male hormone and tested for the display of masculine behavior, or they are administered female hormones and tested for the display of feminine behavior. When tested for masculine behavior, all of the rats, regardless of their genetic sex or their hormone treatment during early development, will display components of the masculine behavior pattern (see Table 1). One might say that they have all developed a masculine-type motivational system quite independent of their genes or hormones.

When we examine the feminine behavior of these animals, we find a different result. Only those animals which developed after birth without male-type hormonal stimulation will show feminine behavior in adulthood. In other words, the male castrated at birth is indistinguishable from the normal female; both show female behavior. The female treated with TP at birth is indistinguishable from the normal male; neither shows female behavior. We have taken these findings to suggest that, in the rat, sexual differentiation is best characterized as a process of *defeminization*. The same appears to be the case in the mouse, while in the guinea pig and monkey early androgen stimulation seems to have a positive masculinizing effect. In these latter species, early hormone treatment increases the chances that the individuals will behave in a masculine fashion. For example, the prenatally androgenized female monkey is less likely to show female presenting responses (defeminization) and more likely to show male-like mounting responses (masculinization) than normal females, although she is unlikely to mount as frequently as does a male.[5]

It would appear from these studies that early in development the male and female organisms possess an undifferentiated nervous system which will later direct sexual responses. This nervous system becomes differentiated because the testes of the male secrete a hormone at a critical period of development. Depending upon the species, the hormonal stimulation will a) masculinize the organism, i.e., increase its propensity to show masculine responses, b) defeminize the organism, i.e., reduce its propensity to show feminine responses, or c) both. Unfortunately, the evidence for man is not clear, but, of course, the sexual patterns of men and women lack the "reflex" characteristics shown by rodents or even other primate species. The adoption by the human of the ventral-ventral mating posture has made it more difficult to specify unique male and female mating patterns.

When we turn to non-mating systems, we also find hormonally controlled sex differences in behavior. For example, the male mouse, unlike the female, readily displays intraspecific aggression. The adult female does not show this behavior even when she is treated with massive doses of male hormone in adulthood. However, if the female mouse is treated with TP at birth and again in adulthood, she readily shows fighting behavior. Similarly, if the male mouse is castrated at birth, he is unlikely to fight in adulthood even when given replacement hormone.[6]

The androgenized female monkey shows a similar enhancement in aggressive behavior. Male rhesus monkeys are much more likely to engage in rough and tumble play and in chasing patterns than are female monkeys. Prenatally androgenized females behave much more like males than females on this dimension. Evidence from Money and Ehrhardt[7] suggests that similar processes may occur in man.

Thus, in both sexual and aggressive spheres, male and female mammals display different patterns of behavior, and they display similar patterns at different intensities. The available evidence would suggest that these differences in behavior reflect permanent differences in brain function, differences which are mediated by hormonal stimulation or its absence during critical periods of brain maturation. This is not to be taken as a denial of the effects of experience in the development of these behavioral systems. Rather, we believe that experience works upon a neurobehavioral substrate which is determined to some degree by hormonal factors. A great deal of additional research is needed before we can partial out the interactive effects of hormones and experience upon behavioral development, particularly in the human species.

Let us now turn briefly to those mechanisms which control the expression of sexuality in adult organisms. These are of three types: sensory (afferent), integrative, and motor (efferent). On the sensory side we may consider those systems which are involved in sexual arousal. What is clear today is that all major sensory systems may, depending upon the species, contribute to the stimulation and execution of sexual responses. In the mouse, hamster and dog, olfactory cues are clearly important. The recent work of Michael in England[8] suggests that the olfactory system may also play a critical role in the control of primate sexuality. Michael has shown that the female rhesus monkey has a hormone-dependent vaginal secretion which stimulates the sexual activity of the male. Application of this substance to a non-receptive female makes her extremely attractive to the male. Possibly such a system is also active in man and accounts for our widespread use of deodorants in spite of adequate bathing practices.

With respect to integrative mechanisms, a variety seems to exist within the central nervous system. The evidence is strong that a number of mammalian species, including primates and probably man, possess central hormone receptor systems which selectively accumulate and bind hormones to cell nuclei as an initial step in their action. In rats, cats, rabbits and monkeys, the direct application of minute amounts of gonadal steroids to limited regions of the brain is capable of activating sexual responses. In addition to these hormone-sensitive systems, there seem to exist hormone-insensitive systems which also play a part in the control of sexuality. For example, in the rat and cat, cortical tissue plays a role, yet our best evidence is that cortical neurons are not particularly sensitive to hormones. In addition to the hypothalamus and cortex, evidence implicates the temporal lobe, the amygdala and particularly the overlying pyriform cortex in the control of sexual responses. Thus, no single brain area seems to be exclusively involved in the mediation of sexual responses. For this reason it is important for us today to dismiss the idea of a "sex center" in the brain, and to conceive of an extensive interconnected system of neurons, some of which are hormone sensitive, some of which are not, some of which are involved in the utilization of sensory input, some of which control the basic motivational state, and some of which are involved in the execution of sexual responses. Finally, we should not forget the role of the spinal cord in sexual systems. In spinally transected animals and man, some sexual reflexes remain, but to date we know surprisingly little about these systems even though they are involved in the processes of erection and orgasm.

In summary, we must ask for an evaluation of our progress toward understanding the biological basis of sexuality. We must admit that it is spotty. In the descriptive aspects of sexuality we know a great deal about the lower mammals, but our simple description of sexual response patterns is terribly inadequate for primates, including man. With respect to hormonal control systems, we have made tremendous progress. We can now measure circulating levels of hormones in all mammals. We now know which hormones are present in the organism and we are in the process of learning about hormonal metabolism and how and where metabolites influence cells. However, we still have a great deal to learn about how hormones affect the nervous system, and how the neuronal systems control sexuality. In this area we cannot answer even the simplest questions. We need and must develop a sexual anatomy of the brain.

Research Perspectives

But, let us be specific. What must the behavioral biologist learn about sexuality? There are two areas which deserve attention: 1) the neurohormonal control of reproduction and 2) the neurohormonal control of sexual behavior. First, reproduction.

During the past 15 years we have made tremendous gains in our ability to control reproduction. The hormone pill and the latest intrauterine devices allow us to prevent conception at will. However, we still do not know how these agents work. We realize that the hormones control fertility by their "negative feedback" actions on those systems which control the secretion of the gonadotropins (follicle stimulating hormone and luteinizing hormone) from the anterior pituitary. We do not know whether the hormones are affecting the pituitary directly or whether they are affecting the brain, which controls the pituitary. We believe that the IUDs prevent fertility by preventing implantation. We do not know the mechanism.

We are also gaining control of fertility through the development of new abortifacients. The prostaglandins appear promising in this regard. Nonetheless, in spite of enormous strides in the past decade, we still know little about these ubiquitous fatty acids or their true potential in fertility control.

Of course, the control of reproduction does not refer solely to the limitation of fertility. We need to know more abut the induction of conception in normally infertile couples. The recent development of clomiphene citrate should be noted in this regard. Clomiphene is an anti-estrogen which has proven effective in inducing ovulation. We are not yet sure whether it stimulates the ovary directly or whether it acts via stimulation of pituitary gonadotropin secretion. If it stimulates gonadotropin secretion, it could do so by acting on the pituitary or by acting on the brain. We do not know.

It should be clear that we need a great deal more research if we are to understand the function of the ovary, the process of implantation, the control of ovulation by the pituitary, and the control of the pituitary by the brain. Until problems in each of these and other areas are solved, we will not understand reproduction.

Let us turn now to sexual behavior. Here our ignorance is deep. We know almost nothing about the psychobiological bases of sexuality. We need a "neurology of sexuality." We need to understand the neural and hormonal determinants of sexual motivation—why is a particular stimulus sexually arousing; what are the mechanisms of sexual satiety; how are the highest neural centers involved in the control of sexual desire? We need to understand the neural and hormonal determinants of sexual performance—what factors are involved in erection in the male and similar vasocongestive phenomena in the female? What role does the spinal cord play in the control of sexual acts? How can one stimulate and inhibit genital reflexes? And we need to understand the neural and hormonal determinants of sexual gratification—what are those multitudinous factors which lead to sexual satisfaction? Finally, we must learn more about the process of sexual differentiation. We must learn the many ways males and females differ in their styles of life and the causes for these differences.

If we had answers to our questions, we would understand more about the sexual development and capacity of retardates. We might be better able to aid them in the understanding of their own sexuality so that they could fulfill their own sexual selves in a way which is appropriate for them and for their communities.

To correct the "sexual disenfranchisement" of the mentally retarded, research must proceed along at least three tracks. One is the psychobiology of sex, discussed above. A second concerns the problems of integrating a minority culture, the mentally retarded, into our modal society. The third is the design, implementation and evaluation of alternative living styles. An oversimplified question that one often hears is, should the retardate learn how to adapt to society, or should the community accommodate to the needs of this subculture? Should the targets for change be individual retardates or environmental institutions? Clearly we need investigative programs in both areas, as illustrated in the following paragraphs.

It is important to note that the excerpts at the beginning of this paper were taken from conversations held five years ago with hospitalized young adults. These mildly retarded individuals are rarely found in total institutions today; current policy reserves institutionalization for only the most extreme behavioral and medical problems. Connie, Dawn and their peers now reside in the community—with their parents, in board and care homes, or perhaps on their own or with a spouse. Thus the needs for social-sexual research are acute and the opportunities plentiful.

At present, it seems particularly appropriate to view the mentally retarded as a minority culture, with current anti-hospitalization and community placement practices seen as analogous to desegregation and school busing programs. Major efforts must be devoted to helping the disadvantaged retardate acquire social survival skills. Information about current living and learning styles would be quite useful in designing community programs. How competently are these new community residents assuming their different roles, particularly in the social and sexual domains? How can they learn to fill in the behavioral steps between where they are now and where they would like to be? We need more information about the developmental tasks and crises they encounter in dating and mating so that preventive training, intervention and support programs can be implemented.

What are the characteristics of those retarded people who do succeed in the community? In his intriguing study of "life on the outs" among formerly hospitalized retardates, Edgerton[9] discovered the importance of a non-retarded "benefactor." We also need to know what internal resources and interpersonal skills differentiate the "successful" from the "unsuccessful" retardate.

We need now, more than ever, information about the community's fears regarding the mentally retarded. How realistic are these concerns, and through which avenues can they be alleviated? Certainly more research is needed on attitudes regarding sterilization, but the problem extends beyond biological sex. How do people feel about living next door to a retarded person or couple? Are there distinctive behaviors (e.g., posture, gesture, facial expression) which signal "retardation" to the public? If so, can these patterns be modified so that retardates are less salient and therefore more acceptable?

The third empirical track might be called "experiments in living." With alternative living styles available, we could talk about individual differences rather than disadvantage. The living arrangement which would require the least "community accommodation" would be sheltered housing units in which retarded individuals could receive help with their budgets, their self-help needs, their interpersonal problems and their use of leisure time.[10] Hunt[11] describes villages in England where retardates can live, learn and love without institutional restriction, shame or stigma. Braginsky and Braginsky[12] propose cooperative retreats offering either temporary or permanent refuge for people "who cannot or do not want to 'make it' in our complex, demanding society." The population might include the poor, the lame, the aged, the retarded, etc. In these societies, would the sexual problems that now exist for the retarded disappear? Would new ones develop? Longitudinal research programs are needed if we are to find answers to these questions.

An experimental strategy that holds great promise—and one

which does not require pervasive changes in institutional structures—involves the elimination of pernicious labeling processes. Once labeled, individuals often lose their individuality. The mentally retarded are construed as members of a homogeneous group with a standard set of characteristics and deficiencies. Would the same people, lacking such labels, be responded to as individuals with varying merits, propensities and problems? Would children who grow up without public labeling and resultant segregation show more, fewer, or just different kinds of competencies and deficits? How will they function in adulthood as social, sexual beings? In a few school districts, programs have been implemented that avoid public labeling of children showing discordant behavior patterns. Perhaps in a few years we will have some preliminary answers to these questions, answers which will support the development of resource centers where people with problems in living can obtain help based on their needs and wants rather than on their labels and diagnoses.

REFERENCES

1. GOODMAN, L., BUDNER, S., & LESH, B.: Parents and sex education. *Ment. Retard.,* 9:43-45, 1971.
2. EDGERTON, R. B. & DINGMAN, H. F.: Good reasons for bad supervision: "Dating" in a hospital for the mentally retarded. *Psych. Quart.,* 2:1-13, 1964.
3. BOWDEN, J., SPITZ, H. H., & WINTERS, J. J. JR.: Follow-up of one retarded couple's marriage. *Ment. Retard.,* 9:42-43, 1971.
4. PHOENIX, C. H., GOY, R. W., GERALL, A. A., & YOUNG, W. C.: Organizing action of prenatally administered testosterone propionate on the tissues mediating mating behavior in the female guinea pig. *Endocrinology,* 65:369-382, 1959.
5. GOY, R. W.: Organizing effects of androgen on the behaviour of rhesus monkeys. In Michael, R. P. (Ed.): *Endocrinology and human behaviour.* Oxford, Oxford University Press, 1968, pp. 12-31.
6. EDWARDS, D. A.: Mice: Fighting by neonatally androgenized females. *Science,* 161:1027-1028, 1968.
7. MONEY, J. & EHRHARDT, A. A.: Prenatal hormone exposure: Possible effects on behaviour in man. In Michael, R. P. (Ed.): *Endocrinology and human behaviour.* Oxford, Oxford University Press, 1968, pp. 32-48.
8. MICHAEL, R. P., KEVERNE, E. B., & BONSALL, R. W.: Pheromones: isolation of male sex attractants from a female primate. *Science,* 172:964-966, 1971.
9. EDGERTON, R. B.: *The cloak of competence: Stigma in the lives of the mentally retarded.* Berkeley, University of California Press, 1967, pp. 233.
10. ELL, J.: Sex and the retarded. *American Association on Mental Deficiency Region II Newsletter,* 17:11-13, 1971.

11. HUNT, N.: *The world of Nigel Hunt: The diary of a Mongoloid youth.* New York, Garrett, 1967.
12. BRAGINSKY, D. D. & BRAGINSKY, B. M.: *Hansels and Gretels: Studies of children in institutions for the mentally retarded.* New York, Holt, Rinehart and Winston, 1971.
13. WHALEN, R. E.: The ontogeny of sexuality. In Moltz, H. (Ed.): *The ontogeny of vertebrate behavior.* New York, Academic Press, 1971, pp. 229-261.

18

Some Socio-Cultural Research Considerations

ROBERT B. EDGERTON
Mental Retardation Center
The Neuropsychiatric Institute
University of California (Los Angeles)

MAN'S CONCERN WITH THE FUTURE has led him to use a wondrous array of divining tools—from the bones or entrails of chickens, the behavior of microcephalics or poisoned chickens, to the position of heavenly bodies. As scientists, we too have a vital interest in the future, although we must (publicly, at least) disavow divination. Unfortunately, our various scientific trades provide us with a minimum of prognostic tools. As a result, like the generals who regularly prepare to fight the last war, we are very often conservative in our views of the future. Especially in the social sciences, we tend to foretell the future by harkening back to the more stable and understandable patterns of the past. To be sure, we have an adequacy of self-proclaimed visionaries—and doomsayers—but how many of these, for example, predicted the changes in sexual beliefs and behaviors that have occurred in the latter half of the past decade? Very few, indeed. Like Alice, most of us have had all the running we can do to keep up with what has already occurred, and when we are called upon to look into the future, we have done so with a singular lack of prescience.

I do not exempt myself from this criticism, nor do I offer any assurance that my views about research on mental retardation and sexuality are necessarily the best ones. Instead, I am acutely aware that I have no idea what the 1970's will bring.

Will sexual liberation continue so that we can expect by 1980 to see the entire nation engage in a massive orgy? Or can we expect the Hegelian dialectic to prevail, bringing sexuality back to less permissive patterns?

How will the economy behave? Will research funding continue at the present reduced rate or can we expect even shorter rations? Will there be jobs available for the retarded? Will public welfare support those without jobs?

How will schools change? Will they have better ways of integrating the retarded or of providing sex education?

Will legal decisions alter American sexual behavior, for example, by further liberalizing abortion laws? Will our technology produce more effective contraceptive devices or will we learn that present devices such as the pill or the IUD are hazardous?

These are neither idle nor rhetorical questions. Any research proposed for the '70's is at the mercy of their answers and of many other broad social, political and technological considerations.

Nevertheless, research is badly needed, and guidelines for such research could be valuable. Before I suggest some possible guidelines, however, I will attempt to take a comprehensive view of the subject, submerging my special predilections as I do so.

As an anthropologist, I have done research in mental retardation since 1959, some of it explicitly focused on sex. For over a year I studied the sexual conduct of patients in a large state hospital for the mentally retarded.[1, 2] I not only interviewed patients and staff, I saw, time and again, what really went on. I did the same with 50 former patients of the hospital who had been discharged to live in the community.[3] I have done research among American Indians, Hawaiians, and Africans and I know something about the sexual lives of normal and retarded persons in these societies.[4] I have also made a considerable effort to understand recent changes in sexual behavior in the United States, but I must confess that I do not pretend to have comparable knowledge of what is going on in the United States today, nor do I understand why it is taking place.

At UCLA, where I teach anthropology, I see and hear every day of some "new" achievement in the "sexual revolution" of the "youth culture." Living in Los Angeles, I cannot help being aware of some of the manifestations of commercialized sex, of middle-class swingers, of gay liberation, and the like. I know of some otherwise respectable professional people in my neighborhood who regularly meet, swap wives and then have sexual relations that include the participation of animals.

I mention these things to convey to you my belief that sexual behavior and attitudes in the United States today are enormously varied, that they are changing rapidly, and that our scientific knowledge of what is taking place is at best inadequate.

The first hurdles confronting anyone attempting research relating to sexual behavior and mental retardation are problems of *definitions*. For example, what do we mean by "sexual" behavior? We must mean more than the expressions of genital sexuality, for that is an absurdly narrow definition. We must also mean less than the entirety of human behavior, yet such a definition could be defended very persuasively by someone who took a vigorous ecological perspective. Probably, we would all agree that we mean something in between these extremes, something that includes attitudes and values as well as actual behavior. We would probably include love and marriage as well as physical sexuality.

But we must also learn—and this is the primary research problem—how mentally retarded persons construe *their* sexual domain. Is it a narrowly conceived domain of sexual intercourse and possible pregnancy, or is it a ramified domain in which love, self-esteem and the meaning of life become relevant?

Thus we begin with a basic problem: it is one thing to define sexual behavior as we wish to study it and quite another thing to define it as the subjects in our study do. Important as it is to see our subjects' viewpoint, this goal will be almost impossible to achieve.

The chief impediment to this goal derives from the second

problem of definition: what do we mean by the mentally retarded? As we all know, the concept embraces an almost limitless heterogeneity, including people with all kinds of backgrounds and degrees of retardation, from the profoundly retarded who require constant care to those whose only "problem" is a relatively low IQ and a distaste for schoolwork. This diversity is appreciated by all who work with the retarded, yet we sometimes speak of mental retardation as though it had some etiological or prognostic significance, instead of being a convenient label of the same conceptual order as mental illness.

Therefore, we cannot simply ask how *the* mentally retarded construe sexuality. We must always specify *which* mentally retarded and so extend and complicate our research almost indefinitely. Thus, the questions we ask must differ with the people we are studying and the conditions in which they live. For example, even among non-ambulatory profoundly retarded patients (IQ 20 or below) who spend their lives in hospital cribs there are great differences in sexual activity. Some men masturbate; others do not. Some women menstruate and masturbate; others do neither. Among ambulatory persons with comparably low IQs, the differences in behavior are even more marked, ranging from almost continuous masturbation and predatory sodomy, through an absence of any expressed sexual interest to an almost genteel interest and decorum in the presence of the opposite sex.

Among the so-called moderately retarded (IQ 36-51), the residential environment varies greatly (hospitals, family care homes, halfway houses, and so forth), and so does the sexual behavior. Such persons display every conceivable form of sexual behavior, from the virginal timidity of old maids and gentlemen at the one extreme, to aggressive seduction (heterosexual and homosexual) at the other.

When we consider the more mildly retarded, we may well have lost the possibility of generalizing. These people simply represent too many physical and intellectual problems, too many social and cultural backgrounds, and too many shifting environmental circumstances.

Consequently, our first research priority must be to determine the relationship of various kinds of sexual behavior to different IQ and AB (Adaptive Behavior) levels as these are found in differing social and cultural environments. The magnitude of such an undertaking can be reduced to manageable proportions by means of a research design in which various levels of IQ and AB would be studied in a sample of the most relevant environments. The selection of IQ and AB levels, as well as of environments, might follow the principles of theoretical rather than probability sampling, although the extensiveness of the design would necessarily depend upon the availability of resources. The ultimate goal of such an undertaking would be to describe the actual distribution of sexual beliefs and types of behavior within this diverse population.

Even partial realization of this goal would be relevant to planning for the placement and care of many thousands of persons whose sexual behavior has probably been as important to them as it has been unknown to us. Heretofore, typically, the only professional persons who have known a great deal about the sexual behavior of the mentally retarded have been ward staff members and social workers, and even the most astute among these may have seen only a narrow range of the behavior of which the persons in their care were capable.

Primates, including humans, characteristically display unusual and pathological forms of sexual behavior when in confinement— whether the place of confinement be a zoo or a therapeutic institution. We, therefore, need to study a wide range of potential in human sexual behavior, especially as humans display this potential in "natural" community settings.

In addition to this major research focus, I would suggest six sub-foci, all of which relate to or derive from the principal focus suggested earlier.

1. Sexual Behavior and Self-Esteem

One central finding from studies of the mildly and moderately retarded is that through being labeled mentally retarded, such persons suffer an acute loss of self-esteem. As would be expected, this diminished self-esteem is a fundamental problem for the retarded and for all who must interact with them.

Parents and institutions alike have denied the retarded access to normal dating and sexual relationships. My research suggests that this prevalent policy of sexual *apartheid* has been particularly damaging to the self-esteem of the labeled retardate.[3]

However, the question of how important normal dating and sexual experiences are for retarded persons remains to be answered more explicitly. We might expect that in today's sexually charged society persons who are sexually segregated suffer even greater deprivation and loss of self-esteem than they did a decade ago.[5, 6] After all, even the institutionalized retarded see television and movies.

2. *Self-control of Sexual Behavior*

An assumption that pervades our professional literature as well as common belief is that the retarded are less capable than the rest of us of controlling their sexual impulses.[7] Hence, the need for close supervision, confinement, sterilization and the like. The question in this instance is not whether the mentally retarded *should* reproduce, but rather whether they are capable of the same sort of self-control shown by so-called normals.

Granting that normal men and women have shown that their power of control over sexual desire is not always absolute, what do we know of the retarded? We possess innumerable reports testifying to their impulsivity and inappropriateness in sexual behavior.[7,9] Such reports are not always free of a naive reporting bias, but even if they were authentic (and some of them surely are), we would still need to know how much control the retarded are capable of under different circumstances.

My own research indicates that the mildly retarded, at least, are capable of truly remarkable—almost puritanical—sexual self-control both in a hospital and in a community setting.[2, 3] In the groups studied, such self-control was a product of internal regulation—their own values, if you will—and not of external social constraint. It would be important to learn whether such accomplishments of sexual self-control can be found or engendered among other mentally retarded persons.

It is also important to learn how well the more severely retarded persons can control their sexuality. Perhaps, the application of behavior modification techniques may make it possible for us to relax our worries about the sexual behavior of hospitalized retardates, as Johnson has advised.[10]

3. Population Control

Since contraception is a necessary supplement to self-control even for so-called normal persons, we must also study the ability of retarded persons (again at various IQ and AB levels and in various environments) to use contraceptive devices. Such devices, however, must be free of stigma. Little will be gained by a return to involuntary sterilization or to any other stigmatizing technique. Consideration, however, may appropriately be given to voluntary sterilization, especially if it is reversible, or to devices such as the IUD or the pill.[11]

Several reports have attested to the inability of the retarded to use contraceptive methods that require regular planning or foresight.[7, 10] In my view, such a categorical conclusion is unwarranted. I have known many mentally retarded persons who were irresponsible about contraception, but I have also known others who have used contraceptives responsibly over an extended period of time. The problem, again, is to find out which kinds of retardates can use which techniques under which conditions and then to offer them an educated choice.

For institutionalized retardates at the lower IQ level, such considerations become academic until some decision is made about the right of such persons to engage in sexual relations at all. It is time to ask seriously whether persons whose inadequate intellectual ability compels them to spend their lives in an institution should be denied the right to have sexual relations with a consenting adult. Are we forever to be appalled by the thought of two persons in their 30's with IQs in the 40's cohabiting and having sexual intercourse in one of our state institutions?

In many institutions sympathetic ward staff members have sometimes allowed such persons to meet surreptitiously (properly equipped with contraceptives) because it seemed inhumane to keep them apart. Others have done so for less humane reasons. If the objection to this practice be that the couples are not married, then let us also study the possibility of marriage for the institutionalized retarded.

4. Marriage and Parenthood

We do not know what might result from a policy that would permit certain institutionalized retardates to marry or to cohabit, but we do know that many mildly retarded persons, whether previously institutionalized or not, are capable of maintaining stable, happy marriages with other retarded persons.[3, 12] That such persons would make capable parents is far less clear.[7,8] In addition to the possible consequences in terms of genetic influences, overpopulation, and inflated public assistance rolls, we must consider whether, even in favorable economic circumstances, persons of low IQ and AB levels can be capable parents. Even should it be demonstrated—as I am certain it could be—that *some* persons of low IQ and low AB could be adequate parents, I think this number would be relatively small. I also think that relatively few normal persons make adequate parents, but, nevertheless, I believe it is important to promote research into the parental skills of retarded parents.

Because it is likely that many retarded persons wish to be parents,[3] we should explore various means of providing such persons with opportunities to serve as surrogate parents. The possibilities include supervised assignment of both institutionalized and non-institutionalized retarded persons to child-care responsibilities in day-care centers, boarding schools for younger retardates, or hospitals where children lack parental contact. Some adult retardates might be assigned formal roles as "godparents" for younger retardates in their own institutions and might thereby be given extensive responsibility for child care.

5. Public Attitudes about the Sexual Behavior of the Mentally Retarded

At the same time that we focus research on the retarded themselves, we should also undertake research into the attitudes of the public toward the sexuality of mentally retarded persons. A great many retarded persons have undoubtedly spent their lives in institutions because their parents had fears about their reproductive potential.[13] Does the general public have similar fears? Would the parents or the public at large accede to plans to liberalize sexual conduct in institutions? Do public attitudes in this regard vary greatly by class, religion, or ethnicity? What sort of public education program might be necessary to gain acceptance of such a policy? The answers to these and related questions are important.

6. Sex Education for and about the Mentally Retarded

Past efforts at sex education for the retarded seem to have been useful.[14,15] Such commendable documents as the *Resource Guide in Sex Education for the Mentally Retarded*,[16] however, need to be improved to reflect recent changes in attitudes toward sexual activity and in the technology of contraception. Equally important would be research to determine how to educate the public to the meaning of these changes for the mentally retarded.

Conclusion

One point I would stress as essential to any research: we must keep in mind the social cultural system *as a whole*. This will be especially important in any attempt to understand how changes in our morality are related to changes in our technology and how these changes in turn relate to the mentally retarded.

The history of the social sciences makes it all too clear that when we are confronted by difficult and expensive problems, we tend to define the problems narrowly, study them by the latest neo-positivistic techniques, and reach conclusions in happy isolation. However, neither human sexual behavior nor mental retardation can profitably be studied apart from the social and cultural matrix in which they take on meaning and become problems. Whatever the expense, this holistic perspective must be maintained.

REFERENCES

1. EDGERTON, R. B.: A patient elite: ethnography in a hospital for the mentally retarded. *Amer. Jour. of Ment. Defic.*, 68:372-385, 1963.
2. EDGERTON, R. B., DINGMAN, H. F.: Good reasons for bad supervision: Dating in a hospital for the mentally retarded. *Psychiat. Quart. Suppl.*, 38:221-233, 1964.
3. EDGERTON, R. B.: *The Cloak of Competence.* Berkeley, University of California Press, 1967.
4. EDGERTON, R. B.: Mental retardation in non-western societies: Toward a cross-cultural perspective on incompetence. In Haywood, H. C. (Ed.): *Social Cultural Aspects of Mental Retardation.* New York, Appleton-Century-Crofts, 1970.
5. BHAGAT, M. & FRASER, W. I.: The meaning of concepts to the retarded offender. *Amer. Jour. of Ment. Defic.*, 75:260-267, 1970.
6. CANNON, K. L. & LONG, R.: Premarital sexual behavior in the sixties. *Jour. of Marriage and the Fam.*, 33:36-49, 1971.
7. BASS, M. S.: Marriage, Parenthood, and Prevention of Pregnancy. *Amer. Jour. of Ment. Defic.*, 68:318-333, 1963.
8. JORDAN, T. E.: *The Mentally Retarded* (2nd Edition). Columbus, Ohio, Charles E. Merrill, 1966.
9. ABEL, T. M. & KINDER, E. F.: *The Subnormal Adolescent Girl.* New York, Columbia University Press, 1942.
10. JOHNSON, W. R.: Sex education and the mentally retarded. *J. of Sex. Res.*, 5:179-185, 1969a.
11. DJERRASSI, C.: Birth control after 1984. *Science*, 169:941-951, 1970.
12. MATTINSON, J.: *Marriage and Mental Handicap.* London, Gerald Duckworth and Co., 1970.
13. HAMMER, S. L., WRIGHT, L. S., & JENSEN, D. L.: Sex education for the retarded adolescent: A survey of parental attitudes and methods of management in fifty adolescent retardates. *Clin. Ped.*, 6:621-627, 1967.
14. GORDON, S.: *Facts about Sex for Exceptional Youth.* East Orange, New Jersey Association for Brain Injured Children, 1969.
15. GENDEL, E.: *Sex Education of the Mentally Retarded Child in the Home.* New York, National Association for Retarded Children, 1969.
16. American Association for Health, Physical Education, and Recreation and Sex Information and Education Council of the United States: *A Resource Guide in Sex Education for the Mentally Retarded*, 1971.

19

Mental Retardation and Sexuality: Some Research Strategies

RICHARD GREEN

*Associate Professor of Psychiatry in Residence
University of California
School of Medicine, Los Angeles*

THE TASK ASSIGNED TO ME is to dream. I am to concoct ideas for future research linking the specialties of mental retardation and sexology. Freed from the constraints of reality, unfettered by an abundance of facts, I will proceed.

I will focus on four areas of potential study:

I. Psychosexual Differentiation: Cultural vs Biologic Influences.
II. Prenatal Gonadal Hormones and Intellectual Development.
III. Sex Hormone-Dependent Social Behavior.
IV. Sex Chromosomes, Intellectual Development, and Social Behavior.

I. Psychosexual Differentiation: Cultural vs Biologic Influences

Familiarity with recent advances in neuroendocrinology forces one to concede a role to biology in the development of male-type and female-type behavior. Familiarity with recent findings of developmental psychologists and with sociologists' reports of cross-cultural disparities in "masculine" and "feminine" behavior

250

forces one to concede a role to learning in the development of male-type and female-type behavior. The research task is to design experiments to assess the relative contributions of each.

A provocative laboratory finding bearing implication for understanding human development is that postnatal sex-linked behavior may be related to the prenatal hormonal milieu.[1] While it has long been known that sex hormones differentiate the reproductive structures in a male or female direction, the possibility that some aspcts of non-reproductive behavior may also be so organized is a relatively newer concept.

Research with the rhesus monkey provides a tantalizing model for human behavior. Preadolescent males and females of that species show sex differences analogous to those seen in the human boy and girl. Both rhesus and human male preadolescents show more rough-and-tumble, chasing, and aggressive behavior than females.[2] By altering the prenatal hormonal milieu, it is possible to breed "tomboy" girl monkeys. Administration of testosterone propionate to the pregnant rhesus monkey carrying a female fetus results not only in anatomic virilization, but in behavioral masculinization as well. These tomboy females show levels of rough-and-tumble, chasing, and aggressive play which approach that of the normal male.[1] This finding invites the question: To what extent are the social play differences seen in the human child also dependent on the prenatal hormonal composition?

Prospects for studying that question have come into view with recent methodologic advances:

Formerly, assays for gonadal hormones were crude, requiring relatively large samples for comparatively gross estimates. The science has progressed from milligram to microgram to nanogram to picagram sensitivity (a picagram being 1/1000 nanogram, which in turn is 1/1000 microgram, etc.), and assays may currently be made from far smaller samples.

Amniocentesis, the drawing of amniotic fluid during human gestation, has become a standard procedure in major medical centers. It is being carried out for a variety of reasons, including the diagnosis of a suspected syndrome that results in mental retardation. Pilot data on assays of gonadal hormones from amniotic fluid samples indicate some correlation between levels in amniotic fluid and those in fetal blood.[3]

Thus tools are becoming available for assessing man's prenatal hormonal milieu. Since not all fetuses detected by amniocentesis as potentially retarded are aborted and not all causes of retardation are detectable by examination of amniotic fluid, there could be available for research a population of retarded children on whom data exist with respect to the prenatal hormonal environment.

What kinds of behavior would one be interested in observing in such children?

A variety of differences in behavior between the sexes have been noted in non-retarded children at various stages of development. At 13 months, males and females have been observed to show differences in their style of play, even when given the same toys. Girls tend to sit relatively passively gathering objects about them, while boys tend to move them about more actively, even flinging them about.[4] At 2 years, nursery school children are already inclined to favor playmates of their own sex.[5] At 4, most children can correctly tell the difference between a male and a female doll and identify the one which corresponds to their own sex.[6] By 5, boys and girls differ in the extent of the display of physical aggression and rough-and-tumble play.[7-9] During these preschool years boys surpass girls in restlessness and general activity,[10] use a larger play area,[11] and play more often with blocks[12-15] and all kinds of vehicles.[16-18] When playing with blocks, boys tend to build tall structures, while girls tend to build horizontally.[12]

To what extent are these differences culturally learned, or biologically programmed? If it is legitimate to presume that the mentally retarded child is less receptive than the normal child to the cultural expectations of male-female behavioral differences, as he or she is to other types of learning, then observations of children with varying prenatal hormonal levels (if such data were available), matched for age and IQ, may help us answer that question. The study could include: 1) observations of behavior in play areas providing equipment for gross-motor activity (monkey bars, balls, other throwable objects) ; 2) observations of behavior in settings providing objects for structured play, such as blocks, vehicles, and dolls; 3) collection of time-sample data on activity levels, such as the extent of daily running, walking, and sitting; 4) collection of time-sample data on aggressiveness, with measures of involvement in rough-and-tumble play, chasing activity, and threatening behavior.

Data could be collected on two groups of subjects: 1) children for whom prenatal hormonal data are available; and 2) children for whom no such data exist. For those on whom prenatal hormone data are available, high and low androgen and estrogen subgroups *within* sexes could be generated and behavioral comparisons made. For those on whom no prenatal hormone assays are available, there still remains a clear indicator of whether the children were exposed, prenatally, to grossly high or low androgen levels: whether they are male or female. Thus behavioral comparisons *between* sexes can also be made.

Obviously, retarded children are not immune to cultural contamination. The extent to which attitudes of parents (before the child's institutionalization) influence such behavior must be assessed as must the influence of institutional caretakers. Just as we need more data on differential handling of typical children by parents, as a function of the child's sex, we also need data on the differences in the ways hospital staff members treat young male and female patients. For example, do caretakers in institutions tolerate noise, messiness, and aggressiveness more in boys than in girls? Are girls held or cuddled more than boys? To what extent is behavior shaped by the type of toy or activity made available?

Yet another target of research within this context may be the maturational timetable for psychosexual differentiation. To what extent do indices of maturation appear as a function of chronological as against intellectual age? If a 4-year-old girl with an IQ of 100 chooses a mother doll in response to the question, "Which will you be when you grow up?" at what age will a 4-year-old girl with an IQ of 50 do the same? At 4 years? At 8 years?

II. Prenatal Gonadal Hormones and Intellectual Development

The possible interrelation between prenatal hormones and intellectual development is a provocative new concept. Two studies hint at such a relation. Both are focused on children whose mothers received a progesterone compound during pregnancy.

Study one assessed the IQ of 10 girls, age 3-14, whose mothers had received a synthetic progestin to prevent abortion. The mean score was found to be 125. Six of the 10 girls had an IQ above 130 (compared to only 2 percent of the random population). While suggesting the possible intellect-enhancing effect of the drug, the authors also point to the possibility of a sampling bias in that six of the nine families included a parent who was a college graduate and the six children whose fathers had gone to college were the six with IQs above 130.[19]

In the second study, children whose mothers had received progesterone for treatment of toxemia of pregnancy were compared with control groups. Dosage and time of initiation of the drug were assessed in relation to a timetable for developmental milestones and intellectual and physical capabilities. Intellectual development was determined by asking teachers to rate the children as average, above average, or below average on verbal reasoning, English, arithmetic, and other skills.

At one year of age, there was no difference in verbal development between 29 children who had had progesterone and 31 controls, but significantly more children who had had progesterone were able to stand and walk unaided.

Another 79 children were evaluated at 9-10 years. Twenty-nine had been exposed to progesterone prenatally, another 29 were also products of toxemic pregnancies but had not been prenatally exposed to progesterone, and 21 were normal controls. The ratings of the progesterone children were found to exceed those of the controls by 13 percent in verbal reasoning, 11 percent in English, 14 percent in arithmetic and 10 percent in craftwork. There was no difference with respect to physical education.

When the progesterone children were divided into high (8 or more grams total administration) and low dosage groups, their comparative academic attainments showed a progressive *increase* from the control group, to the low dosage group, to the high dosage group.

Analysis was also made of educational attainment in relation to the time during gestation when progesterone was first received. A significantly better educational performance was demonstrated among children who received progesterone before the 16th week of gestation.[20]

Enthusiasm for the implications of this study should be attenuated, however, by the investigator's failure to include data on the intellectual capacity of the parents of the children in the various groups or on the intellectual performance of the non-exposed siblings of the progesterone-exposed subjects. Nevertheless, the correlations between dosage, time of administration, and intellectual assessment do suggest the possibility of a prenatal hormonal effect that invites consideration of some research questions.

At the clinical level, it would be interesting to study populations of children born with the masculinizing adrenogenital syndrome, caused by an excessive production prenatally of androgenic hormones. I suggest this area of study for two reasons. First, although progestins are "female" hormones, in that they may be necessary for the maintenance of gestation, they are also androgenic and virilizing. Second, a pilot study has already looked at the IQs of 70 children with the adrenogenital syndrome and has found that 60 percent have scores in excess of 110, as compared with 25 percent of the random population.[21]

In the laboratory, experiments can be designed to manipulate prenatal hormonal variables to test their possible correlation with postnatal capacity for learning. Such experiments, for example, might look for answers to the following questions: do nonhuman primates (or other animals) learn to perform tasks in a superior manner when exposed to androgenic hormones, at varying prenatal intervals? If so, which tasks and which hormones? Recent hormonal research indicates that different metabolites are differentially effective at different body sites.[22, 23] Are there metabolites that have a specific intellect-enhancing effect without concomitant side effects such as virilization?

The intriguing possibility arises here that some cases of idiopathic mental retardation may be related to deficiencies of specific components in the hormonal milieu at critical developmental periods. Hormones are pivotally involved in protein synthesis and in a variety of metabolic maturational processes.

III. Sex Hormone-Dependent Social Behavior

Surgical intervention has been used to control sexual aggression and reproduction in the retarded. Its efficacy derives from the hormonal basis of such behavior. Castration of the male not only effectively precludes reproduction but also reproductive-type behavior since sex drive in the male is largely androgen-dependent. In the female, although reproduction may be prevented by tubal ligation or gonadectomy, these operations have little or no effect on reproductive-type behavior.[24]

Sex hormone-dependent activity has more recently come under control by hormonal rather than surgical treatment. While hormonal intervention in the female is widely known and practiced as a method of contraception, hormonal intervention in the male is comparatively rare, particularly in the United States.

The recent introduction of anti-androgenic compounds offers considerable promise for both research and patient management. The most widely used drug so far is cyproterone acetate. This synthetic hormone, which has some progestational activity, has been widely used in animal research to block, at varying developmental periods, the effects of androgen in the male.[25, 26] It has been used in the clinical treatment of men as a chemical castrator. Cyproterone acetate appears to work by interfering with the receptivity of end-organ target tissue to androgenic hormone,[27] and/or suppressing testosterone levels, and is considered to be a reversible form of intervention.

Clinically, cyproterone has been used for the suppression of socially undesirable sexual behavior in human males and for the suppression of androgen-dependent malignancy. Rapists, exhibitionists, compulsive masturbators, satyriasists, and pedophiliacs have been administered cyproterone or some other drug possessing progestational action.[28-33] Reports to date indicate that such drugs are effective in suppressing sex drive in the male without bringing the feminizing physical changes that accompany estrogenic treatment.

The biggest obstacle to an enthusiastic scientific embrace of anti-androgenic treatment has thus far been the absence of controlled studies. Subjects selected for experiments have been men highly motivated to a) experience and b) report diminished sex drive. Typically, they have been incarcerated or incarcerable persons whose prospects for freedom have depended on their sexual control. Moreover, the patients administered these drugs have been told that they were receiving an anti-androgenic substance. Because there are, perhaps, few human functions as responsive to suggestion as male potency and sex drive, some caution must be taken in assessing the reported results. Male rats, presumably less responsive than humans to placebo effects, do not appear to be so readily sexually tamed by cyproterone.[34-36]

A closely observed mentally retarded population, selected for their open display of masturbatory behavior, and less open to the effects of suggestibility (and not informed of the nature of their medication), might lend itself to an objective assessment of the anti-libido properties of anti-androgenic compounds. Raters would, of course, need to be "blind" as to which subjects have received a placebo and which the drug.

Also, for those caretakers concerned not only about the fertility of their charges but also about their sexual behavior, treatment of the male with an anti-androgenic compound would appear to be a better way to control both fertility and sexual activity than the administration of contraceptives to the female.

The possible interrelation between levels of aggressiveness and circulating androgenic hormones might also be accessible to investigation in a population of institutionalized retardates. If baseline data were available on parameters of aggressiveness (rage reactions, physical assaults, property-destroying behavior) the extent to which such conduct is hormonally dependent (at least in the male) could be assessed by administering anti-androgenic agents and observing subsequent behavior. Since anti-androgenic agents do not result in general sedation, they might provide a better way of bringing some aspects of anti-social behavior under control than the use of high dosages of tranquilizers.

IV. Sex Chromosomes, Intellectual Development, and Social Behavior

The normal female chromosomal karyotype is 44 + XX. The normal male karyotype is 44 + XY. A wide range of variations on this basic theme has been reported. Thus, some men have been found to have two or more X chromosomes in addition to a Y and some to have two or more Ys in association with an X, while some women have 3 or more Xs. The picture has been further complicated by reports of XX males.[37] Of interest to our discussion is the effect of atypical karyotypes on sexual behavior and intellectual development.

Earliest reports of men with XXY karyotypes were from institutions for the mentally retarded. The incidence of this atypical karyotype among institutional retardates was found to be higher than in a random population. First reports of males with an additional Y came from studies of inmates of high security prisons. As a result, an instant mythology appeared of an XYY syndrome or "super-maleness." So biased toward pathology were the early reports of atypical karyotypes that a scientific journal considered it appropriate to publish an article entitled "A Normal XYY Man." [38]

Reports of XXY karyotypes also came from medical centers specializing in the treatment of the anatomically intersexed and those men who wish to change sex. Reports describing the overlapping of a few patients into both categories raised the possibility of a link between chromosomally and psychically intersexed states.[39-41]

Larger and perhaps more representative samples that have since been studied leave some unanswered questions.

A monograph-length survey described males in a hospital for the mentally ill, a hospital for maladjusted mental retardates, a hospital for the severely retarded, a miscellaneous series of psychiatric patients, and a control group of military inductees.[42] The incidence of XXY karyotype was 30 in 6,265 mental hospital inmates (0.5 percent), and 19 in 958 inmates of the hospital for the maladjusted mental retardates (2.0 percent). The incidence was 10 times greater among the patients in the hospital for maladjusted mental retardates than among the military inductees.

Of the 6 inductees with XXY karyotype, none had an above average IQ. The male retardates who had two X chromosomes were among the most severely retarded subjects in the survey. However, that the IQ of a person having an XXY karyotype is not necessarily intellectually subnormal was demonstrated by the finding, in another study, of two XXY patients with IQs of 121 and 132.[43]

Among the 30 psychiatric patients with XXY karyotypes, two were predominantly homosexual, one had murdered and raped an 8-year-old girl, four were pedophiliacs, and one was a fetishist.

A survey of all 2,087 males in hospitals for the intellectually subnormal in a geographic zone of England found 17 XXY men (0.8 percent) as against an expected finding of four (0.2 percent). On a Kinsey 0-6 rating scale of sexual orientation, the lower numbers signifying heterosexuality, none of these 17 XXY men was graded below 3, eight were graded 3, two were graded 4, five were graded 5, and 2 were graded 6. Sex drive in 9 of the 17 was considered low.[44]

A more recent investigation compared men showing antisocial

behavior who had either the XXY or the XYY karyotype. Of 876 males, at least 6 feet tall, who were karyotyped in a prison or a facility for the mentally retarded or mentally ill, nine were discovered to be XYY and 14 XXY. The mean IQ of the XXY males was 80 and of the XYY males 84. Examination of the arrest records of XYY males revealed little difference from the records of males with XXY. Sexual assault and sexual deviation were found in both groups. There was one murderer; he was XXY.[45]

Data have recently been collated on the sexual behavior of 35 males with the XYY syndrome. Of these, 30 were imprisoned or had experienced severe behavioral disturbance. Seven were reported as bisexual, seven as homosexual, and two as heterosexual. Nine had records of sexual offense: bisexual child incest (1 case), pedophilia (2 cases), voyeurism (1), exhibitionism (3), indecent assault (1), and one a combination of transvestism, sadomasochism and sex murder.[46]

Sampling problems make interpretation of these reports difficult. The association of two unique phenomena tends to find its way into the literature, particularly when it poses a tantalizing theoretical question. While it may be that there is a significant weighting toward mental retardation and sexual atypicality in association with anomalies of sex chromosomes, the question remains how "significant" is a significant correlation? The great majority of male transvestites, transsexuals, and homosexuals are 44 + XY, and the great majority of XXY and XYY males are neither in prison nor in mental hospitals.

The challenge of gaining more representative data correlating sex chromosome anomalies with sexual and non-sexual social behavior is, however, far from insurmountable. The occurrence of the syndromes is common enough (1 in 500 males is XXY;[42] 1 in 700 is XYY).[47] The procedure for reading karyotypes is easy enough to make it possible to identify comparatively large numbers of infants with atypical karyotypes shortly after birth so that they can be followed developmentally. A study is now under way in the Boston area in which newborn males with XXY karyotypes are being identified and followed.[48] Studies such as this can be expanded to encompass other large metropolitan areas and to include other subgroups, such as XYY newborns.

The special vulnerability of *some* XXY and XYY males to intellectual and sexual disability is not understood. We need to dissect prenatal biochemical and postnatal experimental variables to learn why, for example, only some XXY males are severely retarded and others are of superior intelligence. Can we simply presume that XXY subjects with IQs of 120 would have had 150+ IQs and that XXY subjects with IQs of 60 would have had IQs of 95 without the extra chromosome? Or do we have here a special population with a special vulnerability in which contributing variables may be more easily identified?

Furthermore, as there are some data indicating that XYY males may have higher than normal androgen levels,[49] the question may be raised of whether the use of an anti-androgenic compound might have an ameliorative effect on those who exhibit antisocial behavior. Finally, findings that XXY and XYY males show central nervous system defects, demonstrated by a high incidence of EEG abnormality,[42] and the onset early in life of extrapyramidal symptoms point to the need for research into developmental central nervous system physiology and its relation to anomalies of sex chromosomes and behavior.

Conclusion

In the foregoing dream fragments I have attempted to integrate the research interests of those whose major focus is mental retardation and those whose focus is human sexuality. These fragments are offered to whet a few research appetites and promote a rapprochement between experts in the two fields.

REFERENCES

1. YOUNG, W., GOY, R., & PHOENIX, C.: Hormones and Sexual Behavior. *Science*, 143:212-18, 1964.
2. HARLOW, H. F.: The Heterosexual Affectional System in Monkeys. *Amer. Psychol.*, 17:1-9, 1962.
3. RESKO, J.: Oregon Regional Primate Center, Beaverton, Oregon. (Unpublished report), 1971.

4. GOLDBERG, S. & LEWIS, M.: Play Behavior in the Year-Old Infant: Early Sex Differences. *Child Develop.*, 40:21-31, 1969.

5. KOCH, H.: A Study of Some Factors Conditioning the Social Distance Between Sexes. *J. Soc. Psychol.*, 20:79-107, 1944.

6. RABBAN, M.: Sex-Role Identification in Young Children in Two Diverse Social Groups. *Genetic Psychol. Monogr.*, 42:81-158, 1950.

7. BANDURA, A., ROSS, D., & ROSS, S.: Transmission of Aggression Through Imitation of Aggressive Models. *J. Ab. Soc. Psychol.*, 63:575-82, 1961.

8. DURRETT, M.: The Relationship of Early Infant Regulation and Later Behavior in Play Interviews. *Child Develop.*, 30:211-16, 1959.

9. SEARS, P.: Doll Play Aggression in Normal Young Children. *Psychol. Monogr.*, 65 IV, 1951.

10. ZAZZO, R. & JULLIEN, C.: Differential Psychology of the Sexes at the Preschool Level. *Enfance*, 7:12-23, 1954.

11. OTTERSTAEDT, H.: Investigations Concerning the Play Area of Suburban Children in a Medium-Sized City. *Psychol. Resch.*, 13:275-87, 1962.

12. ERICKSON, E.: Sex Differences in the Play Configurations of Preadolescents. *Amer. J. Orthopsychiat.*, 21:667-92, 1951.

13. FARRELL, M.: Sex Differences in Block Play in Early Childhood Education. *J. Educ. Res.*, 51:279-84, 1957.

14. MONZIK, M.: Sex Differences in the Occurrence of Materials in the Play Constructions of Pre-Adolescents. *Child Develop.*, 22:15-35, 1951.

15. VANCE, T. & McCALL, L.: Children's Preferences Among Play Materials as Determined by the Method of Paired Comparisons of Pictures. *Child Develop.*, 5:267-77, 1934.

16. HARTLEY, R., FRANK, L., & GOLDENSON, R.: *Understanding Children's Play.* New York, Columbia University Press, 1952.

17. MONZIK, M.: Sex Differences in the Occurrence of Materials in the Play Constructions of Pre-Adolescents. *Child Devel.*, 22:15-35, 1951.

18. GREEN, R., FULLER, M., HENDLER, J., & RUTLEY, B.: Playroom Toy Preferences of 15 Masculine and 15 Feminine Boys. *Behavior Therapy*, 3:425-29, 1972.

19. EHRHARDT, A. & MONEY, J.: Progestin-Induced Hermaphroditism: IQ and Psychosexual Identity in a Study of Ten Girls. *J. Sex Research*, 3:83-100, 1967.

20. DALTON, K. Ante-Natal Progesterone and Intelligence. *Brit. J. Psychiat.*, 114: 1377-82, 1968.

21. MONEY, J. & LEWIS, V.: IQ, Genetics, and Accelerated Growth: Adrenogenital Syndrome. *Bull. Johns Hopkins Hosp.*, 118:365-73, 1966.

22. LUTTGE, W. & WHALEN, R.: Dihydrotestosterone, Androstenedione, Testosterone: Comparative Effectiveness in Masculinizing and Defeminizing Reproduction Systems in Male and Female Rats. *Hormones and Behavior*, 1:265-82, 1970.

23. WHALEN, R. & LUTTGE, W.: Testosterone, Androstenedione and Dehydrotestosterone: Effects on Mating Behavior of Male Rats. *Hormones and Behavior*, 2:117-26, 1971.

24. BREMER, J.: *Asexualization. A Follow-up Study of 244 Cases.* New York, Macmillan, 1959.

25. NEUMANN, F. & KRAMER, M.: Female Brain Differentiation of Male Rats as a Result of Early Treatment with an Androgen Antagonist. Proc. 2 Int. Congr. Horm. Steroids. *Excerpta Medica Fden. Int. Congr. Ser.*, 132:932-41, 1966.

26. NERI, R., MONAHAN, M., MEYER, J., ALFONSO, B., & TABACHNICK, I.: Biological Studies in an Antiandrogen (SH714). *Europ. J. Pharmacol.*, 1:438-44, 1967.

27. WHALEN, R., LUTTGE, W., & GREEN, R.: Effects of the AntiAndrogen Cyproter-

one Acetate on the Uptake of 1, 2 ^{3}H—Testosterone in Neural and Peripheral Tissues of the Castrate Male Rat. *Endocrinol.*, 84:217-22, 1969.

28. LASCHET, U., LASCHETT, L., FETZNER, H., GLAESEL, M., MALL, G., & NAAB, M.: Results in the Treatment of Hyper- and Abnormal Sexuality of Men with Antiandrogens. *Acta Endocrinol. Supp.*, 119:54, 1967.

29. LASCHET, U. & LASCHETT, L.: Die Behandlung der Pathologisch Gesteigerton und Abartigen Sexualitat des Mannes Mit dem Antiandrogen Cypoteronacebat. In Das Testosteron. Die Struma. 13. Symposium der Deutschen Gesellschaft für Endokrinologie. Berlin, Springer, 1968.

30. SERVAIS, J.: A Clinical Study of Cases of Psychosexual Disturbances in Men Treated by a Libido Inhibitor: Methylestrenolone. *Acta Neurol. Belg.*, 68:416-29, 1968.

31. MONEY, J.: Discussion. In R. P. Michael (Ed.): *Endocrinology and Human Behavior.* London, Oxford, 1968.

32. LASCHET, U.: Die Anwendbarkeit von Antiandrogen in der Humanmedizin Saarlaendisches Arzteblatt (Vol. 7), 1969.

33. MONEY, J.: Use of an Androgen-Depleting Hormone in the Treatment of Male Sex Offenders. *J. Sex Res.*, 6:165-72, 1970.

34. ZUCKER, I.: Effects of an Antiandrogen on the Mating Behavior of Male Guinea Pigs and Rats. *J. Endocrinol.*, 35:209-210, 1966.

35. BEACH, F. & WESTBROOK, W.: Morphological and Behavioral Effects of an "Antiandrogen" in Male Rats. *J. Endocrinol.*, 42:379-82, 1968.

36. WHALEN, R. & EDWARDS, D.: Effects of the Antiandrogen Cyproterone Acetate on Mating Behavior and Seminal Vesicle Tissue in Male Rats. *Endocrinol.*, 84:155-56, 1969.

37. NEUWIRTH, J. & RABOCH, J.: Two Men with 46, XX. *Endockrinologie*, 57:29-36, 1970.

38. WIENER, S. & SUTHERLAND, G.: A Normal XYY Man. *Lancet*, 2:1352, 1968.

39. MONEY, J. & POLLITT, E.: Cytogenetic and Psychosexual Ambiguity. *Arch. Gen. Psychiat.*, 11:589-95, 1964.

40. BAKER, H. & STOLLER, R.: Can a Biological Force Contribute to Gender Identity? *Amer. J. Psychiat.*, 124:1653-58, 1968.

41. DAVIDSON, P. W.: Transsexualism in Klinefelter's Syndrome. *Psychosomatics*, 7:94-98, 1966.

42. HAMBERT, G.: *Males with Positive Sex Chromatin.* Göteborg, Akademiforlaget, 1966.

43. MONEY, J.: Cytogenetic and Psychosexual Incongruities with a Note on Space-Form Blindness. *Amer. J. Psychiat.*, 119:820-27, 1963.

44. HUNTER, H.: A Controlled Study of the Psychopathology and Physical Measurements of Klinefelter's Syndrome. *Brit. J. Psychiat.*, 115:443-48, 1969.

45. BAKER, D., TELFER, M., RICHARDSON, C., & CLARK, G.: Chromosomal Errors in Men with Antisocial Behavior. *J.A.M.A.*, 214:869-878, 1970.

46. MONEY, J.: Impulse, Aggression and Sexuality in the XYY Syndrome. *St. Johns Law Review*, 44:220-235, 1970.

47. RATCLIFFE, S., MELVILLE, M., & STEWART, A.: Chromosome Studies on 3500 Newborn Male Infants. *Lancet*, 1:121-122, 1970.

48. WALZER, S.: Harvard Medical School, Personal Communication, 1971.

49. RUDD, B., GALAL, O., & CASEY, M.: Testosterone Excretion Rates in Normal Males and Males with an XYY Complement. *J. Med. Genet.*, 5:286-289, 1968.

BACKGROUND PAPERS

20

Development of Sex Education in Denmark

HENRIK HOFFMEYER
*Head, State Psychiatric Hospital
Glostrup, Denmark*

The Cultural Background of Sex in Scandinavia

Over the years the Scandinavian countries have been the subject of lurid speculation. The popular press has created an image of Scandinavia as rife with promiscuity. Thus, it is appropriate to describe a few important historical and cultural features of Scandinavian behavior.

The peoples of the North can trace their history back some 10,000 years when the peculiar pantheistic religion of Wotan first developed. Integral to the whole Nordic culture, this religion implanted itself on the consciousness of much of the rest of the world, especially during the so-called Viking boom from about 800 to 1100 A.D. To the rest of Europe, the Vikings appeared to be wild gangs of robbers. At home, however, Viking culture was sophisticated and remarkably liberal.

Distinctive characteristics of this culture were the liberty of the individual farmer and the dependency of chief and king on the *thing*—a democratic gathering or council of free men. Another interesting characteristic was the status of women. Broendsted notes: "The woman's position is thoroughly esteemed and honored. She is free and independent. She carries the keys and her dowry is her private property." [1]

Around the year 1000, the North was Christianized by the Roman Catholic Church. However, the ideals of individual liberty carried over from the old heathen culture perhaps gave force to the Lutheran Reformation of 1533, which was characterized by a democratic personalization of relations to God. The old ideals of independence of interpretation also influenced the strong religious movements that swept Denmark during the 19th century. These movements asserted the right of the individual—however low his economic or social status—to maintain relations with God as a personal responsibility.

In general, Scandinavians today are not agnostics. They do, however, tend to be cool to the institutionalized churches. Moreover, even today Scandinavians are influenced greatly by modern theological theories that make relationships to God a matter of privacy, loosen religion from civil morality, and make both religion and morality a matter of personal responsibility.

When Christianity reached the North, it was not accompanied by great immigrations or enormous social upheaval as it was in so many other parts of the world. Thus, its influence on manners and customs was relatively superficial. For example, the Church was allowed to bless ceremonies that in many places retained the ancient, traditional customs.

As Troels-Lund describes the marriage contract during the 16th century: "the main decision took place at the meeting where the couple was fastened together and the actual betrothal was established." Further, he points out, all the legal duties and rights of marriage were tied to the betrothal. The wedding was merely considered an affirmative festivity which would take place when opportunity offered, but which might not take place at all.[2]

A special system of relations between young people was at one time practiced throughout Scandinavia. This system is best translated as "night proposals." The Danish phrase can be directly translated thus: "to lie on truth and love." This means to stay in the girl's bed overnight on "faith and promise." In this custom, the young men of the village visited the girls on Saturday night. The boy lay dressed on the bed with the girl of his choice. Publicly acknowledged, the practice was encouraged by the village elders, who usually saw to it that outsiders were excluded from participating. In the early stage of boy-girl relationships, boys changed girls every Saturday night, and couples often switched partners during the same night. Sexual intercourse was not the custom during this stage. Gradually a couple would decide to stay together and betrothal usually ensued. At this stage, intercourse became the established pattern. The wedding was a secondary matter.

We must realize, however, that during those days of low mobility this custom was usually a closed system. A young man could not just drive into town, pick up a girl, impregnate her, and then leave never to be seen again. Betrothal brought both parties prescribed obligations, which could not be easily evaded in a village where everyone's actions were known. In some places betrothal was not affirmed until intercourse had begun, and sometimes it was not maintained if the bride proved to be infertile. Fertility played a decisive role in ancient rural society.

Many times since the fall of Wotan, Church and State have conspired to stamp out the idea that marriage is a secular arrangement. Despite periods of drastic punitive legislation, these efforts have succeeded to only a limited degree. The Reformation and Renaissance, taking place simultaneously, counteracted this form of repression by paying homage to "natural man" and praising marriage as a state of unfolding naturalness. Lutherans, however, agreed with Catholics that premarital sex was "the work of the devil," but this idea did not change customs in the North, where premarital sex continued to be encouraged by village elders.

Nevertheless, in 1799 the Danish government abolished betrothal as a legal beginning of marriage. Only the wedding was officially acceptable. According to Georg Hansen, church records from this period show a great number of applications for legitimation of children born during betrothal.[3] Betrothal was now replaced by engagement—legally far less binding. Because legal obligations were minimal, the practice of announcing an engagement has eroded to the point where it now is not particularly common. Today marriage is preceded by different styles of relationships. On the one hand, this has caused considerable confusion among some people about the rights and obligations that go along with premarital relations. On the other hand, the ancient code is still a force in Denmark today—a fact that contradicts the idea that modern sex relations are loose.

The Present Situation

Hertoft has reported a series of recent studies on frequency of male premarital sexual activities in Scandinavia and in the United States.[4] Among the groups he surveyed in both areas, premarital intercourse had generally taken place sometime during adolescence. Among males between the ages of 16 and 21, 65 to 85 percent had experienced at least one coital act.

In a representative study of 400 18- and 19-year-old Danish men, Hertoft found that 32 percent had had intercourse before age 17; 31 percent had first experienced intercourse between ages 17 and 19; and 37 percent had still not had intercourse by age 19. Similar studies of Danish women are somewhat less reliable. Available statistics, however, indicate a slightly lower level of premarital activity, a slightly later start in sexual relations, and a smaller number of partners.[5] Thus, it seems a smaller number of very active women are available for a larger number of men. Prostitution does not seem to play a major role.

In a study of pregnant girls under 18 in Denmark, I found that only few could be considered to be free from mental or emotional pathology, and many appeared to come from noticeably disorganized environments. They represented a socio-medical pathology that does not generally apply to the rest of the population.[6]

Of Hertoft's 400 young men, 201 were going steady with a girl at the time of the interview. Of these couples, 138 had had intercourse—almost exclusively in the home of either the man or the girl. Also, 108 of the 138 characterized their relationship as "rather stable," regardless of whether they were formally engaged or just "going steady." Hertoft emphasizes the striking conservatism of the young men who had steady girls. Their life pattern is established and they anticipate staying with the same girl throughout life. Ninety percent of the 138 young men said that if their girl were to become pregnant, they would marry her and would not expect her to have an abortion.[4]

Thus, in a population where young people throughout childhood have opportunities to meet the opposite sex, some start sexual relations before or at about age 16, but by the age of 18, half the young people have had sexual relations. A limited exchange of partners takes place, but a fairly large proportion progress to a permanent relationship. The relationships are often not formalized, but engagements do occur. However, formalities do not seem to be required for family acceptance of sexual relationships. The mere fact that the partner has been presented to the family and has been received in the home seems to be enough. If pregnancy results, it will be followed by marriage in the overwhelming number of instances.

This pattern demonstrates that the existing norms are deeply rooted in Northern traditions. They cannot easily be transmitted into areas with a different historical and cultural background.

Sex Education

In 1961 the Danish government appointed a Committee on Sex Education. In its first report, in 1968, the Committee gave an account of present conditions.[7] It included the following findings:

—As in the rest of Europe, fertility has been decreasing in Denmark for the past 100 years. However, while fertility decreased among the older age groups, it increased in the younger groups. The age groups below 18, however, still contribute only very modestly to the fertility of the society as a whole.

—The age of marriage has been decreasing during the same period.

—Out-of-wedlock births decreased during the first half of this century, but have since increased slightly. Still they account for only 10 percent of all births. In this regard, Denmark does not differ markedly from other European countries. Today, approximately 50 percent of first-born children are conceived before their parents' marriage.

—Abortion figures have not changed much during the last 3 decades.

—Divorce is more common among marriages contracted early in life.

—Incidence of venereal disease increased in Denmark as in most other countries during the fifties, especially among the younger female population. Since then incidence decreased slightly through the years until the report appeared (1968).

Relevant Legislation

Since 1763, Danish children born out of wedlock have had legal claims on their fathers. Under Danish law, when a child is born out of wedlock, the doctor or the midwife is required to report the birth to the authorities, and this obligation is rarely evaded. If the father does not accept paternity, a lawsuit will usually ensue. If the father does not pay the mother directly, she will get an allowance from the State—which later will demand payment from the father. If no paternity is established, the State will pay the allowance. Originally there was concern that such provisions might lead to promiscuity. Such has not been the case.

The pregnancy laws are also significant. All women have a right to a certain number of free consultations with a doctor during pregnancy. They are also entitled to contraceptive services. If an unmarried woman voices anxiety at the beginning of pregnancy about her ability to bring up a child, the doctor is obligated to refer her to a Mother's Aid Institute. There her personal, social, and health conditions are examined to determine whether she needs help. If she insists on having an abortion, her case will be assessed by a board consisting of a gynecologist, a psychiatrist and a social worker. The board decides whether her case meets the legal requirements for an abortion. The law differentiates between medical, socio-medical, eugenic and ethical indications for abortion, one of which is rape. The present law was meant primarily for the relief of older women worn out by childbirth, but it is about to be liberalized to include purely social reasons.*

About 6000 legal abortions—or five per 1000 women—are performed each year. To keep the number down, the Mother's Aid Institutes make a great effort to teach women contraceptive techniques.

The History of Sex Education

Sex education in Denmark is not new. A series of sex education books were published in Denmark at the end of the 18th century. The books were based on Galen's teachings about liquids and were characterized by their stern warnings against masturbation. They were not, however, hostile to sexuality. They supported the Lutheran concept of cohabitation within marriage as useful and natural, but of unchastity before marriage as the Devil's work. During the first half of the 19th century, however, censorship was introduced, and the literature on sex disappeared. Later in the revolt against Victorianism, a move toward sexual freedom flared up in the general literature. Ibsen discussed free love and Strindberg the tyranny of the Victorian marriage. In the field of psychology the controversy over whether children should be told the "facts" began.

However, apart from the fact that some biology teachers dealt with reproduction, sex education in the schools got started only after World War I and then only on a small scale.

During the thirties, various government committees discussed the place of sex education in the schools. A committee preparing the first legislation on legal abortion considered the question of whether the government ought to support or arrange for the dissemination of medical information that would reduce unwanted pregnancies.[8] Although, in those crisis-ridden years, the birthrate was declining, a Danish "population committee" recommended that the schools provide sex education.

In 1945, the schools of Copenhagen issued a circular saying

---

* Autumn 1972: The government proposes free abortion.

that all pupils who had received no sex education before puberty ought to have the opportunity to attend two lectures on sex education before leaving school. In 1946 the Copenhagen school authorities inaugurated a program to provide sex education beginning in the first grade. The program included information about the differences between the sexes, the genital organs, intercourse, and conception. The existence of contraceptive devices was mentioned, but not in detail.

During the fifties, Danish abortion laws were amended and a new committee recommended that general sex education programs be established in all Danish schools.

In 1958 the Ministry of Education appointed a curriculum committee to discuss program content. This committee decided that information about reproduction should be a mandatory part of biology studies. Thus the biology of reproduction was separated from the subject of sex education. The schools were left to decide whether or not they wanted to include sex education in the curriculum. The individual teacher could decide whether he wanted to participate, and, furthermore, the parents had to consent to their child's participation.

In 1961 a government pamphlet, "Guidance on Sex Education in the Primary Schools," urged the schools to hold parent-teacher meetings as a means of explaining the aims of sex education. The pamphlet says:

> The education shall aim at forming the character of the children and contribute to harmonious development. Thus, the education ought not only to impart knowledge of the anatomy and the function of the sexual organs, but must be founded on an ethical basis and be as close to reality as possible according to the age level. At younger age levels the education consists of conversations on occasions when the children ask questions which lead to mentioning human reproduction in a natural way. At older age levels the teacher ought not confine himself only to lecturing, but should discuss sexual maturation and sexual responsibility with the pupils openmindedly and without prejudice. The individual school decides on whether boys and girls are to be co-edu-

cated. Information about puberty phenomena like menstruation, masturbation and homosexuality are included in this education. The aim is to further independence and personal responsibility.

About sexual intercourse the pamphlet states:

The school has to be a preserving factor in society and thus has to stress the fact that sexual intercourse belongs to marriage. Only in marriage can sex life find mentally ideal conditions, and marriage creates the best conditions for rearing children. This has to be emphasized, but in his education the teacher has also to recognize studies which demonstrate that most people begin their sex life before marriage.

About contraception it advises:

Since the abortion problem is so serious, the school must counsel youngsters on more than only responsibility. However, information on contraceptive measures normally ought to be undertaken by a physician. But, if the principal is agreed, a teacher might give the orientation.[9]

The guide counsels against prohibitions that will make sex terrifying to young people.

In 1960 the National Council of Danish Women and the Mother's Aid Institutes asked the Prime Minister to appoint a committee to investigate what could be done to ensure the population's getting sound information about sex. Such information, they said, should include contraceptive knowledge as well as a sense of responsibility in sex life. The request was motivated by what seemed to be an increasing number of unmarried, young— many very young—pregnant women who were applying to the Mother's Aid Institutes for support. Furthermore, the number of out-of-wedlock births was thought to be increasing, as were the number of arrivals of first-born before the ninth month of marriage. Unplanned pregnancies, it was thought, might be forcing many young people into ill-advised marriages. Reference was also made to increases in gonorrhea cases among girls aged 15 to 19 and in legal and illegal abortions.

The Committee on Sex Education

As a result of this request, a large committee, consisting of educators, physicians, theologians and administrators, was appointed to study the situation. The Committee issued two reports—one on sex education in primary schools[7] and another on sex education and guidance at higher levels.[10]

The Committee organized several field surveys to determine knowledge, behavior, and attitudes about sex in the Danish population. It found that in some respects conditions actually were not as bad as had been supposed. However, the number of abortions, legal and illegal, indicated that preventive measures were urgently needed.

Between 1965 and 1967, I personally noticed a sudden increase in interest in sex education. In 1965 I gave a couple of lectures to the primary schools which were televised through the Danish State TV system. In my lectures I spoke chiefly of the relationships between young adolescents and the ethical problem of mutual responsibility, but I also mentioned abortion legislation and showed contraceptive devices. The lectures were followed by question and answer periods with young adolescents. In a few months before the lectures were actually held, 87,000 signatures were collected protesting against the planned TV sex education program—one of the most extensive signature campaigns ever to take place in Denmark. However, the press took a positive view of the program and the following year the lectures, only slightly revised, were repeated. That year the Danish Gallup Institute found that 73 percent of parents with children between 10 and 15 years of age had their children watch the program. Since that time School-TV has been able to continue sex education with hardly a word of protest.

Books on Sex Education

During the past three decades a number of books on sex education, intended for different age groups, have been published in Denmark. The best known for young children "Peter and Caroline" by the psychologist couple, Inge and Sten Hegeler, has been widely distributed in several countries. It helps parents tell children the basic facts of reproduction. Additionally, a group of Swedish teachers has prepared a workbook about sex.

Books on sex education published in Denmark 20 to 30 years ago were rather cautious in mentioning premarital relations. With a characteristic moral tone, they tended to stress the emotional aspects of sex life at the expense of hard information. However, they all included chapters on contraception and abortion. The more recent publications are much less moralistic; they give more space to what might be called the technical aspects of sex life (for example, the technique of clitoris stimulation). A few use vulgar words. Recently, a young Danish psychiatrist published a book illustrated with photographs showing boys and girls masturbating and young people having intercourse in various positions.

Conclusions of the Committee

The report from the Committee on Sex Education concludes:

"It is considered inexcusable that young people are not supplied with exact knowledge of such a fundamental area of life. Deprived of such knowledge, the consequence is likely to be a sex life replete with anxiety and guilt. The young people must have an opportunity to feel that they themselves will be able to fulfill the expectations of a normal sex life. An early pregnancy might have serious consequences for the mother as well as for the child. In the same way a marriage contracted under unfavorable circumstances has a poor prognosis. For the young, the importance of family planning for a healthy and happy family life is invaluable. Our attention is drawn to the fact that children aged 10 to 15 get most of their information from peers, and such information is nearly always unsatisfying. Since they do get information anyway, it should be given by competent persons." (The Committee realizes that sex education does not solve all problems. Problems like early pregnancy, abortion and venereal disease are to a high degree related to certain social groups with complex problems which are not solved merely by information.) [7]

The report discusses why relatively few schools have so far begun sex education and concludes that the reason is simply that the subject is not mandatory. Apathy is abetted by the teachers' anxiety about not having sufficient training for the task, and their fear of parental reaction. Such anxiety and fear, however, could probably be overcome by making the subject mandatory and by introducing programs for sex instruction in teachers colleges and in-service training clinics.

The Committee proposes an integrated sex education program, one in which the subject matter would be taught not in special lessons but rather throughout the general curriculum, wherever it relates naturally to teaching. Human sexuality, the Committee points out, should be closely related to all aspects of human life. The present system of allowing parents the option of exempting their children from the sex education lessons in their schools would not be possible if the subject matter were integrated into other aspects of the curriculum. The Danish administration has proposed legislation to Parliament to require compulsory sex education in the schools according to the committee's recommendations.

Objectives of the Reform

Unfortunately, there has been no research on the effects of sex education. It has frequently been observed that children whose parents have pursued sex education energetically, perhaps imprudently, live a rather complicated sex life. It has also been observed that children who have grown up under secure and satisfying emotional conditions, but without any particular sex education, achieve a natural and harmonious sex life. Sex education, as such, is seemingly not the decisive factor in the quality of a child's future sex life. Sex education as carried out by parents might in some cases express balanced, openminded and confident relations between adults and youngsters; however, in others it might express incestuous family patterns or perhaps represent projections of the parents' own conflicts.

The Danish Sex Education Committee rejects the position that sex education is stimulating to young people. Its philosophy is based on the assumption that having received simple information, children will develop appropriate sexual behavior and attitudes. Of course, information is never plain information; it is always accompanied by value judgments. This was so even during the Enlightenment 200 years ago when the information given about the harmfulness of masturbation was based on Galen's teachings. Until recently in this century, sex education has been for the most part characterized by moral admonitions and vivid descriptions of the dangers of venereal infection or abortion.

Contraception has been a central theme in modern sex education. In today's overpopulated world this is to the interest of society since it is imperative to limit the birthrate, preferably not by abortion.

Some people who would reform sex mores talk of greater naturalness. When we consider that virtually every human being is civilized (that is, bound to a culture), such talk can only be considered an ideological slogan. The question is about reform of the sexual norms and not about reverting to "naturalness."

The contours of the new sex morality are still vague, but the following features can be observed: greater permissiveness in attitudes toward youth; equally polygamous standards for men and women, an equality made possible by contraception and greater access to abortion; and more uniform sexual experiences between men and women, with woman's orgasm ensured through an energetic teaching of the importance of the clitoris.

The objective of sex education in Denmark has clearly changed within the past decade. The first guide published by the Ministry of Education, in 1961, stressed the value of sex life for the individual's personal development. In Sweden, as well as in Denmark, the most advanced sex education literature for youth, published by responsible teachers, psychologists and psychiatrists, now have a slight tendency to be beginning textbooks on the art of love and erotic techniques.

Psychological Aspects of Sex Education

Man is a very flexible specimen, but he has an elasticity limit and will react with inner conflict and symptoms of psychological disturbance if these limits are strained. A society whose ideology is naturalness might be thought to be straining such limits. At varying times, different cultures have assigned man and woman either relatively uniform or very diverging roles. Today's pressure toward uniformity in the holy name of feminism might in fact be regarded as a push toward pseudo-feminism, for it brings pressure to bear on the woman to take on a role equal to the man in sexual behavior. This may be very convenient to the man, but perhaps it is not at all in accordance with fundamental qualities in the female psyche.

Perhaps the man-like clitoris orgasm, prominently acclaimed in sexual literature, is something obtainable by diligence. The definitive biological differences between the two sexes remains unknown.

The "information-only" way of approaching sex education is really an indirect attempt to influence attitudes. Parents, for example, influence their children's attitudes through their own attitudes toward sexually colored phenomena in the child's world, their way of reacting to questions, and the example they give in their own way of life.

Schools influence attitudes whether the information is given by the teacher immaturely, sentimentally, confidentially, or quite objectively—or with coarse or delicate humor. Many a mental rape has happened through a teacher's emotionally inappropriate way of teaching, as when the teacher projects his own problems on his pupils. On the other hand, a strict matter-of-fact manner of teaching might insult a sensitive child and be an expression of aggression on the part of the teacher.

The introduction of sex education in schools is often justified on the grounds that the school undertakes the subject only be-cause the parents neglect it. Interview investigations suggest that only a small proportion of children are given information at home, and that while these children regard the information they received as satisfactory, they still wish the school to take up the subject.[4]

The ideologists of sex education have been relatively uncon-cerned about the psychological levels at which information about sex influences attitudes and behavior. Although numerous inves-tigations have shown that most pupils are very familiar with the facts about sexuality (at least second-hand), the general consensus seems to be that the more sex education the better. Thus "intellec-tual ripening" becomes the program's only *raison d'être*.

As early as 1907, in his article about the sex education of chil-dren, Freud adapted himself to the rationalistic idea of enlight-enment. However, in 1937 he elaborated his views in the following way:

> It is far from me to maintain that this information is detri-mental or superfluous, but obviously the preventive effect of the liberal enlightenment has been exaggerated to a high degree. The children now know something about what they did not know before, but they do not make use of the new knowledge they have been given. Quite obviously they are not ready so soon to sacrifice the natural sexual theories, so to speak, which they have developed in accordance with, and in dependence on, their imperfect libido organization. In-cluded are theories about the part of the stork, about the nature of the sexual cohabitance and the way children arrive. Even a long time after they have received their sex education, they behave like the primitive people who have been forced to Christianity but secretly continue to worship their former gods.[11]

The Danish psychoanalyst, Vanggard, has gone further in a recent interview, expressing preference for the myth about the stork to detailed explanations about the parents' sexual relation-ship, which might accentuate the perhaps already difficult con-flicts of the child.[12] The scientific explanation about the egg and the sperm cell also might seem to be a myth to the child, the truth of which the child has neither the possibility nor the wish to investigate. A more confident relationship might develop between child and parents, however, if the parents tell the myth that they themselves believe that the child does not have to give up later on.

In an examination of all the educational measures that through the years have followed psychoanalysis, Anna Freud writes that many were disappointing or inconsistent—though some were consistent and for the children's good. She maintains that an analytically oriented upbringing brings greater openness and confidence between parents and children regarding sexual relationships. She also reports, however, an unexpected finding that even the most well-meant and plainly formulated sex information cannot be accepted by small children; instead, they cling to fantasies derived from their own world of experience. Much of their own sexual theory translates adult genital sexuality as a form of cruelty or mutilation.[13]

Let me point out some of the problems that might appear when the inner reality of a child is confronted with an outer objective reality. It is, of course, a fact that parents by their attitudes throughout the oral and anal phases of child development greatly influence the future sex life of the child. Oral frustration makes serious complications for a future partner cooperation. Anal over-control might be the starting point of a serious potency disturbance. But it is important to recognize that in the pregenital stage of development the child's own sexual equipment is immature and that the child has to translate what he is told about sex into something that fits his infantile theories. Many parents who give their children sex education find that the child "forgets" what he was told and is equally surprised each time the same story is repeated to him. In the Oedipal period, however, parents are faced with the necessity of answering numerous questions about the origin of babies, along with problems arising from the inquisitiveness of children toward the naked body.

Studies of primitive peoples as well as clinical experiences seem to indicate that nakedness within a family is not necessarily a part of an incestuous pattern. The incestuous pattern is a more complicated phenomenon in which nakedness might play a part. To determine the effects of nakedness in the family on a child or adolescent, one has to consider the customs of the culture or subculture to which the child belongs. Therefore a clear yes or no answer cannot be given to the question of whether nakedness has a place in sex education.

About the Oedipal period, Ruth Iversen, a Danish psychologist, writes:

> If we consider that in the Oedipal period the child strongly experiences rejection, we can see that the child perhaps has a greater need of its parents' permitted love—in the shape of support and help in developing interests, managing the intellectual functions, mastering motoric functions in play and sports or artistic display, than he has a need for the elaboration of the incestuous binding which takes place when genital sexuality is discussed. To have to give up an object of love is in itself a hard and painful process. And to this might be added the control the children (who at the same time grieve over the fact that the love-object is unattainable) have to perform toward hateful feelings, wishes for their rivals to die, etc.[14]

The child in the latency period, as well as the child in the Oedipal stage, still has the possibility of solving his problems on an imaginary level.

At these developmental stages children are able to contain both violent and prohibited thinking, and at the same time to be open, social and interested in obtaining exact knowledge and social information. The individual child's "mental economy" varies greatly, however, and the sex education in schools ought to pay attention to this. A common opinion has been that sex education in the schools ought to be given during the period of puberty. In fact, during the latency period the child is, in many respects, better able to accept a large amount of sex information. During latency the child can accept in a matter-of-fact way teachings about biological propagation, contraceptive techniques, and the social aspects of sex.

Teachers and parents are often confronted with dangerous misconceptions about sex presented in the form of sober questions. The misconceptions should be corrected before the child enters the chaotic period of puberty. However, teachers should not energetically force the child to accept facts about sex for which the child is not psychologically prepared. It is not mathematics the child is learning. Sex facts should be offered as pieces of concrete information that the child may accept or leave depending on his individual readiness.

During puberty the most serious problems regarding sex education occur. On the one hand, the child has developed a new emotional life giving him a basis for a deeper understanding of the content of sex education. On the other hand, in this period some children must cope with grave inner conflicts and the pressures exerted by the adult world.

When sex education is given in a school, it should be presented as an offer of objective information and not as a compulsory subject. During early puberty, anatomy and physiology are emotionally loaded subjects. The teacher must be cautious. Sex education at this level must deal with the main problems of puberty and thus help adolescents attain a sense of identity, reality-orientation and social skills. The basis of discussion preferably should be the ethical and social relationships between the two sexes during youth—rather than "sexology," which should serve only as background information.

The type of integrated sex education envisioned for the Danish primary schools is intended to be presented in a lenient and meaningful manner with a view of preparing young people for a sexually integrated life.

REFERENCES

1. BROENDSTED, J.: *The Vikings.* London, Pelican Book, Penguin Books, 1960.
2. TROELS-LUND: *Dagligt Liv i Norden* (Daily Life in the North) Vol. IX-X an XI-XII, Gyldendal publ., Copenhagen, 1903.

3. HANSEN, G.: *Saedelighedsforhold blandt Landbefolkningen i Danmark i det 18. Aarhundrede*. (Morality in the Danish Rural Population in the 18th Century), Det danske forlag publ., Copenhagen, 1957.
4. HERTOFT, P.: *Unge maends seksuelle adfaerd, viden og holdning* (Sexual Behaviour, Knowledge and Attitude of Young Men). (English Summary), Akademisk forlag publ., Copenhagen, 1968.
5. AUKEN, K.: *Undersoegelser over unge Kvinders sexuelle Adfaerd* (Investigations on the Sexual Behaviour of Young Women). Copenhagen, Rosenkilde and Bagger publ., 1953.
6. HOFFMEYER, H.: The Psychological Background of Pregnancies in Puberty and Adolescence. *Acta Psychiat. Scand.* 1965, suppl. 180 (ad vol. 40, 1964).
7. *Seksualundervisning i Folkeskolen* (Sexual Education in the Primary School), Ministeriel betaenkning (Danish Government Report), No. 484, Copenhagen 1968.
8. *Lovligheden af Svangerskabsafbrydelse m.v.* (Lawfulness of Pregnancy-Interruption et cetera). Ministeriel betaenkning (Danish Government Report). Copenhagen, 1936, p. 104.
9. *Vejledning i seksualundervisning i folkeskolen* (Guidance for the Sexual Education in the Primary School), Ministry of Education, Copenhagen, 1961.
10. *Seksualundervisning udenfor folkeskolen og individuel vejledning m.v.* (Sexual Education Outside the Primary School and Individual Guidance et cetera), Ministeriel betaenkning (Danish Government Report), No. 532, Copenhagen, 1969.
11. FREUD, S.: *Zur sexuellen Aufklärung der Kinder*. Gesammelte Werke Vil, Imago Publ. Comp., London, 1941, p. 26.
12. VANGGÅRD, T.: *Historien om storken var ikke så dårlig* (The Story About the Stork Was Not So Bad), Vi foraeldre (We Parents), No. 4, Oslo, 1968.
13. FREUD, A.: *Normality and Pathology in Childhood*. New York, Int. Univ. Press, Inc., 1965, p. 3.
14. IVERSEN, R.: *Nogle betragtningern om sexualoplysning til børn* (Some Reflections on Sexual Education of Children). Duplicated Copenhagen, 1969.

21

Changing Trends, Attitudes, and Values on Premarital Sexual Behavior in the United States

IRA L. REISS
Professor of Sociology and Director
Family Study Center, University of Minnesota

THE PAST: MYTH AND REALITY

ONE OF OUR MOST PREVALENT MYTHS is that in past centuries the typical form of courtship was that of two virgins meeting, falling in love, and doing very little with each other sexually. They then married, learned about sex together in the marital bed, and remained faithful to each other until death separated them. I am certain that some couples did have exactly that type of experience and I would go even further and grant that this happens in some cases today. But the key point is that I am sure it was never the common pattern for the majority of Americans. The evidence for this exists in large part in historical records. We know, for example, that in Massachusetts at a well-known church in the last part of the eighteenth century one in every three women who married confessed fornication to her minister. The major reason for making such a confession usually was that the woman was pregnant and if she did not make such confession at her marriage, the baby could not be baptized. Many other girls who were nonvirginal but not pregnant would likely not confess fornication to their minister. This was the time of bundling in New England and many ministers blamed the high premarital pregnancy rates on that custom. It is probable that much of the pregnancy occurred after engagement. Engagements in those days were seldom broken and thus were more akin to actual marriage. In any case it seems clear that at the time of the formal marriage the sexual innocence of many couples was questionable.

The Double Standard

If we look at male nonvirginity, the picture becomes even more extreme. Certainly the history of the western frontier was not one of male virginity. In fact it was quite the contrary. The western frontier was settled largely by males and this male-dominated society had a heavy reliance on prostitution. The term "red light district" comes from the custom of girls in prostitution houses leaving a red lantern in the window so that the cowboys riding into town would know "where the action was." "Gunsmoke" notwithstanding, dance hall girls did more than dance. In the typical case the upstairs rooms were where the girls would entice the customers to take them and then collect a suitable fee for the sexual services rendered.

To further show the mythical quality of our view of the past, let us briefly look back at the 1870s and the women's liberation movement of that time. In New York City we find Victoria Claflin and her sister, "Tennessee," setting up a brokerage business as well as other ventures, including a weekly newspaper. Commodore Vanderbilt took to them favorably and helped considerably in getting them established. Victoria was a left-wing-feminist who favored free love. She believed that a woman should live with a man if she loved him and leave him when she no longer loved him. She practiced what she preached and had more than one man living with her in New York City. The more conservative feminists like Harriet Beecher Stowe and Catherine Beecher attacked Victoria regularly and Victoria was annoyed by their statements. The brother of the Beecher sisters, the Reverend Henry Ward Beecher, lived in New York and was one of America's most famous ministers. Victoria tried to persuade the Reverend Beecher to prevail on his sisters to be less critical but to no avail. Finally, she learned that while she was having an affair with a Mr. Tilton, Mrs. Tilton was having an affair with the Reverend Beecher. She threatened to reveal the adultery in her weekly newspaper if the Beecher girls were not quieted. Either due to inability or lack of effort, the Reverend Beecher did not succeed in quieting his sisters' criticisms of Victoria. True to her word, Victoria publicized the adulterous affair of the Reverend Beecher and Mrs. Tilton in her weekly newspaper on November 2, 1872. Adultery was against the law and a trial ensued. The character of the age was revealed in the outcome of the trial. During the events that followed, the Reverend Beecher was acquitted by a hung jury of the charge of adultery and Mrs. Tilton was charged by a church committee of "indefensible conduct" with the Reverend Beecher. The Beecher-Tilton scandal displayed the nineteenth century's orthodox double standard with its granting of greater sexual privileges to males.

Another example that illustrates the sexual orientation of the nineteenth century is afforded by the Philadelphia World's Fair of 1876. The aspect of that fair that echoed around the country was the display of the first vulcanized rubber condom for males. Previous to that time condoms were made out of animal skins and a vulcanized rubber condom was a notable advance. But in a culture that was largely practicing abstinence, this contraceptive advance would hardly have received so much notice. However, in a society where prostitution was rampant and where people were concerned with avoiding venereal disease and unwanted pregnancy, such an advance was important. About this same time the diaphragm and the pessary cap were invented. A few decades later, knowledge of these contraceptive techniques had spread widely among the wealthier and better educated classes and created an impact of major importance on their sexual behavior.

I have examined the historical and cross-cultural record rather closely and have found no society, at any time in history, in which the majority of even one generation of its males remained virginal on reaching maturity—say age twenty or so. The reason is very likely that since males are in power in almost all societies, it is unlikely that they would structure that societal system so as to deny themselves access to sexual pleasures before marriage.

The major changes in premarital sexual behavior throughout history have been in the partners of men. Such partners have at times come from groups such as slaves, prostitutes, lower-class females, or the girl next door. The basic shift in the partners of men in the twentieth century is toward a majority of the women and away from small select groups.

General Trends

According to our best information, the majority of American women have been entering marriage nonvirginal for at least the past fifty years. Kinsey's findings indicated that about half the women born in the 1900-1910 decade were nonvirginal at marriage.[1] This proportion rose only slightly until the late 1960s, but since then it seems to have risen rapidly. In the fifty years from World War I to the late 1960s, the predominant change was not in the proportion of women nonvirginal but rather in the attitudes of women and men toward premarital sexuality. During the first half of this century, guilt feelings were reduced, the public discussion of sex increased radically, probably the number of partners increased, and the closeness to marriage required for coitus to be acceptable decreased. For males, other changes were occurring. Males were becoming more discriminate; they were beginning to feel that sex with someone they felt affection for, person-centered sex, was much to be preferred to body-centered coitus. The male partners were shifting from the prostitute and the lower-class female to the girl next door. One of the most dramatic decreases that has been in evidence throughout the twentieth century is the rapid decline in the proportion of males,

particularly college-educated males, who have experienced intercourse with a prostitute.

The basic change, then, in premarital sexual ethics during the
past centuries has been from an orthodox double standard that
allowed males to copulate but condemned their partners as "bad"
women, to a more modified version of the double standard allowing women to have premarital coitus, but not quite with the
abandon of men. Of course, this is an oversimplification. Among
the almost 210 million Americans, there are many variations in
standards. There are those who are fully equalitarian in a permissive direction and those who are equalitarian in the restrictive
direction, and those who still have the orthodox double standard.
But the overall shift is toward less dominance of the sexual scene
by males. This by no means indicates full equality of the sexes,
but rather a lessening of inequality.

Full equality in the sexual sphere is not possible today given
the different priorities in roles between males and females. In
agreement with the Women's Liberation movement, it seems sociologically well established that if females think that getting
married and starting a family is their first priority in life and
place occupational ambitions secondary to this, then they will
view sex in terms of these goals. This means that they will consider whether copulating with a boy will waste time in their search
for a mate; whether this boy will tell others what happened and
thus hurt their chances of getting married; whether having intercourse will make a boy more or less seriously committed to marriage, and so forth. These concerns are nowhere near as important
to a male, for he is not so strongly oriented toward marriage as
his primary life goal. In the middle class, the male's primary goal
will be an occupational career, and having premarital intercourse
is not very likely to matter one way or the other in relation to
that goal. Surely men today are oriented toward marriage, but
the immediate pressures felt by such a goal are considerably less
than those felt by females. A male is not that concerned with the
time wasted in an affair, nor is he so worried about the effect of
the word of an affair getting around. In fact, among many women

news of such an affair might enhance his image as an exciting date or a romantic interest.

The Role of Contraception

One of the key factors that encouraged the sexual liberalization of women, particularly in the middle and upper classes, was the contraceptive revolution of the late nineteenth century. Nearly a hundred years ago the vulcanized rubber condom, the pessary cap, and the diaphragm appeared on the scene. To be sure these devices were known and used predominantly by the upper 20 or 30 percent of the population. There had long been contraceptive methods available, from the biblical method of "withdrawal" to Casanova's method of placing a hollowed out lemon rind over the cervix. What was new about the late nineteenth-century methods was that they were very effective in preventing pregnancy and they occurred at a time when there was a large group of well-off people with a strong demand for such techniques.

Ever since Priscilla told John to speak for himself, the American courtship system has been to a very high degree run by the participants in it and not directly controlled by parents. By the late nineteenth century this meant that because of the size and complexity of the new urban centers and the fact that even in 1890 almost 4 million women were working, parents could not possibly know the people their children were dating. This autonomy of dating coupled with the high risk taking and the pleasure emphasis that youth culture has always exhibited meant that the desire for sexual pleasures would be strong. Being alone with an attractive person of the opposite sex for several hours on a date exposed one to high temptation. Yet the upper- and middle-class groups in this country were considerably concerned about having legitimate children. Thus, sexual desires were present, but so was the inhibitory influence of a desire to avoid having illegitimate offspring. In the late nineteenth century the development of very effective contraceptive methods that would avoid pregnancy afforded a way out of the dilemma. By the time of the first World

War, condoms were available in a variety of places and their usefulness was widely known. The better-off male could use them and have intercourse with relative safety from venereal disease and also with the comfort of knowing that he was unlikely to impregnate his partner. This meant that he would be more likely to feel free to copulate with the girl next door. Females, too, became aware that males could avoid impregnating them and this must have had an important impact on their sexual orientation. Married women were the main users of diaphragms, but the knowledge that males could prevent pregnancy with condoms and that females too had available methods lessened the view of pregnancy as an uncontrollable consequence.

Many people believe that the availability of the contraceptive pill, starting about 1960, has had a major impact on sexual beliefs and behavior. I think this case has been oversold. In the past the condom and diaphragm did affect the sexual habits of the middle and upper classes. This was so because these classes previously had no highly effective contraceptive techniques readily available. The doubling of the female nonvirginity rates around World War I was partially a result of this force. Of course, diversity in norms, changes in religious controls, and urban-industrial development also were important variables contributing to the growth of the new permissiveness.

The introduction of the pill in the 1960s was something very different from the introduction of the condom in the 1870s. In the 1960s there already were highly effective contraceptive techniques and the pill was simply another highly effective technique. It is easy to overestimate the pill's effectiveness. It does require a rather routinized, organized, person for it to work. The pill must be taken each day for twenty days a month and any lapses can lead to pregnancy. Also, there are side effects, mostly minor ones such as weight gain and temporary nausea and such, but they too may lead to preference for other methods. Finally, when the pill is used the male will not use a condom, and this radically increases the risk of venereal disease for both the male and the female. I am saying all this not to belittle the pill technique but rather to place it in perspective. It is a valuable method of contraception, but has its limitations as do all human inventions.

More important than its effectiveness is the fact that the pill places the control of contraception in the hands of the female. Furthermore, it does this in a way that allows the act to occur spontaneously since the pill does not have to be taken at the time of the act of coitus. For some women the thought of being constantly ready for coitus is not acceptable. They want to be carried away by romantic feelings of the moment, and they want the male to be the aggressor and for the male to plan to be ready for coitus. Without the pill, this attitude leads to a high risk of pregnancy.

A second result of the contraceptive control being up to the woman is that she comes to value sexuality much more highly than before. Her risks of conception are reduced and her abilities to enjoy the physical aspects of sex and view herself as a sexual creature are increased. This contributes to an increasing similarity between men's and women's views of sexuality. Women today are more likely than before to value sex for its own sake and men are more likely to value sex with affection. The sexes still differ in that women are more oriented to affectionate sexuality and men more to body-centered sexuality, but each sex has increasingly learned to appreciate the major orientation of the other. In sum, the importance of the pill, in my mind, is not that it is so effective contraceptively but that it places the burden of contraception on the female and therefore forces her to think about her own sexuality.

The Legitimacy of Choice

Probably the major characteristic of current attitudes toward the premarital sex scene is the felt legitimacy of the sexual choice. More than any other characteristic this one epitomizes what has changed in the last half century. Whether or not to engage in premarital sex is no longer a choice made secretively with a great sense of guilt if the choice is not abstinence. There is still an element of privacy and often still an element of psychological qualms, but the degree of change is vast. Males have always talked openly with other males about certain aspects of their sexual lives, and this continues. However, there is change here, too, in that more males seem willing to admit they have difficulties sexually, in their thinking as well as in their behavior. The mask of the naturalness of sex for males is increasingly being put aside. Furthermore, the affectionate affair is being protected by privacy except from close friends. Here then is a change for males in the area of sexual communication. Conversely, females do talk more about their affairs, although most fully with their close friends.

I have visited dozens of campuses during the past few years on speaking engagements and over and over have been impressed with the openness of communication about sex on the part of college girls. Very intimate details are kept for close friends, but many other aspects of sex, such as attitudes toward premarital coitus, acceptability of oral techniques, and such, are increasingly discussed. I recall one coed telling about the naïveté of one of her sorority sisters who was soon to be married and was unaware of the very common role of mouth-genital sex in marriage. The coed looked on her friend as being very poorly informed and lacking in experience.

The choice of how to think and behave sexually is now accepted as an important choice for young people to make, and they are seriously exploring the full range of possibilities in their conversations with their friends of both sexes. True, many parents today do not accept the legitimacy of such sexual choices and believe that only abstinence is the proper path. But the majority of young people believe the choice is legitimately theirs in sex as it is in politics, religion, and other personal areas of their existence.

Generation versus Role Changes

The basic change in premarital sex is not, however, a generational one. During the early 1960s I studied several samples of high school students, college students, and one national sample that was chosen to represent the nation. The results of this study were published in my 1967 book, *The Social Context of Premarital Sexual Permissiveness.*[2] One of our most interesting findings was that the difference between 55-year-olds and 25-year-olds was not very dramatic. However, the differences between people of the same age who were single, married without children, or married and parents of dating-age children were indeed dramatic. For example, 45-year-old bachelors were highly acceptant of premarital intercourse, whereas 45-year-old married people without children or with little children were much less acceptant, and 45-year-old married people with teen-age or older children were the least acceptant of premarital intercourse. People of the same age are of the same generation and yet their differences are much greater than people who are of different ages and generations. Thus it is the specific role we play that is most important in how we feel about premarital sexuality.

Persons who have themselves participated in premarital coitus may change and become less permissive as they move into the parental role. The reasons for this are not hard to find. The parent does not experience the pleasures of sex that his teen-age or 20-year-old child is undergoing, nor is he exposed to the temptations of being with an attractive person of the opposite sex on a date. In addition, the parent is held responsible by the community if his daughter becomes pregnant or his son contracts venereal disease. We found that even older siblings were low on sexual permissiveness compared with their younger siblings. As older siblings they were put into parentlike supervisory roles. Thus the roles an individual plays in society play a major part in determining his level of acceptance of premarital activity. It follows then that there are 45-year-old bachelors who are more sexually liberated than some 20-year-olds. Young people are not all involved in the new changes in sexuality, nor are older people excluded from such changes.

The forces that promote premarital permissiveness on the part of young people in their courtship roles are also not hard to understand. If we were to invite a sociologist from another country to visit our country and examine our courtship system and tell us what he thinks it accomplishes sexually and how it operates, what would he say? He would note that the average young person dates for approximately ten years and that at least during the last five years of that period, the typical pattern of dating involves (1) the use of some sort of drug such as alcohol or pot, (2) the occurrence of dancing with movements that are clearly genital and sexual in meaning, and (3) a period of time at the end of each date when the couple is supposed to be allowed privacy. That privacy is very often supplied by the young person's parents. The living room of the girl is a very common place for the last hour of a date to take place. It is also the most common place for a girl to start having intercourse. Her parents are upstairs usually "trusting her to behave properly." It is not typical for parents to spy on their youngsters and try to catch them copulating. Parents also teach that love is a key justification for behavior and that being self-reliant is important. Such values tend to help one accept premarital coitus.

Our foreign sociologist would surely note that this system is well organized to promote sexual intimacies between young people. I feel sure that if we presented him with the figures showing the majority of females and almost all males do enter marriage nonvirginally, his amazement would not be that the figures are so high but, on the contrary, that they are so low. The question that needs answering is not why do so many people have premarital intercourse—that can easily be understood by examining our type of courtship; the key question is why do so *few* people have premarital intercourse. How does anyone go through years of such an intimacy-promoting type of courtship institution and avoid having intercourse? The answer to this question resides in good measure in the basic emphasis by females, and increasingly also by males, on person-centered coitus. Such an emphasis, by stressing the value of close ties to another person, puts limits on casual coitus and imposes difficulties in locating proper sex partners. This is especially true for females. Males are still more body centered and therein lies part of the "battle of the sexes."

In a very fundamental sense, all Americans, regardless of age, are involved in the changes that are occurring in our sexual orientations. How could it be otherwise? Parents of the young people who are engaging in premarital sex cannot ignore the greater openness of discussion of sex, because much of it occurs right in the home. Also, parents themselves are encouraged by sex education courses in the public schools, by courses in adult education, by articles in the popular press, by the mass media, and in many other ways to think more carefully and fully about the meaning of sex. This is not simply a youth rebellion, it is a cultural change rooted in our rapid movement toward a post-industrial society. Further, the stress on examination of premarital sexuality leads to an examination of marital and extramarital sexuality as well. The stress on variety in marital sexuality and the examination of the conditions under which "swinging" or old-fashioned secretive adultery may be acceptable are highly visible phenomena in the lives of millions of people in the over-30 generation. In part this spread of sexual dialogue derives from the fact that when the same young people who have examined their sexuality premaritally do marry, they tend to carry over this rational, examining approach. I find many couples today who are working out agreements on extramarital sex before they marry. Many of these agreements are the conventional ones of being faithful, but others are agreements about under what conditions extramarital sex of various types would be allowed.

Today's "situational ethics" stresses the importance of the particular person and his circumstances. We are becoming more and more aware of the fact that standards may differ and yet be equally "correct" for different persons in different situations. In this view of ethics, absolutes can only hold for all those of a certain type in a certain situation and not for all mankind regardless. Thus everyone must find out who he is and what his situation or life style consists of. Because the stress of our civilization today is increasingly on self-realization, personal fulfillment, and happiness, situational ethics is a very compatible philosophy in allowing for a self-designed ethical system. Large segments of Americans at all age levels are involved in this search for self-discovery and for a more personally designed life style. I am sure that America will still have shared patterns of life styles and will not atomize into over 200 million different life styles. But I am equally sure that the variety of tolerated life styles has increased at all age levels.

Social Class Differences in Sexuality

One other important area of change that was discovered in my national research during the 1960s concerns social class differences in premarital sexual attitudes. It has long been believed that the lower classes were most permissive in both attitude and behavior, and that the upper or college-educated group was the least permissive of the social classes. There is good historical evidence to support this proposition. But sometime during the twentieth century, probably about the time World War II was ending, this situation was no longer so true. When we took our national sample in 1963 and examined it for the expected relation between social class and premarital sexual permissiveness, we found no relationship at all. We also looked at four college samples and two high school samples and found no relationship between social class and level of premarital permissiveness. After very elaborate computer checks, we discovered, in relation to sexual orientation at least, there were two radically different social class systems. We divided our sample into thirds and labeled each third either "lower," "middle," or "upper" class. If among all the respondents we looked only at conservative people—that is, people who were conservative in politics, education, and religion—then we would indeed find that the lower-class people in this conservative group were the most permissive. However, if we look only at liberal people—that is, liberal in politics, education, and religion—then we find that the lower-class people are the least permissive and the upper-class (college-educated) people are the most permissive.

Thus there are two opposite types of people in each social class level.

The aspect of this situation that is new is the presence of a highly permissive group among the upper third of the social class hierarchy. This group, I believe, has emerged gradually but became noticeable only during the past twenty-five years or less. It includes members of the largest growing occupational groups —professionals and managers. It was among the professionals, particularly, that highly permissive individuals were found. This group, I would argue, has been most influenced by the contraceptive revolution begun with the introduction of the rubber condom at the Philadelphia World's Fair of 1876. They have the highest educational level, the highest incomes, and the greatest amount of time to think about things other than food, clothing, and shelter. I believe that the possibility of avoiding consequences like pregnancy and venereal disease has led them increasingly to be sexually permissive. For a long time many professional people have been politically, educationally, and religiously liberal. The possibility of controlling negative consequences of sex has led to their also becoming sexually liberal. There are, of course, professionals who are rather low on permissiveness, but compared to other groups who fall into the top one-third of our status hierarchy, the professional group contains a relatively larger proportion of persons who are highly permissive sexually.

This growth of a permissive upper class is a very important occurrence, because if the leaders of this country are permissive in the area of sex, some more liberal legislation in this area should be forthcoming. We have already seen some radical changes in the past five years in abortion laws, contraceptive distribution, and censorship decisions. I believe this trend will continue because of the influence of this powerful professional group. The new sexual orientation is exactly what would be expected from a college-educated group in that it emphasizes control of pregnancy and venereal disease and stresses person-centered sexual encounters. In short, it differs from the older, lower-class permissiveness which was based on economic reasons and a fatalistic philosophy.

THE NEXT DECADES: THE LIKELY OUTCOMES

What can we say about the future during the balance of this century? First, let us examine the notions of some people that full sexual equality is coming and males and females will be identically oriented to sex. The worth of such an outcome is not the issue, merely its likelihood. We have already noted a trend toward greater similarity in sexual orientation between males and females. That trend is shown even more specifically by the results of one of the studies done by Gunter Schmidt and his colleagues at the University of Hamburg concerning the impact of pornography.[3]

Using volunteers for subjects, Schmidt measured both the verbal response and the physiological response of men and women to pornographic materials. The males' verbal responses agreed with the physiological responses and both sources showed arousal from seeing the pornographic materials. The women's verbal responses indicated that they were more likely to be "shocked, irritated, or disgusted." However, their physiological responses were very similar to those of the men! Thus it seems that cultural training inhibits women from full conscious enjoyment of the erotic materials. I am assuming that there was little cover up by the women and that, despite their erotic physiological response, they at times also responded with feelings of distaste owing to their training as females in a double-standard society. The level of similarity and yet the clear difference between men and women in the Schmidt study make my point precisely. Clearly, there are strong areas of similarity between males and females, but equally clearly there are still vast areas of difference. The next few decades should reduce these differences, but since they are rooted in the primacy women give to the home, they are not likely to vanish fully.

Possible Limits on Feminist Goals

Alice Rossi and other feminists have suggested that what is needed is perhaps to have 20-hour work weeks for interested people; every husband and wife would work 20 hours a week and spend another 20 hours per week taking care of the home.[4] There are obvious difficulties in restructuring occupations to a 20-hour work week, but the more serious difficulties lie elsewhere. The male group most favorable to this type of proposal consists of the professional and managerial people. We have seen that this group is highly permissive sexually and also liberal in other respects. However, it is precisely within this group that the strongest commitment to career lies and the strongest interest and enjoyment in work exist. Thus it is precisely those men who most accept sexual equality in occupation and home who are often too devoted to their own work to make this sort of change.

Lower down the social class hierarchy we note more patriarchal traditions and more opposition to male-female equality. It should be noted, too, that at these lower levels the interest in work outside the home on the part of women also often decreases. The type of work that blue-collar wives can do is not nearly as challenging or interesting as that available to white-collar wives. Such blue-collar work would involve being a lathe operator, driving a truck, putting fenders on automobiles, and so on. The wealthier woman has ambitions for the professional, managerial, and technical jobs that offer more in money, prestige, and intellectual rewards. Thus there are built-in blocks to any total change-over to a 20-hour work week and a 20-hour home week.

What the feminists will accomplish will be to open up options such as the 20-hour work week for couples who can make a go of it. This in itself will be a major change and an important opportunity to those women who want to escape the full-time housewife role. However, I expect most women will still predominate in the home in the year 2000. Finally, although equality will increase over the next few decades, I expect males will still predominate in most high-prestige occupations, although not to the extent they do today. If I am correct, then there will be greater equalization between the sexes in general and in their view of sexuality, but there will still be recognizable differences.

Physiological Differences

It should be clear that there is no physiological barrier to sexual equality. The data we have from the Kinsey studies[1, 5] and also from the Masters and Johnson studies[6] show clearly that there are more women who can achieve multiple orgasms than there are men and that some female rates of orgasm are far beyond what any male can hope to achieve. The lack of representative samples is not a serious matter in this conclusion, for we are certain that no group of males exists that can achieve orgasm every few seconds over and over again as many females do. The high-performing male is capable of about six or seven orgasms an hour and the few cases that exceed this do not even approach the extreme end of the female orgasm curve. If one were to venture a conclusion, the most probable one would be that women's orgasmic ability is greater on both ends of the curve; that is, more women fall in both the nonorgasmic category and the multiple orgasmic category. Males are more clustered toward the center. Although it is entirely possible that females who are nonorgasmic could be psychologically trained to be orgasmic, it is not very likely that males could ever be trained to be as capable of multiple orgasms as are some females. Thus, overall, the advantage, orgasmically, would seem to go to the female.

Now, of course, there is more to sex than orgasms. It could still be true that males have some advantage in the ease with which they develop erotic imagery. Kinsey felt the male cortex afforded such an advantage. As a sociologist, I would tend to posit learning as the key factor in determining the sexes' different ability to "turn on," but we cannot be sure at this point. The most important conclusion to draw here is that we know that whatever innate differences exist between the sexes, we can bring up males and females to be relatively equal in their sexual orientation. The evidence for this comes from cross-cultural studies that report societies in which the sexes are relatively equal in their desire for coitus. Also, we know that even within our own society vast differences exist between female groups and these differences would seem to be based on training and experience. In my book I report on a comparison of samples of females from California and New York. Twice the percentage of females in California accepted premarital coitus as did those in New York.[2] I assume that California girls are no different physiologically but rather that something in their life style is different.

Trends in Nonvirginity

What about some of the newer trends? For example, what is likely to be the proportion premaritally nonvirginal of females and males in the remaining decades of this century? First, we should note that the proportion of nonvirginal males has been about 85 to 90 percent for generations and thus there is little room for change here. Nevertheless, there is change going on in respect to attitudes and in the type of partners with whom males have coitus. In the case of females, there was an increase in the World War I period from about 25 percent to about 50 percent nonvirginal by the time of marriage. There has been no indication of any change in this proportion except during the period from the late 1960s to date. During this recent period, reports of studies showing 30 or 40 percent of the 20-year-old college girls nonvirginal have appeared. The Kinsey data from the 1940s showed only 20 percent of the 20-year-old college girls nonvirginal. These data are not conclusive evidence of a sharp increase in female nonvirginity. For example, if such an increase were occurring, we would expect to see some evidence of the female sexuality in an increase in the number of sex partners women have and in the percentage of women who masturbate and the frequency of masturbation. Few such changes have been reported. Thus it is possible that college girls today are copulating earlier than they used to and thereby as a group are reaching the peak percentage of 50 percent nonvirginal before marriage sooner and that they will not exceed that percent. Unless we were to follow a college sample through marriage, it would be hard to draw definite conclusions.

College girls do have a greater likelihood of marrying today than they had in the 1940s, and much of a female's coital performance is related to being in love and engaged. Therefore, it may be that there is more reported coitus among college girls partly because more of them are in the serious courtship process that leads to marriage during their college years. However, the studies by Bell and Christensen and others[7, 8] are so consistent regarding increases in nonvirginity that it is hard to believe that their findings are not valid. Also, if 40 percent of the 20-year-olds are nonvirginal, it is difficult to conclude that by marriage the rate will be only 50 percent. Finally, Bell does find that his more recent sample of coeds had more sex partners per individual and required less affection than his older 1958 sample.[7]

In 1960 I published a book entitled, *Premarital Sexual Standards in America* in which I attempted to sum up what the research evidence told us about sexual orientation in America.[9] I predicted then that by the end of the 1960s we would witness a noticeable rise in the percentage of nonvirginal females. It seemed to me that behavior and attitude were coming into balance around 1960 and, according to my interpretation of the evidence, that usually meant that behavior would then move forward again. Until recently I have held to the belief that the expected increase in nonvirginity had not yet occurred. But the data that are coming in are so consistent in their findings of higher nonvirginity rates at specified ages that I am now willing to assert that the change predicted has occurred and that the actual premarital nonvirginity rate is now probably close to 70 percent for females.

The 1970s, I believe, will be to the last few decades of this century what the 1920s were to the decades of the first half of this century. More specifically, this decade will set the pace for the next few decades and afford clear outlines of the emerging life style. In the decade preceding the 1920s, the older sexual orientations were attacked from a variety of perspectives. A new urban-industrial life style was then emerging and the developing liberal attitudes toward divorce, sex, and women had taken hold and were to evolve gradually during the next 40 years. Then in the 1960s the same process of rapid change that occurred before 1920 was again present. Many alternative approaches to sex and the family were put forth, including suggestions regarding abortion, life-long unions, living together, "swinging," and female sexual orientations. What we are witnessing now is the culmination of the exploration of new life styles. The sixties spelled out many of the new possibilities and the seventies will lead to choices and priorities that will define these alternatives and their estimated worth in a way that will likely last a few decades.

Living Together

Situational ethics has made us aware of the variety of choices that may be viewed as legitimate and has moved us away from the view that only one choice is legitimate. The key characteristic of the seventies will be the awareness and toleration of a larger variety of alternative life styles. For example, living together has recently become a much more noticeable and popular custom on college campuses. Some people have reacted to this custom by viewing it as the death knell of marriage. That view is mistaken on two grounds. First, marriage need not be a legal contract. Indeed, most societies in the world lack a legal system and thus could not have legal marriage. Marriage can be celebrated by a meal together as in the Trobrian Islands, by requesting a common room in some Israeli Kibbutzim, or by an elaborate church wedding as in some segments of American society.

If a new custom of marriage came into America in the form of couples living together, that could still be considered marriage. The test of whether a custom symbolizes marriage is whether the custom sanctions parenthood. If living together were accepted as a way for two people to become parents, then it would indeed be a new marriage custom. From the data I have seen from Michael Johnson[10] and others, it appears that, as a general rule, living together on American campuses is not a substitute for marriage because most of the couples involved do not want children and are careful to avoid them. Most of these couples, however, seem to plan on a legal marriage someday—a marriage that is to take place when they do want children. They seem to be living together as part of a code of honesty and openness in sexual behavior. They regard it as hypocritical to try to cover up a sexual affair by taking the girl home from a boy's apartment. Why not live together and acknowledge that a sexual affair is occurring? For such people living together is simply a new form of courtship and not at all a substitute for marriage.

I expect living together to become more popular as a courtship form, for we seem to be continuing in our greater openness regarding sex. I doubt if it will extend to the sanctioning of children in such arrangements. Our type of society with its inheritance laws, social security laws, and other laws is far too complex to encourage parenthood without a legal ceremony. On the other hand, living together before legal marriage as a form of courtship or preparenthood relationship may have the advantage of avoiding the possible need for divorce in early marriage.

Experimentation in Sex

Actually, a proper perspective from which to view living together is to regard it as one of many developments in the current emphasis on experimentation. We can see evidence of this in the use of drugs "just to see what it is like." We see it in the area of sex in the reduced occurrence of quick self-labeling. For example, people are less likely to label themselves as homosexuals because of one homosexual experience or as loose women because of one affair. Today young people seem to have more of a "shoppers'" attitude toward their sexual lives. They know they will experiment with different kinds of sexual relationships, but they also know that they need not continue any kind of sexuality that they find not to their liking. They reduce thereby the stigma of one type of sexual encounter and increase the importance of experimenting in order to find which sexual life style suits them best. The prevalence of young couples living together without marriage is one outcome of such a philosophy. Other outcomes are the increased openness of the Gay Liberation Movement and the increased attempt at getting societal legitimation for homosexuality. Cases are now in the courts to allow two homosexuals to marry. The economic advantage to homosexuals of such an arrangement is but one motivation for such legal action. My own feeling is that the main motivation is to gain approval in a legal and social sense for homosexuality by public acceptance of the marriage of homosexuals. Homosexuality is thus another one of the avenues that young people may experiment with. However, the vast majority of young people who have a homosexual experience develop into persons who strongly prefer heterosexuality. The homosexual experimentation for most of these young people is simply a phase in their search for sexual identity.

We can be easily misled into thinking that experimentation with all possible varieties of human sexuality is very widespread in our society. Such a view would be a serious error. Most people in any society have very limited and restricted areas that they feel are open to rational examination. In our society, technological areas are open to rational examination, for they are viewed as instrumental to important goals. Areas of life that embody society's basic values are most often not examined. For example, ordinarily the worth of mothering infants is not questioned. Even women's liberation groups usually discuss this topic in terms of who will do the mothering and not *if* mothering of newborn infants is important.

More is now open to questioning in the area of sex than formerly. It is now legitimate in the minds of young people to decide if they want to have premarital intercourse. But note what a small range of alternatives is actually being explored.

The debate in America centers heavily on whether premarital sex, with or without affection, is worth seeking and under what conditions. Incest, rape, pedophilia, and voyeurism are rather minor or rarely discussed segments of the debate. For most people even homosexuality enters into the dialogue as peripheral—something to be tolerated, perhaps, but not as something at the heart of their sexual identity. Homosexuality, however, does enter into the dialogue on sex in America more than any other so-called deviant form of sex but, for most people, it is still not one of the central issues.

In short, then, we have opened up premarital sexuality for public debate, experimentation, and moral examination to a much greater extent than any previous generation in America. But in terms of the possible areas that such a debate could consider, it is still a rather narrow dialogue. Nevertheless, in order to keep our perspective it is important to add that most European countries have not opened up their debate on sex even to the extent that we have.

Control of the Consequences of Sex

One issue that has been central in the new openness regarding human sexuality is that of abortion. Since the late 1960s, the amount of legal change in abortion legislation has been remarkable. However, while the amount of change is unusual for a society such as ours, it is not extreme in any logical sense, for, after all, only 16 states have changed their abortion laws and in many of these 16 the change is not to the point of allowing "abortion on demand." It is likely that such changes will continue, although I doubt if all states in the union will have open abortion laws as does New York State. However, enough states will have such laws so that the single or married woman who wants an abortion (and it most often is a married woman) will be able to have it with much greater ease than ever before. For college girls, who generally can afford the abortion fee, this means an added feeling of control over the consequences of premarital coitus. Like the pill, the liberalization of abortion laws puts the control of sexuality more in the hands of females and thereby helps the female in the development of her own sense of sexuality. Women are no longer so likely to regard sex as something that happens to them and over which they have little control. They now have control over their own sexuality and its consequences to a degree unmatched in Western history. This situation will continue in the remaining decades of the twentieth century.

A qualification is in order here. The changes I have noted should not lead to the view that young people today are always clear-thinking people who carefully reason out their sexual identities. A recent experience of mine may help achieve perspective. A short time ago I visited one of our major universities to participate in a colloquium on sexuality. During my stay there, one of the male students told me of a recent sexual experience. He had been dating a coed for about a month and they liked each other a great deal. One night they both got drunk and went up to his room and had sexual intercourse. He felt certain that she would never have done this unless she was on the pill and she felt certain that he would never have done this unless he used a condom. They continued to copulate for about five weeks more until they realized that the girl was pregnant. Only then did the fact come out that she was not on the pill and he was not using a condom. I asked him why he never spoke to her about contraceptive measures and he replied that he felt that it was too personal to be discussed. This incident reveals how sexual intimacies may well occur before other levels of self-revelation have taken place. Further, it illustrates the nonrational, emotional aspect of human behavior in the sexual realm. We should not expect knowledge of how to avoid unwanted consequences such as pregnancy to guarantee that such knowledge will be properly utilized. The above case illustrates the fallibility of humans.

This case also illustrates the potentiality of sex to interfere with the full development of a love relationship. Love relationships involve high levels of self-revelation. Clearly, sex is one level of revelation that is present in courtship relations; but we are still learning how to keep the sexual revelation from blocking other areas of revelation. Many people in love have found out how to do this but many others have failed. Males, for example, may focus their energies on "scoring" and not bother to try to get to know the other potential rewards of a particular relationship. Females may stress their sexual attractions to the point where they fail to develop or present other aspects of themselves. Or as in the case cited, carelessness regarding pregnancy may make an otherwise developing relationship undergo a crisis that may lead to its termination. In many ways sex can act as a block to the growth of a relationship and this can be the case whether the couple is kissing or copulating. This is not an argument against copulation—it is a statement of the fit of any type of sex in a relationship. Many couples seem able to place sex in perspective and develop other aspects of their relationship, and some couples can do this by having intercourse and thereby relieving that tension, whereas others are able to do it by sexual behavior short of coitus. The point I am making is that this generation seems to value honesty, complete relationships, and "telling it like it is," and such open relationships can best be achieved if we know how to keep sex from interfering with that growth and, equally important, how to utilize sex to help in developing a complete relationship.

One indication of our "hang up" regarding sexuality is our "touch inhibition." Our preoccupation with sex is such that when a male touches a female our immediate thought is that such contact implies a sexual advance made by the male. This type of orientation to touch means that many people cannot harmlessly release sexual tension by, say, putting their arm around a person. This further implies that we may well have people who feel they ought to go further once they start to touch because they define touching as a sexual advance preliminary to full sexual relations. Carolyn Symonds and others have set up encounter groups in which couples are taught how to touch each other without any necessary implication that coitus will follow.[11] My observation of young people today is that they are more accepting of touching than were previous generations, and I expect this acceptance to grow during the next few decades. Such a natural attitude toward sexually related activities increases the ability to utilize sex to help develop a relationship rather than allowing it to be a preoccupation.

CONCLUSIONS

We are entering a new historical phase. We are entering into the post-industrial society just as around World War I we had clearly entered into the modern phase of the industrial society. Note that this entry into the modern type of industrial society occurred in conjunction with a major war. The same sort of situation prevails today. The Viet Nam War has been a major factor in the change to a post-industrial society. As a very unpopular war it has caused us to bring into question much of the political, religious, economic, and educational systems that support the war.

The Post-Industrial Society and Sex

However, the basic forces moving us toward a post-industrial society were present before the war. By post-industrial society, I mean a society in which the industrial output is no longer problematic and thus the means of increasing productivity becomes secondary to questions concerning equity in distribution of wealth and power and concern with the quality of our life style. Certainly, the high level of affluence of the past thirty years has been a major factor in this change.

When most people have no real problem in obtaining food, clothing, and shelter, and even many of the luxuries, then the stage is set for them to devote their energies to issues concerning the quality of life in our type of society. It is no accident that the leaders of the post-industrial life style are the children of upper middle-class parents. We have discussed before how these upper middle-class parents are often permissive sexually and liberal in general. They are the leaders in the change to a post-industrial society for they are the most involved in the affluence that makes this change possible.

Our sexual customs are changing in accord with the emphasis in the post-industrial society on the quality of human relationships rather than on material things. We can most often avoid, if we are careful, the unwanted consequences of sex such as pregnancy and venereal disease and thus we cannot use them as final reasons for our sexual decisions. We must delve deeper into the sexual relationship and decide whether we feel that our personality growth and that of our partner will be helped or hindered by having a sexual relationship of one sort or another. We can examine the potential effect of the relationship upon ourselves and the others who are involved. It is just such an examination that has led to the popularity of situational ethics, for it is abundantly clear that for some people having premarital coitus would contribute to the development of responsibility, the ability to relate to people, a sense of integrity, and self-realization; for other people having premarital coitus might lead to an exactly opposite set of consequences. As Alex Comfort, a British physician, put it a few years ago, this is the first generation that Western society has called upon to make a truly moral, intelligent choice of sexual life styles.[12] Other generations were spared the choice by virtue of the social straitjackets they were wearing.

Mental Health and Choice

The question arises regarding the effect on mental health in the next few decades of today's orientation toward premarital sexuality. What will be the rewards and the costs? These questions are, of course, difficult to answer in any general way. However, it seems that we can already discern a different type of cost. Psychiatrists report that whereas generations ago people used to seek help because they could not get started sexually, today more and more people seek help because they cannot stop sexually. The fact that the individual now has the responsibility for determining the specific controls of his sexual life style means that outside societal support is not as ever-present or so narrow as it once was, particularly for females.

I believe that in a very few years there will be a noticeable increase in the *closure* we reach on sexual questions.[13] The 1960s opened up the doors on a wide range of possibilities. The early 1970s are going to reach closure on many of the issues raised by this wider range of possible sex behavior. We will have learned to live with a greater range of choice and we will learn more about the consequences of the new choices confronting us. Let me illustrate by discussing hard-core pornographic movies. For those who have not seen pornographic movies before, such an experience may be sexually exciting. Nevertheless, I would expect that most college-educated youngsters would soon tire of the heavy genital focus of such material. I expect more movies to be made that involve explicit scenes of sexual intercourse but that focus on a plot concerning human relationships rather than on the genital aspect of the sex act. Let me add, however, that the increased freedom of choice also implies that despite the trend toward person-centered sex, there will remain a visible amount of body-centered sex. Such body-centered sex is part of the experimentation process and for some people it is a preferred life style.[14]

The new sexual morality offers a variety of forms of sexual expression and individualizes choices and this should be a mental health advantage. The older sexual morality was a procrustean bed.[15] If an individual did not fit, the society did not offer alternatives but rather tried to cut the individual down to size. The key advantage of the new sexual morality is also its key disadvantage, namely, the increased possibility of choice. The advantages of choice are obvious—a person can choose a sexual life style more suited to himself. The disadvantages of greater freedom of choice is that we run the risk of choosing "fools' gold." In short, we may choose some course of action that yields temporary satisfaction but in the longer run destroys more valuable aspects of our life style. For example, we may choose to have a weekend with a sexually attractive person we just met and thereby alienate a person we love. Freedom of choice imposes the responsibility for restraint on the individual. The social restraints must be minimized for the freedom to be more than a facade, and this means that the possibility for individual error must be accepted.

In some areas the evidence on which way to choose is far from in. For example, there are proposals that young people be encouraged to live in mixed sex communes for a year or so before settling down. Such communal living could be a rite of passage into the adult society; it would provide a supportive communal group but one without very narrow structures of relationships and thus it would allow for experimentation to help in personal development. I am not making such a proposal but rather suggesting it as one of the many doors that the 1960s opened and that the experience of the next few years will help clarify.

Another recent proposal is for parents to teach erotic behavior to their children—to teach them as they grow up how to derive erotic satisfactions from their own bodies through masturbation. Proponents of this suggestion believe that just as parents have a responsibility for the spiritual development and intellectual development of their children, they also have a responsibility for their erotic development. Most people I have heard discuss this proposal have been opposed to it. Part of the opposition may derive from incestuous taboos, part from fear of "too much" erotic arousal or "too much" body-centered sexuality. I feel certain in predicting that this proposal will be acceptable to far fewer people than the "temporary commune" proposal. It is the present developing consensus on evaluation and ranking of various sexual possibilities that makes me predict that the 1970s will witness *closure* on many of these issues and the forming of more socially shared conclusions.

Summation

We are witnessing the growth of a new, integrated post-industrial type of sexuality. The key characteristics of the current sexual life styles are the emphasis on personal choice and the greater tolerance for experimentation. More than at any other time in our history we now tolerate a variety of sexual life styles. We are far too varied and large a nation ever to expect to find one life style best suited to all people. Thus this development toward tolerance of alternative life styles is functional for our society.

Tolerance of alternatives does not mean acceptance of all alternatives, nor even acceptance of all alternatives as equally good. Some life styles will still be viewed as beyond the pale and some as not to be preferred, but there will also be a variety of accepted life styles.

An examination of alternatives need not weaken our belief in our own ultimate convictions. It can, by the knowledge and understanding it gives, afford us a firmer basis upon which to find ourselves. We shall all be increasingly more aware of this aspect of our post-industrial society as the years tick away in the remaining decades of the twentieth century. As the young people today become parents, we will witness the typical change toward less tolerance of risk taking that occurs as people become parents. But I believe there will be less of this sort of parent-child gap than ever before. This should be so because this generation has gone on record as supporting the legitimacy of choice in the area of sex. I believe that we shall soon see they not only have made such choices themselves but they will allow the same privileges to their children to a greater extent than has any previous generation.

REFERENCES

1. KINSEY, A. C., POMEROY, W. B., MARTIN, C. E., & GEBHARD, P. H.: *Sexual Behavior in the Human Female.* Philadelphia, Saunders, 1953.
2. REISS, I. L.: *The Social Context of Premarital Sexual Permissiveness.* New York, Holt, Rinehart and Winston, 1967.
3. SCHMIDT, G. & VOLKMAR, S.: Sex differences in responses to psychosexual stimulation by films and slides. *J. of Sex Res.,* 6:268-283, November, 1970.
4. ROSSI, A. S.: Sex equality: The beginnings of ideology. In Thompson, Mary Lou (Ed.): *Voices of the New Feminism.* Boston, Beacon Press, 1971, pp. 59-74.
5. KINSEY, A. C., POMEROY, W. B., & MARTIN, C. E.: *Sexual Behavior in the Human Male.* Philadelphia, Saunders, 1948.
6. MASTERS, W. H. & JOHNSON, V. E.: *Human Sexual Response.* Boston, Little, Brown, 1966.
7. BELL, R. R. & CHASKES, J. B.: Premarital sexual experience among coeds: 1958-1968. *J. of Mar. and the Fam.,* 32:81-84, February, 1970.
8. CHRISTENSEN, H. T. & GREGG, C.: Changing sex norms in America and Scandinavia. *J. of Mar. and the Fam.,* 32:616-627, November, 1970.
9. REISS, I. L.: *Premarital Sexual Standards in America.* New York, Macmillan-Free Press, 1960.
10. JOHNSON, M. P.: Courtship and commitment; A study of cohabitation on a University Campus. Master's Thesis, Unpublished, University of Iowa, 1969.

11. SYMONDS, C.: A nude touchy-feely group. *J. of Sex Res.*, 7:126-132, May, 1971.
12. COMFORT, A.: *The Anxiety Makers*. London, Nelson, 1967.
13. REISS, I. L.: *The Family System in America*. New York, Holt, Rinehart and Winston, Inc., 1971.
14. CUBER, J. F. & HARROFF, P.: *The Significant Americans*. New York, Appleton, Century, Croft, 1965.
15. ULLERSTRAM, L.: *The Erotic Minorities*. New York, Grove Press, 1966.

22

Premarital Sexual Experience and Postmarital Sexual Behavior

ROBERT ATHANASIOU

and

RICHARD SARKIN

The Johns Hopkins University

IT IS DIFFICULT, if not impossible, to assess accurately changes in sexual behavior over time. Sample biases, reporting biases, and questionnaire difficulties make virtually all data suspect. Some remarkable uniformities in the data collected from unrelated studies, however, suggest that it is not impossible to make good guesses about changes in sexual behavior and to predict the course of sexual adjustment for specified groups of people.

Several recent studies converge on a number of findings that confirm the hypotheses that the age of first intercourse is decreasing and that the partner in first intercourse is less and less likely to be chosen for marriage.[1-5] Moreover, the studies indicate not only that the older norms of abstinence and double standard have been rejected by large numbers of people but also that attitudes and behavior are in greater congruence now than they have been at any time in the last quarter century.

These changes do not imply that we are lost in what one writer has called a "sexual wilderness,"[6] but rather that we have entered a period of ethical pluralism and that new patterns of behavior are the natural outcome of the application of new types of normative systems.

TABLE 1

PARTNER IN FIRST INTERCOURSE AS RELATED TO STANDARDS FOR PREMARITAL SEX

WHAT IS YOUR OPINION ABOUT PREMARITAL SEXUAL INTERCOURSE?

PARTNER IN FIRST INTERCOURSE

	SPOUSE AFTER MARRIAGE %	FIANCE %	STEADY DATE %	OCCASIONAL DATE PARTNER %	TOTAL %	(#)
1. It is all right for both young people and adults.	12.5	16.8	39.1	31.5	100	(184)
2. It is all right for consenting adults.	24.4	17.5	30.4	26.6	100	(217)
3. It is all right for couples who share affection.	16.3	19.3	40.0	24.5	100	(135)
4. It is all right for couples who are in love.	19.8	29.1	33.7	17.5	100	(85)
5. It is all right for couples who are engaged.	33.3	51.9	14.8	0.0	100	(27)
6. It is wrong...should wait until married.	63.9	9.6	16.9	9.6	100	(83)
(N)	(177)	(142)	(239)	(174)		(732)

The data in Table 1 reveal the present pluralism in sex ethics as expressed in both attitudes and behavior regarding first intercourse. It is interesting to note at this point that a very substantial proportion of respondents who felt that premarital sex was wrong, waited until after marriage for their first coital experience. Similarly, most respondents who felt that coital activity was suitable for engaged couples had their first coital experience with their fiancé.

The dashed enclosures along the diagonal in Table 1 indicate those points where attitudes and behavior correspond. For the most part, the highest percentages in each row are those at these "congruence points." Respondents whose behavior and attitudes correspond, as indicated at these congruence points, are following a particular sex ethic. Respondents whose attitudes and behavior diverge from these points of congruence are reporting belief in one system of behavior and following another.

What are the implications of this pluralism of premarital sex ethics for postmarital sexual adjustment? Numerous studies have indicated that marriage tends to be rated as more successful when premarital chastity has been maintained.[7-9] Shope and Broderick state, "There has been consistent evidence over the years of a positive relationship between premarital sexual conservatism and successful marriage, although the relationship is not of very high magnitude." They suggest that the existence of the low positive correlation might be due to *intervening variables.*[7]

Reiss has suggested that this relationship may be explained by *extraneous variables:*

> It may be that part of the reason people who have had premarital coitus also engage in extramarital coitus is that they are more liberal; when they fall out of love with their mates, they are more likely to commit adultery before obtaining a divorce. Thus, lack of conservatism may explain some of this behavior.[10]

Reiss is referring here to political liberalism. Data from many studies, particularly those carried out by the National Commission on Obscenity and Pornography,[11] have shown, however, that political, economic, religious, and sexual liberalism are all highly correlated.

The several hypotheses dealing with the low positive relationship between premarital chastity and postmarital fidelity were formed during a period when more people were reporting premarital sexual activity than "approved" of it. It is open to question whether this heretofore reliable correlation between premarital chastity and postmarital fidelity will still exist in a social system that is now in greater equilibrium.

It is a simple matter, with the data on hand, to examine this relationship and explore its implications under new normative systems.

Rosenberg[12] has indicated how one may use survey research methods to approximate experimental design in the analysis of data. In particular, he states that, "The systematic investigation of extraneous variables . . . enables a survey correlation to approximate to some degree the experimental-control group matching of the after-only experimental design."

It is beyond the scope of this paper to consider Rosenberg's entire thesis, but it may be helpful to diagram the differences between intervening and extraneous variables. Figure 1 indicates

FIGURE 1

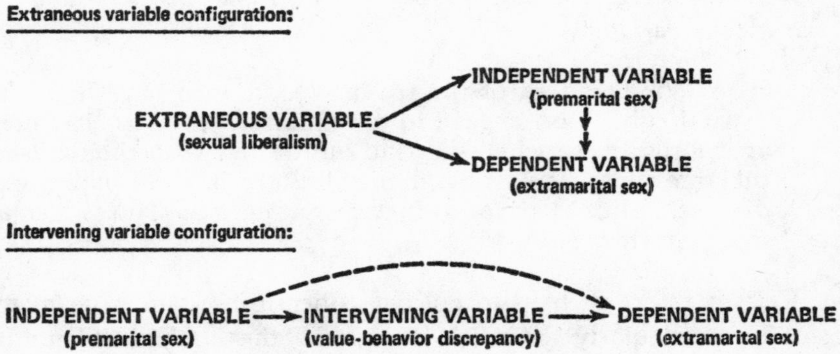

how this may be done for both types of variables with arrows indicating the probable or hypothesized direction of causality. The broken arrow indicates the observed statistical relationship which is presumed to be "not real," that is, to be *caused* by the extraneous or intervening variable.

Rosenberg's approach, while conceptually and logically tighter, is very similar to that of path analysis or causal inference.[13] If a variable in question—a test factor—is an extraneous or intervening variable, then the relationship between the dependent and independent variable will disappear when the test factor is controlled.

One should expect, therefore, that if the set of relationships proposed by Reiss were controlled for degree of liberalism, the statistical association between premarital coitus and extramarital coitus would disappear.

Christensen and others have suggested that premarital chastity as a standard is more likely than other standards to reveal a congruence or discrepancy between values and behavior.[14] That is, if one believes in premarital chastity *and* practices it, then his (or her) values and behavior are congruent. If, on the other hand, one "believes" in premarital chastity and engages in premarital sex, then his (or her) values are discrepant with his behavior.

In discussing this point at length, Christensen has concluded that there are likely to be negative consequences when informal behavioral norms (practices) differ from formal societal norms. He states:

> The functionality or dysfunctionality of *American sex practices* must be seen against *American sex norms,* and unless the latter have been liberalizing as rapidly as the former, there will be an *increase* of strains (dysfunctions) within the personalities and the relationships involved. . . . It could be, for example, that the increasing rates of personal and marital disorganization of recent decades are due in part to an enlarging of sex freedom in the face of a lagging sex ethic.[1]

In this paper we will report on a study to investigate the alternative hypotheses suggested by Reiss and by Christensen[14] and others. Specifically, we have used extraneous variables such as romanticism, sexual liberalism, and attitudes toward separating love and sex in analyzing the relationship between premarital sex experiences and postmarital sex. Additionally, we have examined the possibility that value-behavior discrepancy is an intervening variable between pre- and postmarital sexual behavior.

It was expected that support would not be found for the extraneous variable hypothesis—that even when controlled for "sexual liberalism" the results would still show a low positive relationship between premarital chastity and postmarital adjustment. On the other hand, however, as Christensen has suggested,[14] one would expect that when controlled for value-behavior discrepancy the results would show a reduction in the correlation between pre- and postmarital sexual behavior.

Method

The data for this study represent a 1 in 10 random sample of the responses of 20,000 adults (from a potential population of 250,000) to a sex questionnaire.[15] The questionnaire included a series of items to reveal degrees of romantic, liberal, and conservative sexual attitudes, and an extensive section on demographic variables. The last section of the 100-item questionnaire dealt with types and frequency of sexual behavior.

The sampling accuracy with which the 1 in 10 sample of 20,000 respondents was drawn was better than ± 3% against a conservatively estimated occurrence rate of 50% at the 99% confidence level. This subset of 1,992 respondents was further reduced when all single, widowed and divorced people (and those few who failed to answer the marital status question) were eliminated for the present analysis. A total of 821 currently married respondents remained in the data pool. Eighty-six percent had been married only once, while 11 percent had been married twice and the remaining 3 percent had been married 3 or more times.

The number of respondents for any item, or in any given table in which two items are cross tabulated, will vary according to the number of respondents who actually answered the item or items. This variation is not at all unusual in survey studies when respondents may write in uncodable answers, have no opinion, skip a question, or otherwise end up in missing data code categories.

Although relationships among many of the variables in this total data pool have been found to hold for the general population (see *The Report of the National Commission on Obscenity and Pornography*[11]), this subsample is not representative of the population at large. It is overweighted with persons of higher than average educational attainment: 46.3 percent had done some graduate work after college and another 45.6 percent were either college graduates or had done some college work, making a total of 91.9 percent who had college experience. Similarly, the weighting was toward higher than average income: 37.5 percent had incomes of over $15,000 a year; and another 32.9 percent between $10,000 and $15,000. How far the findings on sexual behavior apply to the population at large is, therefore, open to question.

In this study all the data concerning premarital behavior are retrospective. It is not clear, therefore, whether the attitudes expressed by the respondents are indicative of their premarital behavior, postmarital recall of premarital behavior, or both. The analysis of these data, then, must be viewed for their heuristic rather than deterministic value. Retrospective data are poor substitutes for carefully designed non-reactive longitudinal studies.

Table 2 lists the dependent, independent, and test factor variables used in this study with the percent responses for each category of each item. The items are numbered according to their sequence in the original questionnaire.[15]

The test factor variables, "romanticism" and "liberalism," used in the data analysis in subsequent tables are summative ratings of 8 and 16 items rated on 6-point Likert-type attitude scales constructed on an *a priori* basis. The scale scores were then

TABLE 2

RESPONSE DISTRIBUTION FOR INDEPENDENT,
DEPENDENT AND CONTROL VARIABLES

Independent Variables:

Question	Percent
Q70. With whom was your first intercourse? (N=740)	
1. Spouse after marriage	24.2
2. Fiancé	19.3
3. Steady date	32.8
4. Occasional date or casual acquaintance	23.6
	99.9

Question	Percent
Q71. After the first time, how many times did you have sexual intercourse with that person again? (N=783)	
1. Not again	17.6
2. Once more to 4 times	14.4
3. Four to 10 times	28.6
4. More than 10 times and still having intercourse	39.4
	100.0

Question	Percent
Q72. With how many persons have you had premarital sexual intercourse? (N=816)	
1. None	19.4
2. One	25.7
3. Two-Three	19.7
4. Four-Six	15.2
5. Seven or More	20.0
	100.0

Dependent Variables:

Question	Percent
Q66. Overall, how do you rate your marriage? (N=809)	
1. Very happy	38.0
2. Happier than average	33.6
3. Average	14.6
4. Somewhat unhappy to very unhappy	13.8
	100.0

Question	Percent
Q73. With how many different persons have you had extramarital intercourse? (N=810)	
1. None	60.0
2. One to three	23.6
3. More than four	16.4
	100.0

Question	Percent
Q76. Have you participated in mate-swapping? (N=792)	
1. At least once or twice	6.1
2. Not ever, but I might	29.9
3. Never; would never consider it	64.0
	100.0

Control Variables (Test Factors):

Question	Percent
Q1. How closely do you think love and sex are linked? (N=819)	
1. Sex and love are independent	4.4
2. Love . . . enriches sex but is not necessary	74.0
3. Sexual intercourse without love is not enjoyable	10.5
4. Sexual intercourse should be reserved for expression of serious love	11.1
	100.0

Question	Percent
Q4. If you have engaged in premarital sexual intercourse, how do you feel about it now? (N=631)	
1., 2. Very regretful to somewhat regretful	14.8
3. No feelings	17.5
4. Somewhat glad	27.8
5. Very glad	39.9
	100.0

broken into quartiles based on the entire distribution of responses. These scales have been discussed in considerable detail elsewhere[4] and appear to be adequately constructed for validity and internal homogeneity.

A value-behavior discrepancy index was constructed from the data paradigm illustrated in Table 1. If a respondent indicated that he believed premarital sex was wrong *and* did, in fact, have his first intercourse with his spouse after marriage, he received a score of "0" on the discrepancy index. Respondents whose behavior deviated from their expressed value received a liberal or conservative deviation score different from "0."

Table 3 shows the statistical associations between the independent, dependent and test factor variables prior to applying any controls. All the "correlations" are gamma (γ) statistics and represent proportional reductions in error. The statistics should be read, "knowing how respondents A and B are ranked on one variable allows us to reduce the error in predicting their ranking on another variable by γ x 100 percent."

To control for the effect of test factors, the independent-dependent correlation was examined within each category of the test factor responses. To obtain a single measure of association for the "controlled" relationship, the weighted average of the separate proportional-reduction-in-error (P.R.E.) measures (γ) was calculated and tested for significance by accumulating the Chi-squares and degrees of freedom for each test factor category. These procedures have been described in detail by Blalock.[16] The use and choice of appropriate P.R.E. measures is described by Costner.[17]

A recent article by Curtis[18] has emphasized the necessity for detailed consideration of measures on statistical association.[18] While γ is an excellent P.R.E. measure with a straightforward and conceptually meaningful interpretation in terms of probabilities, its sampling distribution is not well known. For this reason, we have used the Chi-square test to evaluate a departure from randomness and γ to indicate the degree of monotonicity present as well as the reduction in error when predicting one ordinal variable from

TABLE 3

Association Statistics (γ) for Independent, Dependent and Control Variables

Independent Variables	Q66. How do you rate your marriage? 1 = very happy 4 = very unhappy	Dependent Variables Q73. Number of extramarital partners? 0 = none 3 = 4 or more	Q76. Have you participated in mate swapping? 1 = frequently 3 = never
Q70. With whom was your first intercourse? 1 = spouse after marriage 4 = casual acquaintance	.043	.18	−.30
Q71. How many times with that person again? 1 = not again 4 = 10 times and still having intercourse	−.07	−.16	.22
Q72. With how many persons have you had premarital intercourse? 1 = none 5 = 7 or more	.07	.26	−.28
Control Variables			
Quartile of *a priori* Romanticism. Scale: 1 = low 4 = high	−.31	−.20	.23
Quartile of *a priori* Sexual Liberalism-Conservatism. Scale: 1 = low 4 = high	−.03	.25	−.33
Q1. How closely do you think love and sex are linked? 1 = independent 4 = reserved for serious love	−.11	−.44	.67
Q4. If you had premarital sex, how do you feel about it now? 1 = very regretful 5 = very glad	−.19	−.03	−.23

another. Statistics such as Pearson's C or λ would, perhaps, have yielded higher absolute values than γ, but would not be sensitive to the monotonic character of the relationships under consideration and would not have the conceptual relationship to the square of the correlation coefficient which γ has. Further information on the use of γ may be found in Hays,[19] Goodman and Kruskall,[20] and Curtis.[18]

Results

Table 3 contains the association statistics for various types of extramarital and premarital behavior with the extraneous variable controls of "liberalism," "romanticism," "association of love and sex," and "regret of premarital sexual experience." These data combine responses from both men and women. The relationships among the variables listed in Table 3 were examined for men and women separately and no substantial differences in the size or direction of statistical relationships were found.

It is obvious that before partialing out the control variables, the low positive relationships between premarital chastity and postmarital adjustment found in other studies appear in these data as well. The lowest independent-dependent relationship is that in which partialing out the variable "partner of first inttr-course" gives a 4.3 percent reduction in the error of predicting how respondents rated their marriage. In the case of the mate-swapping variable, rather substantial reductions in error of 22 to 30 percent are shown.

As required by Rosenberg's paradigm, the control variables, or test factors,[12] also show adequate relationships with the dependent variables.

The data in Table 4 show that there is little or no effect on the dependent-independent variable relationships when the test factors are partialed out. In general, then, the hypothesis that the relationship among measures of premarital chastity and postmarital adjustment are the result of extraneous variables is not acceptable.

TABLE 4

DEPENDENT AND INDEPENDENT VARIABLE ASSOCIATION STATISTICS WITH EXTRANEOUS VARIABLES PARTIALED OUT

Dependent Variable	Independent Variable	γ Without Extraneous Variable Partialed Out	γ With Romanticism Controlled	γ With Liberalism Controlled	γ With Love and Sex Linked Controlled (Q1)	γ With Premarital Sex Regret Controlled (Q4)
Q66. Overall, how do you rate your marriage?	Q70. First partner*	.04	.02	.04	.03	.13
	Q71. Times**	—.07	—.09	—.07	—.06	—.05
	Q72. Partners***	.07	—.02	.07	.05	.17
Q73. With how many different persons have you had extramarital intercourse?	Q70. First partner*	.18	.17	.14	.12	.15
	Q71. Times**	—.16	—.16	—.15	—.14	—.11
	Q72. Partners***	.26	.26	21	21	25
Q76. Have you participated in mate-swapping?	Q70. First partner*	—.30	—.12	—.28	—.22	—.22
	Q71. Times**	.22	.23	.23	.22	.14
	Q72. Partners***	—.28	—.27	—.24	—.20	—.14

* Partner of first intercourse.
** How many times with that person again.
*** Number of premarital partners.

There are, however, two notable exceptions among the 36 relationships. The measure of romanticism does seem to account for about half the power of the variable "partner of first intercourse" to predict mate-swapping intentions. Regret over premarital sex seems similarly to reduce the relationship between the number of premarital partners and mate-swapping intentions.

In the cases where controlling for regret over premarital sex increases the relationship between marital ratings and the independent variables, regret seems to be acting as what Rosenberg calls a "suppressor variable." [12] This was rather unexpected and will be discussed further.

Tables 5 and 6 indicate the effect of controlling for value-behavior discrepancy while examining the relationships between the dependent variable of number of extramarital partners (Q73) and the independent variables of stability of the relationship with the partner of first intercourse (Q71) and the number of premarital partners (Q72). The other tables for the remaining pairs of dependent-independent variables are not included here since they showed virtually the same pattern with regard to the "value-behavior discrepancy" variable. These data do not provide support for the intervening variable hypothesis, but do indicate that under conditions where behavior and values are congruent, *or* where behavior is more liberal than values, premarital activity is a good indicator of postmarital sexual activity.

In an attempt to assay other possible effects of premarital sexual behavior, we examined the correlations of the independent variables with dependent variables such as orgasm frequency, coital frequency, enjoyment of sex, rating of sex life, and (for males) frequency of impotence. In not one of these 15 sets of data did variation in premarital sexual behavior account for a statistically reliable proportion of dependent variable variance.

Discussion

These data give some further indication of the reliability of findings previously cited in support of the chastity norm.[7] Gen-

TABLE 5

NUMBER OF EXTRAMARITAL PARTNERS BY STABILITY OF FIRST COITAL RELATIONSHIP CONTROLLING FOR PREMARITAL VALUE-BEHAVIOR CONGRUENCE

Type of Congruence	Number of Extra-marital Partners	"After the first time, how many times did you have sexual intercourse with that person again?"			X^2	γ
		Not Again	1-9 Times	10 or More		
Values and Behavior Congruent	None (%)	51.6	54.9	71.6		
	At Least One (%)	48.4	45.1	28.4	11.4	−.3
	(N)	(91)	(82)	(141)	p<.01	
Behavior *More* Liberal than Values	None (%)	65.8	45.2	75.0		
	At Least One (%)	34.2	54.8	25.0	6.3	−.1
	(N)	(38)	(31)	(32)	p<.05	
Behavior *Less* Liberal than Values	None (%)	55.6	55.8	58.6		
	At Least One (%)	44.4	44.2	41.4	.14	N.S.
	(N)	(9)	(43)	(304)		

TABLE 6

NUMBER OF EXTRAMARITAL PARTNERS BY NUMBER OF PREMARITAL PARTNERS. CONTROLLING FOR PREMARITAL VALUE-BEHAVIOR CONGRUENCE

Type of Congruence	Number of Extra-marital Partners	None	One	2-3	4-6	7	X^2	γ
				Number of Premarital Partners				
Values and Behavior Congruent	None (%)	84.6	82.4	55.0	54.4	48.3		
	At least one (%)	15.4	17.6	45.0	45.6	51.7	30.3	.41
	(N)	(52)	(51)	(60)	(68)	(89)	$p<.001$	
Behavior *More* Liberal than Values	None (%)	83.3	68.4	81.3	62.5	30.8		
	At least one (%)	16.7	31.5	18.8	37.5	69.2	16.2	.48
	(N)	(6)	(19)	(32)	(24)	(26)	$p<.01$	
Behavior *Less* Liberal than Values	None (%)	58.4	65.4	53.0	50.0	43.2		
	At least one (%)	41.6	34.6	47.0	50.0	56.8	8.5	.15
	(N)	(101)	(136)	(66)	(30)	(44)	$p<.1$	

erally speaking, respondents who report extensive premarital sexual experience report extensive extramarital activity. Measures of the "partner of first intercourse" (i.e. how far away from a likely marriage choice the first partner was), and "number of premarital partners" show low positive associations with rating one's marriage as less happy than average, "number of extramarital partners," and with "intention to participate in mate-swapping." A measure of the stability of the relationship with the "partner of first intercourse" (Q.: "How many times did you have intercourse with that person after the first time?") was negatively related to these dependent variables as expected.

When extraneous variables such as sexual liberalism, sexual romanticism, and attitudes toward separating love and sex are partialed out, one finds that these independent-dependent variable relationships are essentially unaffected. One cannot, therefore, accept Reiss' suggestion[10] about extraneous variables for *this* set of data.

It is apparent, however, that one dependent variable—participation in mate-swapping—is slightly affected by controlling for romanticism or for regretful feelings over premarital sex. Only a very small proportion of the respondents had actually participated in mate-swapping, but a lot were thinking about it. Our guess is that many of the respondents consider mate-swapping to be something like a "home improvement loan": something you think about, but avoid doing because of the potential high costs.

Romantic attitudes—a belief that "being in love gives life meaning and direction," or that "love is more important than practical considerations"—might reasonably be expected to account for some of the variance in mate-swapping intentions. That is, the more romantic respondents might reasonably be expected to be less interested than others in mate-swapping since they could be presumed to be more emotionally attached to their mates than the less romantic respondents. It is not clear, however, why only mate-swapping and *not* the variables dealing with rating one's marriage or the number of extramarital partners was affected by romanticism.

The degree to which one is happy about or regrets having participated in premarital sex also affects prediction of the mate-swapping variable. The relationships among the dependent and independent variables in Table 4 are greater the happier one is about having had premarital sex. That is, for those respondents who reported that they were "very glad" that they had participated in premarital sex, the number of premarital partners predicted mate-swapping intentions with a gamma = —.25 (the fewer partners, the more likely one would not consider mate-swapping).

Satisfaction with having participated in premarital sex also changed the weighted average for the relationships between marital rating and the independent variables of partner of first intercourse and number of premarital partners. For example, for respondents who were "somewhat glad," or "very glad" about participating in premarital sex, it was possible to predict that their marriage would be rated as less happy the greater the number of their premarital partners (γ = .29 and .19 respectively). For respondents who were regretful about having had premarital sex the relationship between number of partners and marital happiness was near zero (γ = .018).

We are left, then, with a persistence of low positive relationships between the relative degree of premarital chastity and several variables which were chosen to indicate postmarital adjustment. We have assumed that not wanting to participate in mate-swapping is a "good" thing and similarly that having few or no extramarital experiences is "better" than having many or some. We have also assumed that a "very happy" marriage is better than one which is "somewhat happy."

In other analyses of these data[4] it was found that some of the conservative respondents rated their marriages as "happy" or "very happy" even though their coital frequencies and enjoyment of sex were below average. This may suggest a response bias caused by either dissonance reduction or simply lack of perspective. Respondents with an active history of premarital sexual behavior might have more (or better) criteria for comparison of sexual enjoyment. We view the findings with regard to rating of marital happiness as heuristic and feel that further study is required. A single question cannot, of course, adequately sum up the numerous dimensions of marital happiness.

One cannot deny the reality of the empirical relations among these data. If we put aside the question of external validity for the moment, we cannot ignore their obvious implications with regard to the *present* value structure of our society. Given a value structure that defines adultery and mate-swapping as "bad," these data suggest that some respondents adhere to the stereotype that "bad" consequences will arise from premarital sexual activity.

It has been pointed out earlier that American sex norms and practices are changing.[2-5] It may well be the case that the cross-sectional data and conclusions in this study will not survive the leap across the generation gap. That is, we may find that a society that fully accepts premarital sex does not need, want, practice, or accept extramarital sex. In counseling young adults, one most often finds that both men and women expect both partners to adhere to a fidelity norm after marriage even though they condone (or even exalt) a rather wide range of premarital sexual experience.

It is also possible to envisage a pluralism of ethics for extramarital behavior just as we can now see a pluralism of premarital sex ethics. For some people the aphorism, "the family that swings together, clings together," may be a valid expression of a (presently) rather rare sex ethic. It may be that future generations will find extramarital sex (for both men and women) to be an acceptable adjunct to marriage. We may also find that new styles of marriage such as group marriage or polygamy will become acceptable.

All of these changes may be averted if changes take place within marriage. We know, for instance, that while only 50 percent of Kinsey's[21] young, married, college educated sample participated in oral-genital intercourse, fully 75 percent of the respondents in the present study (when matched on age, education, and other demographic variables) report such activities. These data similarly suggest that orgasm frequency, coital frequency, and other sexual responses have increased relative to the benchmark data collected more than two decades ago by Kinsey and his coworkers.[21] If these trends continue *and* if expectations about sex in marriage change, will we still find these correlations between premarital chastity and postmarital fidelity?

If we do continue to find these associations in our data, what will they mean? Without belaboring the issue of situational ethics or cultural relativism, it is possible that these data may be open to a rather straightforward interpretation. Behavioral norms and sexual value systems may be changing. These data may not be an indication of the dysfunctional character of premarital sexual behavior. Rather, they may be the logical, functional, and natural outcome of the application of different normative systems. If one can intellectually accept a pluralism of premarital norms, then one must also be prepared to accept a pluralism of extramarital norms. Theoretically, society should no more insist that *the* premarital norm be "permissiveness with affection" than it should insist that *the* postmarital norm be unflagging fidelity. Norms are often defined as prescriptions for behavior which will lead to the achievement of values. The scientist must always ask whose values and whose norms he is studying before he delivers an opinion on their degree of functionality.

REFERENCES

1. CHRISTENSEN, H.: Scandinavian and American sex norms: some comparisons with sociological implications. *J. of Soc. Issues*, 22:60-75, 1966.
2. CHRISTENSEN, H. T. & GREGG, C. F.: Changing sex norms in America and Scandinavia. *J. of Mar. and the Fam.*, 33:616-627, November, 1970.
3. REISS, I.: How and why America's sex standards are changing. *Trans-Action*, 5:26-32, March, 1968.
4. ATHANASIOU, R., SHAVER, P., & TAVRIS, C.: Sex (a report to *Psychology Today* readers). *Psych. Today*, 4:37-52, July, 1970.
5. ATHANASIOU, R.: A review of public attitudes on sexual issues. A paper delivered at the American Psychopathological Association, 61st Annual Convention, New York City, February 6, 1971. In press.
6. PACKARD, V.: *The Sexual Wilderness*. New York, Pocket Books #78010, 1968.
7. SHOPE, D. F. & BRODERICK, C. B.: Level of sexual experience and predicted adjustment in marriage. *J. of Mar. and the Fam.*, 29:424-427, 1967.

8. REISS, I. L.: The sexual renaissance: a summary and analysis. *J. of Soc. Issues,* 22:123-137, 1966.
9. MUUS, R. E.: Mental Health implications of a preventive psychiatry program in the light of research findings. *Mar. and Fam. Liv.,* 22:150-156, 1960.
10. REISS, I.: *Premarital Sexual Standards in America.* New York, Free Press, 1960.
11. *The Report of the National Commission on Obscenity and Pornography.* Washington, D.C., U.S. Government Printing Office, 1970.
12. ROSENBERG, M.: *The Logic of Survey Analysis.* New York, Basic Books, 1968.
13. BLALOCK, H. M.: *Causal Inferences in Nonexperimental Research.* Chapel Hill, University of North Carolina Press, 1964.
14. CHRISTENSEN, H. T.: Sex, science, and values. In SIECUS (Ed.): *Sexuality and Man,* Chapter 10. New York, Charles Scribner's Sons, 1970.
15. ATHANASIOU, R. & SHAVER, P.: A research questionnaire on sex. *Psych. Today,* 3:64-69, July, 1969.
16. BLALOCK, H. M.: *Social Statistics.* New York, McGraw-Hill, 1960.
17. COSTNER, H. I.: Criteria for measures of association. *Amer. Soc. Rev.,* 30:341-353, 1965.
18. CURTIS, E. W.: Predictive value compared to predictive validity. *Amer. Psychol.,* 26:908-914, 1971.
19. HAYS, W.: *Statistics for Psychologists.* New York, Holt, Rinehart and Winston, 1963.
20. GOODMAN, L. A. & KRUSKAL, W. H.: Measures of association for cross classification. *J. of Amer. Stat. Assn.,* 49:732-764, 1954.
21. KINSEY, A. C., POMEROY, W. B., MARTIN, C. E., & GEBHARD, P. H.: *Sexual Behavior in the Human Female.* Philadelphia, W. B. Saunders, 1953.

Background Papers

GENERAL DISCUSSION

GEORGE TARJAN, *Presiding*

At the final session of the conference, Dr. Reiss, Dr. Athanasiou, and Dr. Helweg-Larsen (substituting for Dr. Hoffmeyer) were asked to summarize the background papers.

Dr. Reiss chose instead to comment on what he as a sociologist had learned at the conference. He made the following points:

There is a need to avoid helping those among the retarded who would get along better without interference. However, the retarded are not a unitary group and includes persons below a certain level of psychological and physiological adequacy for whom society must step in and do something. The question is: *What is that level?* Here value judgments are necessary, but those making such judgments must do so with enough perspective to recognize the basis on which they are being made. This is particularly true in regard to the questions of who should be sterilized and why.

It is also important to recognize the stereotypes that exist about the retarded, who holds them, and which ones are held by the people in power. Comparative studies need to be made of the sexual activities and behavior of retardates (at least of those with IQs above 50) and of persons with IQs of 100. Studies are also needed to check out the indications given at this conference that retardates have need for the two basic human relationships known to all societies: 1) an intimate relationship between adults who give one another an affectionate and psychological response, and 2) an intimate, nurturing relationship between an older person and an infant. The retarded who have these needs to the same extent as other people may be considered within the normal range of human beings under criteria for normality that are sociologically and cross-culturally relevant.

Dr. Athanasiou suggested that his paper had the following implications for the subject of the conference:

The finding that a positive relationship, not based on extraneous variables, exists between premarital and extramarital experiences means that talk about the right of mental retardates to have premarital sexual experience may affect their postmarital style of exercising their sexuality. The finding also means that minds should be kept open to the question of whether or not the monogamous, nuclear family is the most appropriate for retardates. Because today pluralism in premarital sexual styles is becoming accepted, pluralism of styles in postmarital sexual behavior may be expected in the future. Therefore, if it has been found that two mental retardates can live together happily and well, it may be appropriate to consider whether three or four may do so in a halfway house or some kind of communal setting.

Dr. Helweg-Larsen in summarizing Dr. Hoffmeyer's paper made six points:

1. Premarital sexual intercourse is a centuries-old tradition in Scandinavian countries, but it seems to be as common among males in the United States where there is a formal taboo against it.

2. Petting is not known in Denmark, suggesting that as the sanction against premarital sex increases, the greater the tendency to use petting as an alternative.

3. Hertoft's finding in 1964 that 37 percent of a sample of 400 males aged 18 and 19 had not yet had sexual intercourse, and that 20 percent had had intercourse with only one female partner does not indicate a high degree of promiscuity.

4. The recent legislation providing for sex education in Danish state schools explicitly requires that sexual problems should be

discussed in a family context. The content is to include the anatomy and physiology of the genital organs, information about intercourse, abortion, contraception, and venereal disease, and ethical issues. The teaching of sexual techniques is prohibited.

5. Sex education for mentally retarded children will be essentially the same as for other Danish children.

6. It is not known whether the open display of pornography in Denmark has had any effect on sexual behavior or whether there is more or less promiscuity today than 10 years ago.

Closing Summary

GEORGE TARJAN, *Presiding*

In summing up, Dr. Tarjan identified three "clear facts" that came through the conference: 1) that great gaps in knowledge exist in the areas of sexual behavior, reproduction, and mental retardation; 2) that almost nothing that is applicable to the "clinical" types of retardation can be generalized to "social cultural" retardation; 3) that little is known about social attitudes toward mental retardation and sex. Reminding the participants that mental retardation exists in a social matrix that includes such human issues as poverty, overpopulation, unemployment, and care systems, he suggested that anything done about retardation must take this fact into account. Warning against absolutist approaches, he recommended research involving longitudinal, relevant data-collections and, "until all scientific evidence is in," a continuation of the type of dialogue represented by this conference.

Name Index

341

Subject Index

Abortions
   attitudes toward, 198, 202, 212, 308
   in Denmark, 272-273
Adjustment in community. *See* Social behavior
Adolescence, sexuality in, 15-16
Adrenogenital syndrome, 228-229, 255
Age factors
   and homosexual activity, 41
   and masturbation, 33-34
   and orgasm in sleep, 35
   and petting experiences, 36
   and premarital coitus, 38
   and puberty in retardates, 31-32
   and role perception, 23-24
   and sexual knowledge, 46
Alternative living styles
   for retardates, 237-238
   toleration of, 305-306
Amniocentesis, and hormone assays, 251-252
Animals, sexual experience with, 44
Anti-androgenic agents, effects of, 256-258, 261
Attitudes
   of community. *See* Community attitudes
   of parents, and sexual behavior of children, 278, 280, 282-283, 314
   of staff. *See* Institutionalism and attitudes of staff

Background papers, 267-339
   discussion of, 337-339
   on premarital sexual behavior, 286-315
   and postmarital behavior, 317-335, 338
   on sex education in Denmark, 267-284
Behavior patterns, sexual differences in, 229-232, 250-254. *See also* Social behavior
Biological aspects. *See* Physical and biological aspects
Birth rate among retardates, 86-91, 111-116, 179-180, 191
Books, on sex education, 6, 276-277
Brain function, and sexual responses, 233

Catholic attitudes, on sexuality in retardates, 198-199
Child care, capability for, in retardates, 192-194, 247-248
Childhood, psychosexual development in, 15-17
Children of retardates, 189-192
   adjustment of, 217-218
   attitudes toward, 200, 203
   intelligence of, 187-188
   intervention in care of, 200, 210-211
   and special child-rearing programs, 211-212
Chromosome karyotypes, studies of, 258-261

342

and coitus frequency, 40
and employment, 175
and fertility, 86-91, 111-116, 179-180, 191
legal aspects of, 188
offspring of, 189-192
and pooling of resources, 182-183
and social adjustment, 174-175, 187
studies in England, 169-185
studies in Northern Ireland, 186-194
and suitability as parents, 192-194, 247
between tenants of halfway house, 155
See also Children of retardates
Masturbation
attitudes on, 21, 64-65, 68, 148
fantasies in, 7, 35
prepubertal, 33
after puberty, 33-35
Maturation. See Psychosexual development
Mental health, and premarital sexuality, 312-314
Minority culture, retardates as, 208, 236-237
Moral implications of sexuality in retardates, 195-204
Catholic point of view, 198-199
and guidelines for sexual behavior, 199-202
Jewish point of view, 195-198
Mother's Aid Institute, in Denmark, 272, 273, 275

Nervous system
differentiation of, 231
and sexual responses, 233
Nudity, female, responses to, 45

Object relations, in retardates, 18-19
Ovulation, prediction and detection of, 100-101

Parents
attitudes of, and sexual behavior of children, 278, 280, 282-283, 314
of retardates
attitudes and responsibilities of, 74, 221
involvement in sexual problems of children, 73, 81, 105

retardates as, 192-194, 247-248
See also Children of retardates
Personal relationships, and emotional attitudes, 24-25
Petting, premarital, 36-38
Pheromones, 8
Physical and biological aspects, 79-141
and control of sexuality, 232-234
and development of sexual systems, 227-232
See also Psychosexual development
discussions of, 105-107, 139-141
and psychobiology of sexuality, 235-236
and sexual differentiation, 250-254
Pictures, erotic
frank examination of, 11
responses to, 8-9, 44-46
in sex education, 5-9, 277
Polymorphism, balanced, 131-132
Pornography
attitudes toward, 5-9, 11, 61
responses to, 8-9, 44-46, 300
Pregnancy
knowledge of, 46
from premarital coitus, 39
prevention of. See Contraception
Premarital sexual behavior
attitudes toward, 286-315
and coitus, 38-39
with prostitutes, 39-40
and contraception, 291-293
and control of consequences of sex, 308-310
and cultural changes, 294-298
double standard in, 287-289
and experimentation in sex, 306-308
historical aspects of, 268-269, 286-287
and legitimacy of sexual choice, 293-294
and living together, 305-306
and mental health, 312-314
and petting, 36-38
in post-industrial society, 311-312
and postmarital sexual behavior, 317-335, 338
social class differences in, 298-299
trends in, 289-291, 303-305
Prepubertal sexual activity, 31-33
Progesterone, prenatal exposure to, effects of, 254-255
Progestins, for contraception, 98
injections of, 97